CONFEDERATE ★ STATES ★ PAPER MONEY

CIVIL WAR CURRENCY FROM THE SOUTH

12TH EDITION

TEXT BY ARLIE R. SLABAUGH

EDITED BY GEORGE S. CUHAJ

PRICING BY WILLIAM BRANDIMORE

Published by

Krause Publications, a division of F+W Media, Inc.
700 East State Street • Iola, WI 54990-0001
715-445-2214 • 888-457-2873
www.krausebooks.com

To order books or other products call toll-free 1-800-258-0929
or visit us online at www.shopnumismaster.com

ISBN-13: 978-1-4402-3086-8
ISBN-10: 1-4402-3086-2

Designed by Al West
Edited by George Cuhaj and Caitlin Spaulding

Printed in China

CONTENTS

Part II — Historical Data

Part III — Catalog (Southern States)
Paper Money of the Southern States

ABOUT THE 12TH EDITION

This new edition, like previous works, uses the text of the late Arlie Slabaugh. A native of Springfield, Pa., Slabaugh began collecting in 1938 at 16 and grew to become not only an avid collector but a renowned numismatist and author. Slabaugh's career included the publication of his own hobby magazine, *The Hobby Spotlite,* as well as a stint at the Franklin Mint. Slabaugh generously shared his vast knowledge with the numismatic public by writing for publications such as *The Numismatic Scrapbook, The Numismatist, Numismatic News* and *Bank Note Reporter.* His work and involvement earned him many awards and honors, including the American Numismatic Association's Lifetime Achievement Award, Numismatic Ambassador Award, and the Numismatic Literary Guild's Clemy Award.

Slabaugh began compiling his catalog of Confederate currency in 1957, with the first edition published in 1958. By the 10th edition, published in 2000, no Confederate paper money book had been through as many editions. Sadly, after a long and storied career, Slabaugh passed away in September 2007 in Springfield, during the production of the 11th edition of the catalog.

This 12th edition preserves and extends the color images introduced in the 11th edition, but returns to the immensely popular Slabaugh numbering system, at the behest of our readers. Krause Publications is honored and proud to continue to bring Arlie Slabaugh's work to our readers.

INTRODUCTION FROM THE 10TH EDITION

by Arlie R. Slabaugh

I began to collect seriously early in 1938 on a planned basis, not just Confederate currency, but many other things. Of particular value at that time was the publication of *The Standard Paper Money Catalogue* by Wayte Raymond in 1940, which provided me with a list of types so that I knew what to seek. I also learned about the notes from articles published in Raymond's *Coin Collector's Journal* to which I subscribed, as well as purchasing the 1915-1919 years of *The Numismatist,* which contained H.D. Allen's series of articles on the background of Confederate currency (later included in a 1945 reprint of Bradbeer's catalog). By 1946, I had a rather good collection of types as well as some varieties that appealed to me. I was able to assemble all of the types with one exception — the "Indian Princess" note (No. 14) and I could have obtained it, too, but at that time none was offered for sale in better than good condition and I was seeking a better example. (This is still largely true, although higher prices have since attracted better examples to the market.)

The purchase I remember best is that of the $500 Montgomery note (No. 3) that I obtained in XF condition at Kosoff's New York auction in 1942, at what was then said to be a record price of $88. At that time, Raymond catalogued it at $75. Since that note now brings $10,000 or more in similar condition, you can see what unbelievable changes have occurred in the past 50 years. I wish I still had this note, but I sold my original collection many years ago when prices were yet low. In other words, prices listed in this catalog are unbiased, having been obtained from various sources and are not for my personal benefit.

Believing that the approaching Civil War centennial would reawaken interest in Confederate currency (which was not an appreciably active series in the 1950s), I began compiling a catalog 1957, which was published the following year by the Whitman Publishing Co., Racine, Wis. Two further editions (1959 and the 1963 Centennial Edition) were similarly distributed by this company, well-known publishers of the *Guide Book of United States Coins*. The first edition relied on prices that had been current among dealers up to that time. This was to change as both demand and prices rose due to the increased demand for Civil War artifacts during the Civil War centennial. Nevertheless, prices were still restrained compared to those experienced in the 1990s.

Now that the 10th edition of this catalog has appeared, it may be a good time to review the publication of previous editions. As noted, the first three editions were published by Whitman. The fourth edition appeared in 1967 and was published jointly by me and Hewitt Brothers, Chicago, as a part of its "Numismatic Information Series." The same holds true for the fifth edition in 1973 and the sixth edition in 1977. Probably not many collectors own a complete set, but each edition contains price changes or data not in others. The seventh (1991), 8th (1993), 9th (1998) and the 10th edition have been published by Krause Publications, Iola, Wis. No other Confederate paper money catalog has gone through as many editions.

A peculiarity of collecting involves swings in collector interest, whether it be baseball cards, coins, paper money or other subjects. One year, "everyone" is seeking certain collectibles while a year later the same series may be "dead." During the 1990s, interest in paper money of most kinds, not just Confederate, increased greatly, with accompanying increases in prices. Whether future prices will continue to rise, stabilize or drop is unknown, but collectors should be aware of this and collect what they really want to own and not for speculative purposes.

It should be noted, though, that as online auctions and sales via computer continue to grow, the market for Confederate currency may soon exceed its present levels. Should that happen, one is warned that as prices increase, so does the increased likelihood of fakes and modern reproductions being sold as genuine notes that are claimed to be "inherited."

A NATION ASUNDER

With the secession of South Carolina on December 20, 1860, the Union, "one and inseparable," was a Union no longer. The igniting spark was the question of slavery but the North and the South — one industrial, the other agrarian — had been drawing apart in many ways since Colonial times.

By February 1861, six Southern states (South Carolina, Mississippi, Florida, Alabama, Georgia and Louisiana) had seceded from the Union. Delegates from each of these states assembled at the provisional capital in Montgomery, Ala., where a committee of 12 under the chairmanship of Christopher G. Memminger drafted a constitution. Although the Confederacy had its share of radicals, they were overruled by cooler heads and the resulting constitution that was submitted in March to the state governments for approval (but not to public vote), resembled, to a large extent, the U.S. Constitution on which it was based.

Prior to its approval, the Confederate Congress passed an Act on February 9, 1861 that stated, "Be it enacted by the Confederate States of America in Congress assembled, that all the laws of the United States of America in force and in use in the Confederate States of America on the 1st day of November last, and not inconsistent with the Constitution of the Confederate States, be, and the same are hereby, continued in force until altered or repealed by the Congress." After all, not only had Southerners lived for many years under U.S. laws, many of the delegates had served in the state houses or the U.S. Congress and were familiar with the U.S. Constitution. It was not like they were inexperienced men preparing the document from scratch. Rather, they were trying to improve the U.S. Constitution to meet the needs of the South.

Portions of the Confederate States Constitution are identical to the U.S. Constitution except that the words "United States" are changed to "Confederate States." An important difference appears in the preamble, which is also the major weakness of the Confederate Constitution. The preamble states, "We, the people of the Confederate States, each state acting in its sovereign and independent character, in order to form a permanent federal government, establish justice, insure domestic tranquillity, and secure the blessings of liberty to ourselves and our posterity-invoking the favor and guidance of Almighty God-do ordain and establish this Constitution for the Confederate States of America." Note the emphasis on the independence of each state, a feature that undermined the government of the United States under the Articles of Confederation after the Revolutionary War and which would be no more successful for the Confederate States, since it resulted in much bickering between states and President Jefferson Davis, who sought to impose his will upon national affairs and the conduct of the Civil War.

Election, Wednesday, November 6th, 1861.

FOR PRESIDENT,

JEFFERSON DAVIS,

OF MISSISSIPPI.

——:o:——

FOR VICE-PRESIDENT,

ALEXANDER H. STEPHENS,

OF GEORGIA.

——:o:——

Electoral Ticket.

FOR THE STATE AT LARGE,

JOHN R. EDMUNDS, Halifax.
ALLEN T. CAPERTON, Monroe.

FOR THE DISTRICTS.

1st District—	JOS. CHRISTIAN, Middlesex.
2d "	CIN. W. NEWTON, Norfolk City.
3d "	R. T. DANIEL, Richmond City.
4th "	WM. F. THOMPSON, Dinwiddie.
5th "	WOOD BOULDIN, Charlotte.
6th "	WM. L. GOGGIN, Bedford.
7th "	BEN. F. RANDOLPH, Albemarle.
8th "	JAMES W. WALKER, Madison.
9th "	ASA ROGERS, Loudoun.
10th "	S. C. WILLIAMS, Shenandoah.
11th "	SAMUEL McD. REID, Rockbridge.
12th "	H. A. EDMUNDSON, Roanoke.
13th "	JAMES W. SHEFFY, Smyth.
14th "	HENRY J. FISHER, Mason.
15th "	JOS. JOHNSON, Harrison.
16th "	E. H. FITZHUGH, Ohio.

FOR CONGRESS,

ROGER A. PRYOR.

On the other hand, the Confederate Constitution did contain improvements, the most notable of which is found in Section 7 of Article I. Like other portions, it is similar to the U.S. Constitution but contains the provision that "the president may approve any appropriation and disapprove any other appropriation in the same bill. In such case, he shall, in signing the bill, designate the appropriations disapproved." This is the line-item veto that was long sought by U.S. presidents, particularly since so many bills have riders attached that have no relation to the original bills. It wasn't until 1996 that a modified version was finally passed.

Unlike the U.S. Constitution, which added the 14th Amendment (Section 4) to avoid the payment of certain obligations incurred by the Civil War, the Confederate Constitution states that "no law of Congress shall discharge any debt contracted before the passage of the same." While the United States did honor debts contracted prior to the adoption of its constitution, as indicated in Article VI, Section 1, feelings were strong at the end of the Civil War against payment of debts related to the rebellion. Assuming that the paper money of the Confederate States was not already virtually worthless by the end of the war, this amendment had the effect of relieving the United States of having to redeem the Confederate issues.

Other features of the Confederate Constitution included the limiting of the term of office for the president to six years; giving the president authority to remove political appointments at his discretion; and the continuation of slavery, including its protection in any new territory the Confederacy might acquire, while at the same time forbidding the importation of more slaves.

Jefferson Davis, who had served in the Mexican War and was U.S. Secretary of War during 1853-1857, wanted to serve the South as a general but accepted the nomination of provisional president on February 9, 1861, at the Montgomery Convention. Not until November 6, 1861, was he elected president for six years. By that time, the capital of the Confederacy had been moved to Richmond, but not before the Confederate Congress proclaimed (May 6, 1861) that a state of war existed between the Confederate States and the United States. Fort Sumter had fallen on April 14; the next day, President Lincoln declared that an "insurrection" existed and called for volunteer troops. Both sides were girding for a war that they believed would be short, but which lasted four bloody years.

In his inaugural address, President Davis asked that the Southern states be permitted to pursue their own course. That was not to be. When Horace Greeley, the New York newspaper publisher, inquired of Lincoln in 1862 what policy he was pursuing, Lincoln replied, "My paramount object in this struggle is to save the Union, and is not either to save or destroy slavery. If I could save the Union without freeing any slave, I would do it; and if I could save it by freeing all the slaves, I would do it; and if I could do it by freeing some and leaving others alone, I would also do that."

Following the battle of Antietam (September 17, 1862), President Lincoln issued his Emancipation Proclamation a few days later. He had been waiting for a decisive victory to announce it and while Antietam was a draw, his hand was forced by the danger that the British and French governments were about ready to recognize the Confederacy that had until then engaged in a number of successful battles. In other words, the Emancipation Proclamation was at that time primarily a propaganda measure for European consumption since it ordered slaves freed only in areas held by the Confederate States and not in the North or loyal border states. Secretary of State William Seward put it in proper focus when he said, "We show our sympathy with slavery by emancipating slaves where we cannot reach them, and holding them in bondage where we can set them free."

In all fairness to Lincoln, on December 1, 1862, he appealed to Congress for a constitutional amendment that would provide for compensated emancipation to any state that abolished slavery before January 1, 1900, but it was opposed by the border states. As a result, there was none then or later. Lincoln, in his Second Inaugural Address (March 4, 1865) asked for "malice toward none" when the war was over, but his assassination on April 14 changed his plans for reuniting the states to one that was far more vindictive. It would not be far-fetched to say that Lincoln's death was as great a calamity to the South as the loss of the war.

THE COTTON ECONOMY

Much has been made of the fact that the currency of the Confederate States was not "legal tender." It's true that the North did issue Legal Tender Notes during the Civil War but was there really that much difference between these "greenbacks" and the "bluebacks" issued by the Confederacy? The inscription on the U.S. notes stated that "This note is a legal tender for all debts public and private, except duties on imports and interest on the public debt and is redeemable in payment of all loans made to the United States." The Confederate notes stated that they were "Receivable in payment of all dues except export duties." Moreover, the notes of the Confederate States carry the statement that they would be paid six months (or two years) after a treaty of peace. The U.S. notes do not say when they would be redeemed.

Although redemption of the U.S. Legal Tender Notes began after the war, there was considerable opposition against redeeming or discontinuing them, and it was not until 1879, as a political expedient, that specie payments were fully resumed. A Greenback political party was actually formed, which included in its platform the demand that the U.S. government continue to issue irredeemable currency. Both the U.S. and Confederate notes of the Civil War were an emergency fiat currency, not directly backed by coin as were the later gold and silver certificates. In earlier days, governments at war generally suspended specie payments since otherwise people would take all their paper money to the banks and demand coin in exchange, which they then hoarded in order to have something of value in the event that their governments failed. (Nowadays, fiat currency and huge government debts are the rule, war or no war; you know who pays.)

To continue, a bill was introduced in the Confederate Congress to make the currency legal tender but it failed to pass. Secretary of the Treasury Memminger stated that Confederate paper money was "the accepted currency of the whole country" and there was no need to make it legal tender. Actually, the people had little choice since it and the other paper money of the Southern states, banks and local notes was the only money in circulation. Coins and bullion held by the banks at the start of the war had been loaned to the government, which used it where paper money was not acceptable. But for army requisitions and the like, Confederate currency was tendered in payment and the holders could only hope that it would eventually be paid as promised on the face of the notes. Had the South won the war, it is very likely that it would have lived up to its promises although hardly within two years, considering the destruction that had been wrought on the country.

The U.S. Legal Tender Notes held their value better not because they were legal tender but because people had more confidence in them. The North had many times the resources of the South since most of the manufacturing industries were located there. Until the Civil War, even cotton growing was to a large extent at the mercy of Northern bankers (who made crop loans) and Northern mills where the cotton was spun into cloth. Moreover, instead of depending upon more and more paper money to meet the needs of the war, thereby inflating the currency beyond what was actually needed, the U.S. government passed Internal Revenue Acts (income taxes) in 1862 and 1864 and also raised other taxes.

A major failing of the Confederacy was not utilizing its tax base to the extent it should have. Instead, it relied heavily on loans and the sale of bonds. These failed to raise the amount of money expected. In 1861, the Confederate Congress provided for a direct tax on property but it was very lenient (50 cents for each $100 of goods and money) since it was the desire of the government "to get along with as little tax as possible," according to a speech by Vice President Stephens. The government also recognized that each of the Southern states that made up the Confederacy valued its own sovereignty almost as highly as its unification against the North. For that reason, the tax was levied through the states, each of which was permitted to meet its quota by paying the tax instead of obtaining the money from its citizens. Thus, this tax had little effect on the people, while the states increased the inflationary trend by raising the money through the issuance of their own bonds and paper money.

Not until 1863 and 1864, when it was late, did the Confederate States begin serious taxation. One measure affecting banks, shipping, manufacturing and business firms was a tax of 25% on all profits exceeding 25%. Farmers and planters were affected by a tax of an unusual nature — tax-in-kind. After reserving a stated quantity for their own use, they were required to deliver to government depositories one-tenth of their production of various things, ranging from hay to sugar. This helped to support the army, but did little for the currency that had by then increased from two to four times what was needed for general circulation, an amount that translates into an incentive for inflation in any economy. (The accompanying illustration shows a tax-in-kind receipt for the delivery of bacon.)

Had the plans of the Confederacy worked as anticipated, the necessity of taxes would have been immaterial. Cotton was expected to be the equivalent of gold to the Confederate States. To understand this better, consider the role of cotton in world trade at the time the Civil War began. In 1860, the value of cotton exports from the South exceeded the combined total of all other commodities and manufactures shipped from the United States. More than 4 million 500-pound bales of cotton were grown each year, which was 80% of the world's supply. In the aftermarket, thousands of people, from shippers to spinners, depended upon cotton for a livelihood. Thus cotton had a similarity to the concentration of petroleum in the Middle East today, and the Confederacy expected to exercise the same economic leverage with it. England imported two-thirds of the South's cotton, another 10% went to France with the balance going primarily to the Northern states and other countries. In 1861, Southern planters were asked to "loan" half of their cotton production to the Confederate government for which they would receive 8% bonds in exchange. This amount of cotton (2 million bales) would have brought the Treasury $100 million, a strategy that would presumably have covered the interest on the bonds, government expenses and supplied the troops, while encouraging planters to continue the procedure each year.

However, instead of shipping cotton, the Confederacy decided that the best way to gain quick recognition from England and France was to withhold it. Unfortunately for the South, this caused no hardship in 1861 since there was then a cotton surplus. A shortage did not develop until the summer of 1862 and by 1863, cotton yarn production in England had dropped from nearly 500,000 tons to 200,000 tons and many workers were unemployed. By then, instead of an embargo of their own making, the Confederacy found that the North had established a fairly tight blockade along the coast. Thus, when they were ready to ship cotton, it was no longer possible to export it in large quantities. As a result, cotton failed to produce the income that could have gone a long way toward preventing the depreciation of the currency.

Some cotton was sent to Europe and supplies received in return through the use of blockade runners. But the amount was not great because the blockade runners were normally small ships built for speed in order to elude the naval patrols of the North. These blockade runners were very profitable (when successful) but of the estimated 8,250 runs they made during the war, they managed to transport less than 2 million bales of cotton to the West Indies from where it was shipped to England. This was only a little over 10% of four years' production in normal times and less than half of the amount the Confederate government had planned to sell each year. (The illustration shows a rare stock certificate of one of the blockade runners). Accordingly, cotton production was reduced and replaced by corn. One major result was an increase in cotton growing elsewhere in the world, such as in Egypt and India.

There is still another facet of the cotton-into-money story. This involved the sale of Confederate bonds. The first $15 million loan under the Act of February 28, 1861 was raised through the sale of 8% bonds primarily to Southern banks that were to be paid from a duty of 1/8 of 1 cent per pound on all cotton exported by the Confederate States from that which had been received from the planters. By the end of the war, more than twice as many kinds of bonds had been issued as there are types of paper money but the majority of them make no mention of cotton. However, in addition to using bonds to reduce the amount of currency in circulation, the government made extensive efforts to exchange bonds for cotton, which was then placed in warehouses for future shipment to Europe. (Due to the closure of ports and the inability of the small blockade runners to carry large loads, a considerable amount of cotton remained in the warehouses at the end of the war.)

Under the Act of April 21, 1862, Cotton Certificates were issued for future delivery of 20 bales of cotton (i.e. $1,000 bonds) to foreign buyers. Still another Act of April 30, 1863 authorized an issue of bonds payable in coin or cotton. However, the most famous of the cotton bonds was the Erlanger Loan that originated in France and got its name from Emile Erlanger, the French banker who devised the scheme that he sold to John Slidell, the Confederate commissioner in France. Slidell, who had a great deal of personal vanity and a daughter with a romantic interest in the French banker's son, allowed himself to be deluded into believing that in addition to raising a great deal of money, here was finally the chance of French recognition for the Confederate States. (Slidell had meetings with the vacillating French emperor, Napoleon III, who used the opportunity of the American Civil War to establish an empire in Mexico under Maximilian and then failed to support him.)

Unlike other confederate bonds, those for the Erlanger Loan were printed in Europe. Issued under the Act of January 29, 1863, these bonds had 40 coupons attached (not shown in the illustration) and were in the denominations of 100, 200, 500 and 1000 pounds sterling or their equivalent in francs or cotton. The sale of the bonds was handled by Emile Erlanger & Co. in France and J. Henry Schroder & Co. in England and was expected to realize 3 million sterling ($15,000,000). Interest was 7% payable semi-annually over 20 years, but the attractive part of these bonds was the expectation of being able to obtain cotton at the rate of six pence sterling per pound after the war ended or if during the war, delivery was to be made "at a point in the interior within 10 miles of a railroad or steam navigable to the ocean."

Erlanger expected to make a great deal of money since he received the bonds at

£77 per £100, which meant that any money obtained over £77 went to him. He also received a commission of 5%. The bonds were placed on the market at £90 and were oversubscribed in less than three days. At first they commanded a premium of 5% since buyers were in a position to make a considerable profit on cotton, but when reality emerged, the price dropped and the Confederacy was forced to support it by transferring money to Erlanger from its funds in London. After the fall of Vicksburg and Port Hudson (July 1-8, 1863), which effectively ended any possibility that the Mississippi River might soon be reopened to commerce (cotton deliveries) and cut the Confederacy in two, the price of the bonds dropped to 36. In the end, only one-third of the total amount was ever realized and of this Erlanger obtained, through buy-backs and commissions, as much as the Confederate States. It was another misguided episode of Confederate finance.

First issue of Confederate currency from Montgomery, Alabama.

Part I — Catalog
CONFEDERATE STATES

Collecting Confederate Currency

This catalog has been written with the idea of conveying as much information as possible in a handy size volume. All notes are listed by types and major varieties. This is the ideal way to collect these notes due to the rarity of many minor varieties and the difficulty of obtaining them. In supplying the large quantity of paper money required by the Confederacy, not only different papers but many different plates were required to print the notes. The result was many different varieties and plate letters.

While there are many major varieties that are of interest and worthy of collecting, the fallacy of going to the extreme was pointed out as early as January 1877 when "An Observer" wrote in the *American Journal of Numismatics* under the title of "Collecting Run Mad" that "an altered portion of a letter, numerical character or design; a little shading more or less; or two or three marks of the graver, indicating that no two engravers make their note plates alike, or that the same engraver is liable to make varieties of his own work (was) a direct perversion of the higher and more aesthetic objects of numismatic science." The number of minor varieties is given in this catalog as a matter of record, but the numbers continue to change for the reason that some, originally listed in William W. Bradbeer's 1915 catalog, have since been determined to be alterations or counterfeits while in other instances, additional varieties have been added through the discovery of previously unlisted printing varieties. It is possible that the writer in the *American Journal of Numismatics* had in mind certain collectors of that time who were so avidly seeking additional varieties of Confederate notes that unscrupulous persons went so far as to manufacture new varieties for them to purchase. This was accomplished through counterfeits or alterations of genuine notes. As noted, some of these have since been identified as not being genuine, but it is possible that others still remain in Bradbeer's book and Criswell's revision.

While I personally prefer to collect Confederate notes by type, the collecting of varieties does hold a certain fascination and I believe in the freedom of everyone to collect in the manner that gives the owner the greatest satisfaction. I must warn you, however, that variety collecting, particularly minor varieties, will probably have to be limited for most collectors to the more common notes due to the prices having increased tremendously over the past 50 years. Today, 100 times the cost of the same notes in 1940 is not unusual. Moreover, even forming a type collection can be difficult and expensive since only 50 to 100 specimens exist of several major types, which means that one must wait until specimens come on the market and then compete against other collectors for the same notes.

Although this may sound discouraging, collecting Confederate notes is certainly no more expensive than that of assembling complete collections of U.S. type coins. Not only that, with Confederate notes, one is able to literally "hold history in your hands." Moreover, there is great flexibility in building a collection — one may limit oneself to major designs, or a note from each issue, or the whole works, as far as you want to go. Plus, there are many collateral items, some of which appear in this catalog.

Catalog Prices

It is hardly news that authors stick their neck out when they price catalogs. In that respect, I am not an exception. Although due care has been exercised in arriving at the prices for each of the Confederate notes included in this catalog, it is very seldom (if ever) that collectors or dealers agree 100% with the valuations quoted in any work that covers a considerable number of specimens of any kind. While I have depended largely on prices submitted by dealers or obtained from price lists, advertisements and auctions, as well as considering the comments of collectors, there will be complaints that the prices for certain notes are "too high" or that they are "too low." On the other hand, if a catalog doesn't include any prices at all, there is even greater complaint, if collectors even purchase it.

While it is unfortunate that greater emphasis is given to prices than should be the case, being one of the symptoms of our civilization, it is nevertheless desirable to have a fairly good idea what something is worth. In that respect, I feel that this catalog is "close to the mark," bearing in mind that between the time this catalog was compiled and the time you may purchase or sell a given note, that the market may have changed, upward or downward.

It hardly needs to be said that practically everyone wants to buy coins or paper money at the lowest possible price. This includes both collectors and dealers. Bear in mind, though, that a dealer can't very well claim to pay the "highest" prices and then turn around and sell for less than you would be willing to sell the same items. In other words, perspective may be as important as price.

Buying and Selling

The prices listed in this catalog are retail, which means that if you are selling notes to a dealer, you will receive a lower price, just as any merchant must buy his goods at less than his selling price if he is to stay in business. Buying prices will probably average about 60% of the listed price. Rare notes and those that are popular and in demand may realize nearly full retail but worn notes, especially of the more common kinds, may not realize 50%. At times, this may even be true of notes in better condition if a dealer already has a sufficient quantity. In that case, it is advisable to "shop around" since someone without any of the notes, or only a few, may be willing to pay a better price. Conversely, this also holds true when buying. A dealer with twenty specimens of a given note may be willing to sell them for less than someone else who has only one, simply because he is "overstocked."

In addition to buying at a stated price from dealers, it is also possible to purchase Confederate notes (and other numismatic material) at coin and paper money auctions, which are held frequently. These sales are usually public or by mail bids, and nearly all have printed catalogs. Auction sales permit one to buy at your bid, providing someone else doesn't bid higher, but you must remember that if you are the successful bidder on any lot, that auction sales are not approval sales. This means that if you are bidding by mail instead of viewing the lots in person at a public sale, you should have a good idea what you are bidding on. Auctions and direct purchase from dealers give collectors a choice when buying or selling notes and many use both methods.

Remember that prices are not etched in stone and those asked by dealers or obtained at auction are likely to vary somewhat due to a number of factors including competition and the desire of a collector. Economic conditions and fluctuations of the market also influence prices. When something is "hot," it is not unusual for prices to rise rapidly. On the other hand, if business is at a standstill, prices may drop. In any case, it is wise to recall an old adage — "Opportunity is often the best bargain."

Grading

Grading is very important aside from aesthetic considerations because the grade and the price of a note is so closely intertwined. A note offered for sale as "Fine" is no bargain if the condition is actually only "Good." What may sound like a nice specimen in the everyday world (such as someone offering a used lawn mower for sale in good condition) has an entirely different meaning in the collecting field. Therefore, it is suggested that if you are not already familiar with bank note grading, that you either visit coin shops that sell paper money, numismatic conventions, or receive bank notes on approval by mail to familiarize yourself with what each grade looks like before buying anything really expensive. Bear in mind that there is no cut and dried rule for grading — there will be variables from note to note within a grade, but they should approximate the descriptions given here. Grading unfortunately does not work like a color chart where one can simply hold up some object against the chart and determine the exact shade of color. To a large extent, it is experience and personal opinion based on the parameters established for each grade, and once you become familiar with grading, your opinion may be as good as that of others. There may be a science of numismatics but grading is more of an art.

Having said this, let us proceed to a description of the major grades.

Uncirculated. An uncirculated note has never been in circulation as money, is new and unused without any folds. It should appear fresh and crisp, like it has just been printed. But Confederate notes, which are now well over 100 years old, frequently show signs of aging, even if they are new. Moreover, many of them have poor margins due to having been cut apart unevenly. The prices in this catalog are for Uncirculated specimens that are of average nice grade. Those with defects such as a bent corner, are worth a little less. Exceptionally fresh looking specimens ("Gems") are worth more, especially those of the first three issues of Confederate currency.

Extra Fine specimens are nearly Uncirculated and crisp, but have a few light folds or minor smudges and the like that indicate that they have seen a little circulation or handling.

Very Fine notes have more light folds, or one or two heavier folds, but are still clean and are not torn or badly aged. More evidence of circulation but design is still sharp. Very Fine notes retain considerable crispness.

Fine specimens are of a grade that resembles many of the bills you are likely to find in your pocket. Notes in this condition show considerable circulation with many folds or creases. Design details are still clear but becoming less sharp. The paper is beginning to show signs of soiling and the edges may show signs of handling or have a few tiny nicks. Fine notes still have some crispness except where creased.

Very Good notes have seen extensive circulation and are completely limp. The note is still complete but some details in the design may no longer be clear due to wear or soiling. The corners may be rounded somewhat and there is an increasing number of small tears in the edge. Still reasonably attractive.

Good notes are heavily worn but should be basically complete except possibly for very small parts. The soiling is much heavier and generally covers the entire note.

Less than Good notes are badly worn, torn or repaired, and pieces of larger size may be missing. Notes of these lower grades are considered acceptable for those that are of very rare types of which it may be very difficult to obtain better specimens. Although they may not be beautiful, don't shun them — sometimes these low grade notes turn out to be the only example you will ever see. If a better example turns up later, you can then buy it to upgrade your collection.

Cancellations. Notes that have been cancelled are usually worth somewhat less, depending upon how the overall appearance is affected. Unlike cut-out cancels, neat "X" cut cancels, such as those found on First Issue notes, have little effect on the value if the notes are otherwise in the indicated grade.

FIRST ISSUE — 1861

The Act of March 9, 1861 "authorized Treasury notes to be issued for such sum or sums as the exigencies of the public service may require, but not to exceed at any time one million dollars, and of denominations not less than fifty dollars for any such note." Payable "Twelve months after date" with interest at 1 cent per day for each 100 dollars. Redeemed notes could be replaced with new notes so long as the total sum of this issue outstanding did not exceed $1,000,000. Accordingly, a totaling of the number of each denomination issued under the Act shows an aggregate sum of $2,021,100 although not all in circulation at one time. This Act expired March 1, 1862.

MONTGOMERY

The first notes of $50 to $1000 are dated from Montgomery, Ala., which was the Confederate capital until after Virginia seceded and the capital was moved to Richmond on May 24, 1861. This move was made because of the desire to have the capital closer to the field of operations and because the Old Dominion had great prestige among Southern states.

This issue was engraved and printed by the National Bank Note Company in New York. The South, lacking skilled engravers, arranged to have its first notes printed in the North and shipped by express to the South. This was not too difficult considering there were many Southern sympathizers (including Mayor Wood) in New York. Besides, bank note companies have tended to have a business rather than a political basis. As long as the printing is paid for, it does not matter whether the government is an old established one or has just revolted.

Surprising as it may seem, the vignettes used on Confederate notes were not wildly patriotic designs — many notes did not even picture Southern scenes but were vignettes used before in the North. For example, the central design on the $500 note had appeared only a short time before on a $1 note of the North Western Bank of Warren, Pa., so that the design was circulating in the North at the same time it appeared in the South. Vignettes took long hours of engraving work; they could not be lightly cast aside. Each company copyrighted its designs and used them in various combinations on notes of different banks. The first four series of Confederate issues contain many Northern vignettes or copied vignettes.

These notes bear various written dates (usually May or June 1861) and are usually endorsed on the back. They bear the signatures of Alexander B. Clitherall as Register and E. C. Elmore as Treasurer of the Confederacy except for a small number of $500 notes that were signed by C. T. Jones, Acting Treasurer, after Clitherall resigned. First issue notes are on bank note paper and are of only one major variety for each note. This issue is often found cut cancelled, including crisp specimens. Surprisingly, these notes are found in all conditions, although they were intended to be held for the interest they paid. In this connection, they are somewhat in the nature of bonds, but are not bonds (coupon bearing bonds were issued by the Confederate government at the same time), being correctly described as "interest bearing paper money," many examples of which have been issued before and since by various banks and governments.

Engraved by National Bank Note Company

1. $50— Three slaves in cotton field. Black and green. Series A. 1606 issued. Rare.

GOOD	VG	FINE	VF	XF	UNC.
$5,000	$8,000	$12,000	$20,000	$30,000	$100,000

Center vignette later used by Keatinge & Ball on $100 interest-bearing note of 1862 (see No. 42).

More of the $50 note and other denominations may have been printed but the U.S. government seized the plates from the National Bank Note Company.

About Prices

Genuine Confederate and Southern states currency in exceptionally choice condition may command a higher price than indicated by the valuations. General economic changes or the popularity of certain notes may also affect prices.

2. $100— Railroad train at station, Columbia at left. Black and green. Series A. 1606 issued. Rare.

GOOD	VG	FINE	VF	XF	UNC.
$4,000	$6,000	$9,000	$15,000	$20,000	$93,500

The center vignette was being used on a $3 note of the American Bank, Baltimore, Md., at about the same time it appeared on this Confederate note. Both printed by the National Bank Note Co. After the war the train vignette on this note and the $500 denomination counter of the following note were used on a bond of the New Haven, Middletown & Willimantic Railroad Company of Connecticut, dated 1871. The National Bank Note Company also used the Columbia vignette in the 1870s on a $10 Arkansas State note and a modified version on a 10 pesos bank note of the 1870s for El Banco del Pobre of Chile.

3. $500— Cattle being driven down lane to brook as train crosses bridge. This vignette by James Smillie shows his mastery of detail. On sign at left of rider appear the words "Look out for bell rings" (i.e. on approaching trains when using the crossing). Ceres in oval at left. Black and green. Series A. 607 issued. Very rare.

GOOD	VG	FINE	VF	XF	UNC.
$10,000	$13,000	$20,000	$30,000	$45,000	$100,000

The center vignette was in use in the North at the same time on a $1 note of the North Western Bank, Warren, Pa. It was also used on a Little Rock (Arkansas) City Bond $2 note during the 1860s. In the 1870s, the vignette was copied on a $5 note of Bridgeport Furnace Store, Tennessee. Still later, the vignette was copied on checks. One of the most interesting uses of this vignette appears in altered form on a 5 Soles note of La Compania de Obras Publicas y Fomento del Peru, July 4, 1876, which bears the signature of Henry Meiggs, the railroad builder. Several stock certificates and bonds, both U.S. and foreign, have also used this vignette.

The small Ceres vignette was used after the war on a $1.00 Florida State note dated March 1, 1870.

4. $1000— John C. Calhoun at left; Andrew Jackson at right. Both are prewar vignettes, best known in South Carolina and Tennessee. Black and green. Series A. 607 issued. This is the highest denomination of Confederate notes. Very rare.

GOOD	VG	FINE	VF	XF	UNC.
$12,500	$15,000	$20,000	$35,000	$45,000	$95,000

RICHMOND

The Confederate Treasury needed more $50 and $100 notes to be held for their interest by the smaller planters instead of the $500 and $1000 notes that were largely held by banks. Secretary of the Treasury Memminger desired the National Bank Note Co. to print more of the lower denominations, but before this could be accomplished, hostilities broke out. In order to produce notes a Confederate agent was to go to New York to obtain the plates, but the U.S. Government seized them from the National Bank Note Co.

Secretary of the Treasury Memminger thereupon turned to having the needed notes printed in the South. After contacting Samuel Schmidt, manager of the New Orleans branch of the American Bank Note Company, a contract was made on May 13 for the production of $50 and $100 notes. They were completed on August 26, 1861.

In the meantime Schmidt changed the name of the branch to the more agreeable "Southern Bank Note Company" and this imprint appears on the notes that were printed on red fibre paper under the same Act as the Montgomery issue. Written dates (usually August or September 1861). Written signatures of Robert Tyler as Register and E. C. Elmore as Treasurer. Robert Tyler succeeded Clitherall as Register on August 13, 1861. Tyler was a son of John Tyler, 10th President of the United States.

Engraved by Southern Bank Note Company

5. $50— Industry and Agriculture seated on cotton bale. Justice at left, Washington at right. Black and green. Series B. 59=798 issued. Very Scarce.

GOOD	VG	FINE	VF	XF	UNC.
$350	$750	$1,500	$3,500	$4,000	$5,000

Earlier the center vignette had appeared on a $5 note of the Bank of Lexington, N.C. (also others) and after the war on the 10 Fare Ticket issued by the South Carolina Railroad Company, July 1, 1873. Both of these notes bear the imprint of the American Bank Note Company, which indicates the true source of this and other "Southern Bank Note Co." notes.

6. $100— Railroad train rounding bend; Justice at left, Minerva at right. Black and green. Series B. 5798 issued. Very scarce.

GOOD	VG	FINE	VF	XF	UNC.
$500	$1,000	$2,000	$4,000	$5,000	$6,000

The train is a prewar vignette as are others used on the First Issue. Later it was used by Keatinge and Ball on $2 Florida State notes, 1863-64. It is somewhat ironic that this and other Confederate notes depict trains since the railroads were a major weakness of the South. Not only were large sections of the Confederate States without railroads, those that existed used different widths of track. All, of course, were subject to Federal military forays, and as early as June 18, 1861, General Robert E. Lee stressed, "that proper and easy connections of the several railroads . . . should be made as promptly as possible. The want of these connections has severely retarded the operations so far, and they may become more important."

The Southern Bank Note Company had insufficient equipment and only a couple of men for the production of Treasury notes on the scale needed by the Confederate States. To remedy this situation, agents were sent to Europe to procure plates, stones, inks, papers and machinery needed for the production of notes. In addition, engravers, lithographers, and printers were employed.

In the meantime, until enough smaller denomination notes could be produced under the Act of May 16, 1861, the Treasury arranged with Southern banks for a loan of their notes (most banks had their own notes, in use before the war began) for which the Government deposited large denomination Treasury notes of the Montgomery issue or bonds. Under this arrangement the banks loaned over $10,000,000.

Prices of Rarities
Rare notes that are in strong demand tend to rise continuously in price. This is particularly true of the Montgomery issue and certain other notes.

SECOND ISSUE — JULY 25, 1861

The Act of May 16, 1861 authorized treasury notes not exceeding a total of $20 million "fundable in Confederate States stock bearing eight per cent interest," which was payable "two years after date." The Act of July 24, 1861 authorized the Secretary of the Treasury to appoint clerks to assist the Register and Treasurer in signing notes since the quantity was too great for these two men alone. Apparently part of the notes were already printed as some varieties have "for" before "Register" and "Treasr." written instead of printed.

There are many minor varieties and plate letters. Valuations are for notes of the more common varieties. Quantities issued are given as a matter of record, but are not a true indication of value as the paper used in many notes did not wear well; many notes were used in purchase of government bonds, others were replaced by later issues, while still others were simply lost or destroyed.

Engraved by J. Manouvrier

After Secretary of the Treasury Memminger found that Schmidt's Southern Bank Note Co. was inadequately equipped to produce currency quickly or on a large scale, and until engravers and equipment could be obtained from Europe, he turned to what was supposed to be a temporary expedient — the use of lithographic notes. Jules Manouvrier of New Orleans received a portion of the printing work but "flunked" the test. The notes were plainly designed and the banks complained that they were too easily counterfeited. In addition, when the notes were snipped to Richmond, they were carelessly packed and some were stolen. As a result, a $10 note that Manouvrier also prepared was never released for circulation and the Confederate government gave him no further contracts for Treasury notes. He did, however, produce several North Carolina State and Southern bank issues. Manouvrier continued in business after the war, having formed a partnership with P. Snell.

7. $5— Called the Manouvrier note because it is the work of J. Manouvrier, a small printer in New Orleans. Design without illustration. Vertical FIVE at left end. Blue tinted paper. "For" before "Register' and "Treasurer" written. Reverse has plainly printed "Confederate States of America" and value at corners in blue. 15,556 notes of this type were issued. Difficult to obtain better than Fine.

GOOD	VG	FINE	VF	XF	UNC.
$500	$2,500	$4,000	$7,000	---	---

This note was printed in four plate letters: F, G, H and I.

Trying to salvage something from his loss of the Confederate Treasury note business, Manouvrier shortly afterward used the reverse design of this note on the back of a $5 note of the Bank of Whitfield, Ga.

Engraved by Hoyer & Ludwig

All of the following notes of this issue were engraved and printed by Hoyer & Ludwig of Richmond, Va., producer of many of the Confederate postage stamps. Previously engaged as card and poster lithographers, they brought assistants from Baltimore from where they also smuggled paper, and were soon deeply immersed in government work. All printed in black with plain backs.

8. $5— Liberty and eagle in center behind scroll upon which is superimposed the figure "5." Sailor leaning on capstan at lower left. 72,885 notes of this type issued, but not many exist due to poor quality of paper. Price speculative on better grades, which are rare.

GOOD	VG	FINE	VF	XF	UNC.
$300	$500	$2,000	$8,000	—	—

This note comes with two plate letters (B and Bb) with "For" before "Treasr." printed. Existence of these plate letters with "For" written is considered doubtful. Also known stamped with "P" (See No. 11).

Hoyer & Ludwig used a similar central vignette (with figure "2") on a City of Norfolk, Va., note of June 1, 1861. The sailor on the $5 note and Hope with Anchor on the $10 note below were used together by Hoyer & Ludwig on a $1 Traders Bank, Richmond, note of 1861.

9. $10— Center design similar to $5 but with shield containing Confederate flag instead of "5." Hope with Anchor at lower left. The central design is an old one that appeared on many state bank notes and contained the seal of the state in which the bank was located. Hoyer & Ludwig used a similar design on City of Norfolk $2.50 note of June 1, 1861. Total issue was 170,994.

GOOD	VG	FINE	VF	XF	UNC.
$140	$250	$750	$1,500	$4,000	---

There are over 40 minor varieties of this note representing combinations of different plate letters (A, B and C), "For" Treasr. either printed or written, number of stars on flag, bond or plain paper, and differences in the "10" in upper corners. Varieties of this note are very difficult to distinguish.

10. $20— Three-masted sailing ship in center, figure 20 at left. Another old design. Total issue was 264,988.

GOOD	VG	FINE	VF	XF	UNC.
$70	$95	$135	$225	$500	$700

There are 13 varieties of this note due to differences in plate letters (B, C, Cc, Ccc and D), "For" printed or written, plain, bond or thin papers, and differences in the denomination vignettes. Also known stamped with "P" (See No. 11).

11. $50— Bust of George Washington center. Tellus seated at lower left. Total issue was 123,564.

GOOD	VG	FINE	VF	XF	UNC.
$90	$140	$225	$300	$350	$500

Prior to producing this note, Hoyer & Ludwig used these same vignettes in a similar arrangement on a $1.50 note of May 1, 1861 printed for the Southern Manufacturers Bank in Richmond. Subsequently, the vignettes were again used, but in a transposed arrangement on State of Florida notes issued during the fall of 1861.

This note is occasionally found stamped in green with a "C" inside an oval as illustrated. Its exact use is unknown. While several explanations have been advanced, none answer the question of "Why this issue only?" A small capital "P" in green also appears stamped on some of these notes, as well as Nos. 8 and 10. Varieties of this marking and others such as CST and GIC exist, which raises the question of whether they are contemporary markings by Confederate officials. In any case, the most commonly seen are notes stamped with a "C," which increases the value approximately 15% to 20%, while those with "P" are worth an additional 25% or more.

There are nine varieties of this note not including markings described above. These result from differences in plate letters (B, Bb, C), plain, thin or bond papers, and "For" written or printed. There is also a difference in the location of the oval frame of Washington's portrait over the "5" — some 5s are more completely covered. This makes additional minor varieties.

12. $100— Ceres and Prosperine flying to left. Bust of Washington lower left. The central design was used on some prewar state bank notes. Total issue was 37,155.

GOOD	VG	FINE	VF	XF	UNC.
$500	$750	$1,500	$2,000	$2,500	$3,500

There are 7 varieties of this note due to plain, bond or thin paper, varieties of plate letters (B and C) and "For Treasr."

13. $20— Female riding deer. Seated Indian smoking at lower left. Signatures printed instead of written. This is a bogus note and is included in this listing as it is often collected in the Confederate series. There are several varieties. It comes in black printing with shading in red, orange or green, with or without one of seven types of reverse design. See the section on Bogus Notes in Part II for additional information on the background of this note.

GOOD	VG	FINE	VF	XF	UNC,
$60	$90	$150	$200	$275	$375

The above listed prices are for contemporary or early printings, not modern reproductions that show a vertical white line across the center of the note.

About Sizes

The sizes of Confederate States notes may vary slightly, due to differences when the sheets were cut apart, but most are approximately 3 to 3¼ inches by 7 to 7¼ inches in size except Nos. 43-46, which are 2¾ by 61/8 inches. The 50-cent notes (Nos. 57 and 65) are approximately 2¼ by 4¼ inches.

THIRD ISSUE — SEPTEMBER 2, 1861

This series of notes was authorized under the Act of August 19, 1861 and was not to exceed $100 million "outstanding at any one time, including the amount authorized under former acts." This was supplemented by an additional $50 million authorized by the Act of December 24, 1861 while a third Act of April 18, 1862 increased the total by an additional $50 million without reserve, plus $10 million more as a reserve fund, a total of $60 million and a grand total of $210 million. Section 21 of the Act of August 19, 1861 takes cognizance of making or passing counterfeits.

Encouraged by the rout of the Union forces at the First Battle of Bull Run on July 21, this issue states that it is payable "six months after the ratification of a treaty of peace" instead of two years as on the previous issue.

Outside of the difficulty of obtaining competent engraving, the greatest problem of the Confederate Treasury was to obtain sufficient paper. The Confederacy had paper problems from the first and they became greater with this large issue. It is, perhaps, not so remarkable that the treasury issued such a great quantity of paper money, but that it was able to obtain sufficient paper to print all of it. In this day and age when we see new printed matter every day, we are likely to overlook that at the time of the Civil War, paper was not produced in large quantities by present-day methods. Instead of using wood pulp, most paper was made from linen and cotton rags. An editor in Georgia thought it likely that paper could be made from wood pulp, but no one in the South acted upon the idea at the time, although the process had earlier been invented in Europe and had been adopted in the North for envelopes, handbills, and the like. So the 20 paper mills in the South (circa 1863) continued to call for rags, of which they never received enough. Some paper was captured or smuggled from the North, but I mention the matter of paper at this time because the greater part of the smuggled paper came from England and makes its appearance with this series of notes.

In addition to plain and red fibre paper, this issue of notes is found with watermarked paper bearing the following watermarks, several of which identify English-made paper: CSA in block letters; CSA in block letters with wavy borderline; CSA in script letters; J WHATMAN 1862; HODGKINSON & CO WOOKEY HOLE

MILL; FIVE; TEN. There is also a rare watermark of J. Green & Son 1862 (not shown). The NY script is not the usual watermark, but is formed by a thickness in the paper. Reduced size tracings of watermarks are shown below.

In this catalog, notes are grouped by engravers rather than following the sequence of denomination and mix the various engravers' work together. However, except for the multitude of printers for the Third Issue, the arrangement is similar to that of other catalogs arranged by denomination (except that some catalogs start with the highest denomination and work down). Since the Confederate issues do not appear in rigid order until the Fifth Issue, no arrangement is 100% satisfactory.

In grouping notes by engravers, it should be pointed out that by engraving it is meant the firm that engraved the design upon the lithographic stone or plate. Except for the engraved plate work of the National Bank Note Co. and the Southern Bank Note Co., most Confederate notes are printed by the lithographic process, either by the original engraver or by other printers who received plates or transfers from the engravers and helped with the printing. Such notes are not usually distinguishable (especially from the Fifth Issue on) except for imprint of the printer and minor differences. It was comparatively easy to "sublet" the work since most Treasury note printers were located in the same city. With this issue printers began removing their operations from Richmond to Columbia, South Carolina so as to be safe from possible Northern capture of Richmond.

Engraved by Hoyer & Ludwig

14. $5— Slaves loading cotton on steamboat at lower left; "Indian princess" at upper right, by which term this bill has become known. The Indian girl earlier appeared on a $1 note of the Bank of Saline, Mich., in 1837. However, its source was an 1850s note of the Bank of Charleston, S.C. Plate letter Ab. 7,160 issued. Very rare. Usually very worn.

GOOD	VG	FINE	VF	XF	UNC.
$14,000	$25,000	$37,000	$50,000	—	—

15. $10— Liberty, shield and eagle upper left. Shield is blank. (See Nos. 8 and 9.) Another old design is seen in the train and cars at right. Very rare. Usually worn.

GOOD	VG	FINE	VF	XF	UNC.
$6,000	$5,000	$10,000	$45,000	—	—

7,160 were issued of plate letter Ab. Plate letters A9 to AI 6 also exist but were never regularly issued as this type was changed to note No. 20.

16. $20— Ceres seated between Commerce and Navigation. Liberty standing left. Both vignettes are prewar and were also used on several state issues. Black and green. The design generally has a "muddied" appearance, as the green overprint of cherubs becomes worn. Plain and watermarked paper (Ten). Serial letter A. "For" before "Treasr." printed or written. Three varieties. Total issue was 43,732.

GOOD	VG	FINE	VF	XF	UNC.
$350	$600	$1,000	$1,500	$2,300	$4,500

17. $50— Moneta seated beside open treasure chest (another prewar design). The vignette came from plates furnished by the Bank of Charleston, S.C. Two sailors at lower left. Plain paper. 47 minor varieties, which result from plate letters A to E, AD to AL, AI to AI6 and printing differences. 469,660 notes.

GOOD	VG	FINE	VF	XF	UNC.
$40	$260	$450	$100	$250	$500

18. $100— Slaves loading cotton bales on wagon (another old design). Sailor at lower left. Plain paper. Printing differences plus plate letters A to E, CA to OA, AC to AK and Al to A8 account for more than 60 minor varieties. 607,227 notes.

GOOD	VG	FINE	VF	XF	UNC.
$60	$80	$120	$170	$220	$500

For other Hoyer & Ludwig notes, see Nos. 19A, 20A, 21A and 40. Also No. 47. Ludwig did not wish to make the move from Richmond, Va. to Columbia, S.C., figuring to do better at job printing work and such contracts as the Confederate Government might let him have for miscellaneous printing. His major work ends with the Third Issue. In any case, he still had plenty of work producing Virginia bank notes and local script. The partnership of Ludwig Hoyer and Charles L. Ludwig ended in 1865 and shortly afterward a partnership was formed between Ludwig and Edward Keatinge of Keatinge & Ball, which lasted only until 1867, when Keatinge returned to New York.

Engraved by J. T. Paterson

James T. Paterson was a man of varied interests. When the Civil War began he was a dentist in Augusta, Ga. However, when Ludwig indicated his unwillingness to transfer from Richmond, Paterson contacted Treasury Secretary Memminger as to the advisability of purchasing the currency production facilities of Hoyer & Ludwig and whether contracts would be continued on the same terms. After Memminger replied favorably, the purchase was made, and Paterson obtained equipment, engravings and transfers from Ludwig that explains the similarity of their work. Paterson then made the desired move to Columbia, S.C., while maintaining operations in Augusta, Ga. After the war, he engaged in the lumber business.

19. $5— Commerce seated on bale of cotton; sailor at lower left. Another old design. Plain and watermarked papers (CSA block, CSA script). 48 plate letter varieties, A9 to A16. Without series and "Second Series." Beware of alterations of "Third Series" notes, which are rare. See chapter on Counterfeit and Altered Notes. The total issue was 3,694,896 notes.

GOOD	VG	FINE	VF	XF	UNC.
$20	$55	$75	$100	$150	$300

A. Same type by Hoyer & Ludwig. Plain paper, 8 plate letter varieties, A9 to A16.

GOOD	VG	FINE	VF	XF	UNC.
$25	$35	$45	$70	$125	$275

20. $10— Ceres holding an urn, with Commerce seated at left. Paterson had earlier used this pre-war design on a Confederate Certificate under the Act of May 16, 1861. The rest of the design, including the train at right, is identical to No. 15 of Hoyer & Ludwig, showing the close connection of their work. Plain and watermarked paper (CSA block). The watermarked version is scarce. 40 plate letter varieties, A9 to A16. Total issue of both printers was 1,076,738 notes.

GOOD	VG	FINE	VF	XF	UNC.
$25	$40	$50	$90	$175	$400

A. Same type by Hoyer & Ludwig. Plain paper. 48 plate letter varieties, A9 to A16.

GOOD	VG	FINE	VF	XF	UNC.
$30	$45	$60	$650	$850	$1,100

Hoyer & Ludwig had used the Ceres and Commerce vignette on a City of Norfolk, VA. $1 note of June 1, 1861. The Confederate Treasury was not happy about having to use prewar vignettes that were available in the North and this situation was further aggravated by its printers using the same vignettes on other work. But this situation would not change until the Fifth Issue.

21. $20— Three masted sailing ship in center. Sailor leaning on capstan at lower left. (See designs of notes Nos. 8 and 10.) Paterson had used this ship vignette on a Certificate issued under Act of August 19, 1861. Plain paper. 16 plate letter varieties, Al to A8.

GOOD	VG	FINE	VF	XF	UNC.
$75	$125	$200	$350	$700	$1,150

A. Same type by Hoyer & Ludwig.

GOOD	VG	FINE	VF	XF	UNC.
$25	$35	$45	$65	$125	$250

Over 150 minor plate letter varieties with and without flourishes between "Confederate" and "States". The total issue of all varieties of both printers was 2,366,743 notes.

Engraved by Southern Bank Note Company

Although the work of the Southern Bank Note Company was of a superior quality, the rate of production was so slow that the Confederate Government asked that the work be speeded up or move to Richmond and join the other printers. When Schmidt (the manager) failed to do this, his equipment and plates were seized and shipped East under the declaration that the American Bank Note Company was an enemy alien of which the Southern Bank Note Company was a branch. Accordingly, the following notes were the last printed by this firm for the Confederate Treasury.

22. $5— Seated women center representing Commerce, Agriculture, Justice, Liberty and Industry. Minerva at left. Statue of Washington in the state capitol at Boston, Mass., at right. Red and black. Red fibre paper. Three plate letter varieties, A, B and C. 58,860 printed.

GOOD	VG	FINE	VF	XF	UNC.
$250	$400	$800	$2,000	$3,500	$9,000

Prewar vignettes are used on this and the $10 note.

23. $10— Family group of Indians in center. Thetis at left, Indian woman at right holding ear of corn and "X" (for 10). Printed in red and black on red fibre paper. Three plate letter varieties, A, B and C. 58,860 printed.

GOOD	VG	FINE	VF	XF	UNC.
$350	$600	$900	$1,500	$3,500	$6,000

24. $20— Navigation seated beside globe and charts. Minerva at left. Blacksmith at right. Red and black on red fibre paper. Series A. 14,860 printed.

GOOD	VG	FINE	VF	XF	UNC.
$2,500	$3,500	$5,000	$6,000	$10,000	—

The center design earlier appeared on a $5 note of the Ship Builders Bank, Rockland, Maine during the 1850s that was printed by New England Bank Note Co. and Rawdon, Wright, Hatch & Edson (later part of the American Bank Note Co.). Also used on a few other bank notes. The side vignettes are also prewar. After the war, the American Bank Note Co. used the Navigation vignette on exchange drafts of the bank of California. (See illustration on page 76.)

25. $50— Train. Hope with anchor at left. Justice at right. Printed in red and black on red fibre paper. Series A only. 14,860 printed. Very scarce.

GOOD	VG	FINE	VF	XF	UNC.
$2,500	$3,500	$5,000	$9,000	$16,000	—

Surprising as it may seem, the train design was in use at the same time on a $2 note of Westmorland Bank of New Brunswick, Canada. The vignette of Justice is equally surprising since this was subsequently used by the American Bank Note Co. on the back of National Bank Notes of the First Charter Period issued by the U.S. government to represent the arms of the State of Maryland. Because of such recurring use of vignettes owned by the private bank note firms, and other abuses, the U.S. government discontinued their contracts and began printing all of its currency in 1877 at the Bureau of Engraving & Printing.

Engraved by B. Duncan

Col. Blanton Duncan secured engravers and workmen in Europe and opened a printing establishment. His work is not of first quality, but is somewhat more original than that of Hoyer & Ludwig and Paterson. Originally located in Richmond, Duncan shortly afterward moved to Columbia, S.C. As a result, additional varieties were created through the use of both imprints. No. 28 was printed at Richmond, Nos. 27 and 30 bear imprints of both cities, while Nos. 26, 29, 43, 44, 45 and 46 are from Columbia, S.C.

26. $2— Allegorical representation of the Confederacy striking down the Union. Bust of Judah P. Benjamin, Confederate cabinet member, at upper left. 10 plate letter varieties, 1 to 10. These notes are usually found worn.

GOOD	VG	FINE	VF	XF	UNC.
$500	$1,000	$2,250	$8,000	—	—

The date of September 2, 1861 on this note is an error. It should be June 2, 1862 (see No. 45). The date resulted from confusion with the September 2 date on the $5, $10 and $20 notes (Nos. 27-30), which Duncan was then producing. That the date was soon corrected accounts for the scarcity of this note although there are ten plate number varieties. The exact quantity is uncertain, but it is estimated that the issue totals 35,000 or 36,000 notes.

27. $5— Sailor and cotton bales center. Bust of Christopher G. Memminger, Confederate cabinet member, at lower left. Justice and Ceres right. The sailor is a prewar vignette. 16 plate letter varieties: A to H without series from Richmond; 1 to 8 Second Series from Columbia, S.C. 1,003,289 printed.

GOOD	VG	FINE	VF	XF	UNC.
$30	$50	$75	$220	$500	$2,000

28. $10— Slave picking cotton. Landscape and boat scene at right. 8 plate letter varieties (A to H). 286,629 printed.

GOOD	VG	FINE	VF	XF	UNC.
$150	$250	$1,000	$1,500	$2,000	$5,000

29. $10— General Francis Marion offering dinner of sweet potatoes to Sir Banistree Tarleton during Revolutionary War. This vignette is based on the fanciful painting (1836) by John Blake White (1781-1859) entitled "General Marion Inviting a British Officer to Dinner." Bust of Robert R.M.T. Hunter, Confederate cabinet member, at lower left. Minerva at right. The central design earlier appeared on notes of the Bank of the State of South Carolina. During the Reconstruction it was used on the $5 South Carolina state note of 1872.

GOOD	VG	FINE	VF	XF	UNC.
$25	$40	$60	$120	$350	$900

Issued in First, Second, Third and Fourth Series with a total of 34 plate numbers. Second and Third Series lack engraver's imprint. 1,949,465 notes.

About Prices

Genuine Confederate and Southern states currency in exceptionally choice condition may command a higher price than indicated by the valuations. General economic changes or the popularity of certain notes may also affect prices.

30. $20— Industry seated behind large 20 with Cupid and beehive at sides. Vice President Alexander H. Stephens at lower left. Hope with anchor at right. Plain and watermarked paper (CSA script). Counterfeits exist on J Whatman 1862 watermarked paper.

GOOD	VG	FINE	VF	XF	UNC.
$25	$40	$50	$100	$250	$400

Issued in three different series that account for 47 plate number varieties. 2,835,285 notes.

Engraved by Keatinge & Ball

Keatinge & Ball (Richmond, Va., later Columbia, S.C), the firm that eventually became the leading engravers and printers of Confederate notes, began work with this issue. Edward Keatinge was a vignette engraver from Great Britain who was employed by the American Bank Note Co. of New York. Upon offers from the Confederate government, he established a firm in partnership with Thomas A. Ball for the purpose of engraving and printing Confederate money. Since more men were needed, Confederate agents sought experienced lithogravers from England who were given 40 to 60 pounds for travel expense to the British West Indies from where they were brought to the South by blockade runners. The inducements were many, for until Columbia was burned in February 1865, the English lithographers and engravers were among the favored few who were paid in gold under contracts that stipulated $20 per week, plus additions for extra work. By crossing the lines, Keatinge managed to get other printers and equipment and was then in the position to produce a good grade of work, mostly of original designs. The firm concentrated on currency and was a source for many of the notes issued by Southern states and banks during the Civil War, in addition to its work for the Confederate government.

Initially, this firm was a partnership named Leggett, Keatinge & Ball, but on March 12, 1862, Secretary of the Treasury Memminger informed them that Leggett had been seen with a spy and if he were not immediately removed from the firm, the Confederate government would suspend their contract and remove all materials over which they had control. The order was complied with and thereafter the firm was known as Keatinge & Ball. Nos. 31 and 34 of this issue bear the Leggett, Keatinge & Ball imprint; Nos. 32 and 35 bear both imprints; Nos. 33, 36, 37, 38 and 39 bear the Keatinge & Ball imprint. It is thus possible to determine the approximate time of printing.

31. $5— Blacksmith with anvil and tools at right. Boy in oval at lower left. This design is a close copy of a prewar $5 note of the Mechanics Savings Bank of Savannah, Ga. Printed in black and orange/red on plain or red fibre paper. 20,333 printed. Four plate letter (A, AA) and paper varieties.

GOOD	VG	FINE	VF	XF	UNC.
$750	$1,250	$2,000	$4,000	$6,000	—

32. $5— Bust of C. G. Memminger in center. Minerva at right. Ornamentation printed in blue/green or yellow/green. With "V" in lower right corner for 5. Plain and watermarked papers (CSA block, Five, J Whatman 1862). 136,756 notes.

GOOD	VG	FINE	VF	XF	UNC.
$175	$250	$450	$1,200	$2,000	$5,000

Well over 100 plate letter, paper and imprint varieties. Notes with the J Whatman 1862 watermark are scarcer.

About Prices

Genuine Confederate and Southern states currency in exceptionally choice condition may command a higher price than indicated by the valuations. General economic changes or the popularity of certain notes may also affect prices.

33. $5— Similar to No. 32 in black only. "Five" in lower right corner. Plain and water-marked papers (CSA block, CSA script, J Whatman 1862, Hodgkinson & Co. Wookey Hole Mill). 228,664 notes.

GOOD	VG	FINE	VF	XF	UNC.
$75	$125	$200	$350	$600	$1,500

With and without engraver's imprint. 32 plate letter, paper and imprint varieties. Notes with the J Whatman 1862 watermark are scarcer. The Hodgkinson & Co. watermark is rare.

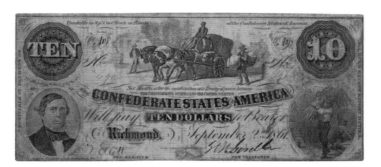

34. $10— Wagon load of cotton bales. Bust of John E. Ward at lower left. Corn gatherers at lower right. This design is copied from a prewar $10 note of the Mechanics Savings Bank of Savannah, Ga. It was not a wise choice, as John E. Ward (who had been bank director, etc.), pictured on the note, was not in favor of the Confederacy and left the South. Possibly the explanation of the use of the $5 and $10 designs of this bank lies in the fact that these notes were produced by predecessors of the American Bank Note Co. by whom Keatinge was formerly employed. It is conceivable that he had transfers of these designs or perhaps they were obtained from the bank. Printed in black and orange/red on plain or red fibre paper. 20,333 printed. Three plate letter (A, A 1) and paper varieties.

GOOD	VG	FINE	VF	XF	UNC.
$1,000	$1,700	$2,700	$4,500	$7,000	—

35. $10— Bust of R. M. T. Hunter at left. Vignette of child at right. Printed in black and orange/red on plain, fibre or watermarked paper (CSA block, CSA script, Ten, J Whatman 1862, NY).

GOOD	VG	FINE	VF	XF	UNC.
$140	$250	$350	$750	$1,1500	$2,500

The child vignette was later used by Keatinge & Ball on a couple of Florida State issues. This vignette has been identified as being that of Dr. Alfred L. Elywn, a Philadelphia minister who was also an abolitionist. Of course, that was when he was no longer a child. 48 plate letter (H to K), paper and imprint varieties. 278,400 notes. Notes with the NY watermark are very scarce.

36. $10— Hope with anchor. Bust of R.M.T. Hunter at lower left and C.G. Memminger at lower right. Plain and watermarked paper (CSA block, J Whatman 1862, Hodgkinson & Co. Wookey Hole Mill). Notes with the J Whatman 1862 watermark are scarce, those with the Hodgkinson & Co. watermark are rare.

GOOD	VG	FINE	VF	XF	UNC.
$40	$150	$225	$350	$600	$1,250

There are 16 plate letter (W to Z) and other varieties of this type. 178,716 notes were issued.

37. $10— Similar to No. 36 except overprinted "X-X" in red or orange. The X (for 10) is shaded in three ways: A. Solid; B. Web; C. Embellished. (See illustrations below.) Printed on plain or watermarked paper (CSA block, CSA script, J Whatman 1862 and Hodgkinson & Co. Wookey Hole Mill). The J Whatman watermark is rare while the Hodgkinson & Co. watermark is very rare. 562,800 notes.

GOOD	VG	FINE	VF	XF	UNC.
$65	$100	$200	$275	$700	$1,500

Variety C (Embellished) is worth 10% more.

| **A. Solid** | **B. Web** | **C. Embellished** |

Specialist's delight. Without series and 2nd Series. There are over 70 varieties due to combinations of "X-X" overprints, plate letters (W to Z), papers, missing dashes, etc. Many of the 2nd Series notes are alterations or counterfeits. Genuine notes of the 2nd Series exist of the variety with Embellished overprint, serial numbers 1 to 12,100.

Important

Where more than one variety was issued of a note, the prices listed are for the more common kinds, not a rare minor variety. Where no value is indicated, the price is speculative due to such notes being rare in higher grades and seldom offered. Most of the illustrations in this catalog are either larger or smaller than the actual specimens.

38. $20— Bust of Alexander H. Stephens against a background representing industry and agriculture. Printed in black and dark or yellow/green. Plain or watermarked paper (NY, CSA block, CSA script, J Whatman 1862). Notes with the J Whatman 1862 watermark are scarce, those with the NY watermark are rare.

GOOD	VG	FINE	VF	XF	UNC.
$150	$250	$700	$1,000	$2,000	$3,000

Unlike all other notes on which the date and capital (Montgomery or Richmond) are clearly indicated, on this note one must search to find it in the small shield at the lower center. 26 different varieties due to plate letter (W to Z), color shade and paper combination. 164,248 notes issued.

39. $50— Bust of Jefferson Davis, President of the Confederate States. Printed in black and green on red fibre or watermarked paper (CSA script, CSA block, J Whatman 1862). The J Whatman 1862 watermarked notes are scarcer. 424,988 notes.

GOOD	VG	FINE	VF	XF	UNC.
$75	$125	$200	$350	$700	$1,500

56 plate letter (WA to ZA), imprint, paper and series varieties. Notes printed on plain paper are counterfeits while the rare notes with plate letters 1A to 4A are believed to be alterations.

FOURTH ISSUE —1862

This issue authorized by the Act of April 17, 1862 contains several interesting features. Section One authorized notes in the denominations of $1 and $2 although by error some $2 notes contain an earlier date of September 2, 1861 (See No. 26). Section Three authorized the $100 interest notes that paid interest at the rate of 2 cents per day or double that of the 1861 Montgomery issue. This was an attempt to reduce circulation as these were held as a temporary investment. Later, by the Act of February 17, 1864, the 100 notes had their status changed to that of bonds. Another oddity of this issue is the $10 note dated September 2, 1862 as well as $10 and $20 "essay" notes of the same date, none of which were authorized by this Act. $165 million of the $100 interest notes, and $5 million of the $1 and $2 notes were authorized. The Act of September 23, 1862, increased the amount of the $1 and $2 notes by an additional $5 million. Due to the lack of coinage, these $1 and $2 notes (and the later 50-cent note) were greatly needed to make change, but the Secretary of the Treasury was reluctant to issue currency in denominations of less than $5. For that reason, there was a large number of state, bank and local issues in fractional denominations.

Engraved by Hoyer & Ludwig

40. $100— Railroad train in center with straight white steam issuing from locomotive. Milkmaid at left. Hoyer & Ludwig earlier used this train design on a Confederate bond, Act of August 19, 1861. Situated in Richmond, they sold out in 1862, so the bulk of this type was printed by J.T. Paterson in Columbia, S.C. Written dates of May 5 to May 9, 1862. 15 plate letter varieties (A, Ab to Ah).

GOOD	VG	FINE	VF	XF	UNC.
$25	$35	$60	$150	$200	$300

A. Same type by J. T. Paterson. Various written dates of 1862. 48 plate letter varieties (Aa to Ah).

GOOD	VG	FINE	VF	XF	UNC.
$15	$30	$50	$65	$80	$100 UPDATE????

The train design is a prewar one used on several notes. It was originally copied from an N. Currier lithograph titled "The Express Train." This print showed the train passing under a bridge, and this vignette may be seen on a $5 note of the Bank of Columbus, Ga., dated 1856. On other notes, the background has been removed or altered to contain a ship, as on these notes.

Engraved by J. T. Paterson

41. $100— Similar to No. 40 except diffused steam issuing from locomotive. New engraving by J. T. Paterson (& Co.). Various written dates of 1862 up to January 8, 1863. Plain and watermarked paper (CSA block, CSA script). 48 plate letter varieties, Aa to Ah. The script CSA watermark (in reverse) shows through the illustrated note.

GOOD	VG	FINE	VF	XF	UNC.
$20	$30	$50	$100	$150	$300

The train design on these notes was also used on Civil War period notes of Corporation of Charlottesville, Va.; Virginia Central Railroad; New Orleans, Jackson & Great Northern Railroad; a $20 note of North Carolina, March 1, 1862; and $1 of Georgia, January 1, 1863 and April 6, 1864. Last was printed by Howell. The total issued of both types (Nos. 40 and 41) was 559,200, fairly evenly divided. These notes are sometimes found with a plate engraver's name such as Cammann in the margin. This also occurs on certain other notes but most frequently on Nos. 40 and 41. The value of notes bearing engraver's name is increased by 10%.

Engraved by Keatinge & Ball

42. $100— Slaves hoeing cotton. John C. Calhoun at left, Columbia at right. The central design is copied from the $50 note of 1861 (No. 1). The scrolls in the upper corners come in two different styles, vertical and horizontal (see illustration). Black with "Hundred" in orange/red. Various written dates August 1862 to January 8, 1863. Plain and watermarked paper (CSA block, CSA script, J Whatman 1862, Hodgkinson & Co. Wookey Hole Mill). The J Whatman 1862 and Hodgkinson & Co. watermarks are scarcer. The scroll varieties are of approximately the same value.

A. Vertical Scroll   **B. Horizontal Scroll**

GOOD	VG	FINE	VF	XF	UNC.
$40	$55	$100	$150	$200	$250

Over 70 plate letter (W to Z), scroll, date and paper varieties. If frame line varieties are included, the number increases considerably.

An example of the CSA block watermark shows through the back of the $100 note pictured below.

    All of the $100 interest-bearing notes generally bear interest paid markings on the back, usually straight line type with or without a rectangular border. Prices are listed for this type. Markings of certain cities that are infrequently seen are worth somewhat more. Notes bearing postmarks on the back are worth double or more (Charleston, S.C. is the most common) while other circular depository markings raise value of notes up to 25%. Notes bearing Army or Navy markings on back are worth triple. Some notes bear no markings on reverse, but they command little over the listed prices. Notes with printed bogus backs, which are described in Part II of this catalog, are worth about double in nice condition. Thian gives a total of 670,400 notes of this type, a figure that appears to be greater than it should be for this type since it is somewhat scarcer than the train types, although all are common.

Engraved by B. Duncan

43. $1— June 2, 1862. Steam-sailing ship. At left a figure said to represent Liberty but which is more likely a nondescript product of the artist's imagination. Lucy Holcombe Pickens at lower right. Mrs. Pickens was the wife of F. W. Pickens, governor of South Carolina during 1860-62, and widely known in the Confederacy.

GOOD	VG	FINE	VF	XF	UNC.
$40	$50	$85	$140	$200	$400

First, Second and Third Series (32 plate number varieties).

44. $1— Same type as No. 43 but overprinted "1" and "One" in green.

GOOD	VG	FINE	VF	XF	UNC.
$50	$85	$200	$500	$1,100	$2,000

First and Second Series (20 plate number varieties). Thian's Register gives a total of 2,102,200 notes of Nos. 43 and 44 of which about one-fourth have the green overprint. This note is usually found worn.

45. $2— June 2, 1862. Allegorical representation of the Confederacy striking down the Union. (Actually, Hercules liberating Prometheus by killing the vulture that was eating his liver — from Greek mythology.) Bust of Judah P. Benjamin, Confederate cabinet member, at upper left. (See also No. 26.)

GOOD	VG	FINE	VF	XF	UNC.
$25	$40	$60	$100	$160	$300

43 varieties in First, Second and Third Series.

46. $2— Same type as No. 45 but with overprinted "2" and "Two" in green. Usually found worn.

GOOD	VG	FINE	VF	XF	UNC.
$40	$150	$400	$1,500	$9,000	$14,000

11 plate number varieties (Second Series). Thian indicates that 1,749,600 notes were issued of Nos. 45 and 46 of which more than 85% were of No. 45.

The Enigmatical Issues

The following three notes are called the "enigmatical issues" because there are many unanswered questions concerning them. All three notes are dated September 2, 1862 but no notes of that date were authorized. It probably should have been September 2, 1861. The $10 (No. 47) was regularly issued, but the $10 and $20 (Nos. 48 and 49) were not. Therefore, like No. 13 (Female Riding Deer note) need not be included in a type set of regularly issued notes. This is probably just as well as Nos. 48 and 49 are rare and difficult to obtain. They are included in this catalog due to their interest to collectors. For a discussion of these notes see Part II of this catalog.

47. $10— September 2, 1862. Commerce reclining on cotton bale; ships in background. Bust of R. M. T. Hunter, Confederate cabinet member, at lower right.

GOOD	VG	FINE	VF	XF	UNC.
$30	$50	$90	$150	$300	$600

635,250 notes issued. Variety (A) reads "Six Month after"; Variety (B) reads "Six Months after." Eight plate letters (I to P) used for each. Same value for both.

The center design is an earlier vignette, an example of which may be seen on a $1 note of the Bank of Chicago, Illinois. Printed by Hoyer & Ludwig although the note does not bear their imprint. However, the name Ludwig is concealed beneath the cotton bale.

48. $10— September 2, 1862. Ceres seated amid agricultural produce. Bust of R. M. T. Hunter, Confederate cabinet member, at lower right. Plate letter N. Rare.

GOOD	VG	FINE	VF	XF	UNC.
$3,500	$5000	$6,000	$8,000	—	—

The center vignette is an old one, examples being a $3 note of the North River Banking Co. of New York, 1840, the work of Durand and Co., and a $6 note of the Peoples Bank of Patterson, N.J., produced by a later Durand firm. At about the same time Endicott and Clark used the vignette on $1 Republic of Texas notes, 1839-41. It is also to be found on a $3 note of the Merchants Bank, Salem, Mass., October 8, 1854 that is said to be a spurious note made up from cuts sold by W. L. Ormsby.

49. $20— September 2, 1862. Liberty with shield. Bust of R. M. T. Hunter, Confederate cabinet member, at lower right. Plate letter N. Rare.

GOOD	VG	FINE	VF	XF	UNC.
$2,000	$3,000	$4,000	$6,000	—	—

The engraver may have obtained the inspiration for the central design from the Liberty seated vignette prepared by Paquet for U.S. pattern coins in 1859. Although Liberty faces in the opposite direction on the coins, there is a great deal of similarity, including the shield and fasces. However, acceptance of a design bearing the U.S. shield hardly seems likely. This vignette was copied about 1865 by Henry Seibert & Bros. on a stock certificate of the First National City Bank of Brooklyn.

Nos. 48 and 49 bear the erroneous imprint of Keatings and Ball, Columbus, S.C., instead of Keatinge and Ball, Columbia, S.C. The notes are not believed to have been printed by them.

Both notes are printed on a bluish parchment-like bank note paper that may turn brownish with age. Also noted on a thin rice paper, similar to some prewar bank notes, which appear to be of the same printing. The use of these distinctive papers, rather than paper generally used for Confederate notes, tends to indicate that these notes were originally prepared for some special use. The quality of the engraving and printing compares favorably with other Hoyer & Ludwig, Paterson and Duncan notes. I have, however, seen Nos. 48 and 49 on which the printing presents a ragged appearance. This is either from having been wet at one time, or the notes may be reproductions made in recent years to sell at a high price.

Nos. 48 and 49 have printed signatures. Usually they bear serial numbers written in red, of approximately the 2,500 and 5,600 range, but generally in the 5,000s. Interestingly, only about thirty of these notes were known in the 1960s. Since then, more have been reported, bringing the total to approximately one hundred for the two notes. The majority are $20 notes.

FIFTH ISSUE — DECEMBER 2, 1862

Under the Act of October 13, 1862, $90 million in Treasury notes were authorized, but upward of $140 million were actually issued by utilizing previous legislation. By having all denominations engraved by Keatinge & Ball instead of each printer originating their own designs, the Confederacy finally had a uniform currency that was less subject to confusion (and counterfeiting). Part of the lithographic and printing work on the lower values continued to be done by other firms. B. Duncan helped produce the $1, $10 and $20; J. T. Paterson & Co., $2, $5 and $ 20; and Evans & Cogswell, $5 and $10. Notes produced by these firms carry their imprint in addition to that of Keatinge & Ball. Some lower denominations with only the Keatinge & Ball imprint are believed to have been printed by Hoyer & Ludwig and George Dunn of Richmond. There are certain inconsistencies since portions of some denominations may have been printed by firms other than those named on the notes.

With the addition of Evans & Cogwell to its printers, the Confederate government enlisted the aid of one of the largest publishing houses in the South. Located in Charleston and Columbia, S.C., they had 76 printing presses plus other equipment for book publishing as well as their printing work for the Confederate Army and Treasury. Over 300 persons were employed of whom 74 were from Europe. This number apparently included officers and workmen in addition to printers since it has been stated that each press was operated by a printer who had two slaves as helpers.

(Unlike many firms in the South that were ruined when the Civil War ended, Evans & Cogswell continued in business under the name of Walker, Evans & Cogswell until 1990 when they became bankrupt.)

Engraved by Keatinge & Ball

50. $1— Bust of Clement C. Clay, Confederate senator. Plain back. Pink paper.

GOOD	VG	FINE	VF	XF	UNC.
$40	$60	$125	$175	$200	$250

A total of 1,141,200 notes were issued. Imprinted 1st and 2nd Series and without series. 35 or more plate letter varieties (A to 1). Both the $1 and $2 notes were to have reverse designs but this would have required additional press work and expense while the Confederacy was already hard pressed to meet the demand for currency.

51. $2— Large "2" in center. Bust of Judah P. Benjamin, Confederate cabinet member, at right. Plain back. Pink paper.

GOOD	VG	FINE	VF	XF	UNC.
$30	$50	$100	$130	$150	$200

Imprinted 1st and 2nd Series and without series. 60 or more plate letter varieties, A, B to I. 603,000 notes.

52. $5— Capitol of the Confederate States (Virginia State Capitol, Richmond). Bust of C. G. Memminger, Confederate cabinet member, at lower right. Blue ornate reverse with denomination. Pink paper.

GOOD	VG	FINE	VF	XF	UNC.
$20	$40	$50	$90	$125	$175

Imprinted 1st, 2nd and 3rd Series. 90 plate letter (A to H) and printing firm varieties. 2,833,600 notes. 1st Series notes with J. T. Paterson & Co. imprint on white paper, unsigned, and without numbers are considered samples.

53. $10— South Carolina State Capitol, Columbia. Bust of R. M. T. Hunter, Confederate cabinet member, at lower right. Blue ornate reverse with denomination. Pink paper.

GOOD	VG	FINE	VF	XF	UNC.
$20	$40	$50	$90	$125	$175

Issued in four series with a total of 90 or more plate letter (A to H) and printing firm varieties. 3,060,000 notes. The view of the State House was based on the architect's design. Due to the Civil War, the tower had not yet been added. After the war, a dome was substituted.

54. $20— Tennessee State Capitol, Nashville. Bust of Alexander H. Stephens, Vice-President of the Confederate States, at lower right. Blue ornate reverse with denomination. Pink paper.

GOOD	VG	FINE	VF	XF	UNC.
$100	$200	$350	$500	$750	$1,150

1st Series only. Face of tower on capitol with and without shading. 56 plate letter (A to H) and printing firm varieties. 707,200 notes. This note (and those of the same design issued in 1863 and 1864) picture a capitol building that was not in Confederate hands. Nashville was occupied by Union forces on February 25, 1862 and held throughout the war.

55. $50— Bust of Jefferson Davis, President of the Confederate States. Printed in black and green. Green ornate reverse with denomination. Plain and watermarked paper (CSA script, CSA block, CSA block with wavy borderline, J Whatman 1862, Hodgkinson & Co. Wookey Hole Mill). The J Whatman 1862 watermark is scarce, the Hodgkinson & Co. watermark is rare on this note.

GOOD	VG	FINE	VF	XF	UNC.
$75	$200	$300	$450	$800	$1,300

56 varieties resulting from different plate letters (WA to ZA), papers, flourishes in design, and position of printer's imprint. 364,800 notes. All are 3rd series.

56. $100— "Women of the South" as represented by Lucy H. Pickens. Two soldiers at lower left. Bust of George W. Randolph, Confederate Secretary of War during 1862, at lower right. Interestingly, Randolph was no longer a cabinet member by the time this note appeared. Not only that, the portrait is on the $100 denomination, placing him "above" President Davis. Plain and watermarked paper (CSA block with wavy borderline, J Whatman 1862, Hodgkinson & Co. Wookey Hole Mill). The J Whatman 1862 and Hodgkinson & Co. watermarks are rare.

GOOD	VG	FINE	VF	XF	UNC.
$100	$200	$250	$350	$450	$600

Without series and 2nd Series. 20 plate letter (A to D) and paper varieties. 609,040 notes.

For years the woman appearing on the $100 note was called Mrs. Jefferson (Varina) Davis and, occasionally, still is since it was so listed in Bradbeer's book (1915), which is still being used. Then, in 1917-19 H.D. Allen published a series of articles on Confederate currency in *The Numismatist,* which contained much research into sources of designs, The result was that he pronounced the lady appearing on the $100 note as being Mrs. Lucy H. Pickens.

Why was it, then, that such early researchers and authors as Lee, Haseltine, Massamore and Thian, so soon after the Civil War, all called the portrait Mrs. Davis? As they had access to much original material, it stands to reason that if the portrait was generally known as Mrs. Pickens, they would have listed it as Mrs. Pickens as they did the $1 note (Nos. 43 and 44). Since they did not, I believe that people in general did not know who the vignette represented.

H.D. Allen's research discloses that Mrs. Pickens' relatives and friends recognized her on the $100 note but others must have named the subject as being Mrs. Davis unless these first researchers simply deduced it to be her from portraits. For, while Mr. Allen appears overly determined to prove that the portrait is that of Mrs. Pickens, he may be correct. Nevertheless, in fairness to those who considered the portrait to be that of Mrs. Davis, there are photographs of her that show features that could be confused with the one on the $100 note that has been identified as being Mrs. Pickens.

As a part of my continued research, I have tried to locate a photograph of Mrs. Pickens that shows her wearing a wreath, but so far I have not been successful. I did locate a photograph of Mrs. Virginia Tunstall Clay with a similar hair arrangement and wearing a wreath, except that it is a frontal view rather than a profile. It's unfortunate that H.D. Allen never sought to question her since she and her husband, Clement C. Clay, were close friends of President Davis and his wife. Mrs. Clay, who became known as "A Belle of the South," was strongly opposed to the North and lived until 1915, shortly before Allen's articles were published. While this may not alter the proofs obtained by Allen, Mrs. Clay's portrait does show that the wearing of a wreath for some special purpose was not unknown in the South. Should it ever be proven that the portrait is really Mrs. Clay, "A Belle of the South," then I wouldn't be far wrong having claimed for years that the portrait represents "Women of the South."

There were many patriotic Confederate women who were highly esteemed. All the tales of Southern chivalry are not figments of the imagination, And why not? Besides helping the army in various ways, notably by making clothing, women even raised money to build gun boats. Some signed themselves as "Daughters of the Confederacy." Inasmuch as a study of the period will show them to have been quite worthy of recognition, I do not consider it unlikely that while Mrs. Pickens was used as a model, she was really intended as a personification of "Women of the South."

I offer an example by quoting a letter from a Confederate military company in Virginia that was published in the Camden (S.C.) Confederate newspaper early in 1863: "Ladies: Your much needed present of blankets and clothing was received on the third of January. Again we have the pleasure of returning our thanks for so kindly remembering us, far away from you and our homes. After this war is ended, whenever we shall think of the hardships and dangers we have gone through, we will ever recollect with grateful hearts the noble devotion of the women of our land, in behalf of the poor private soldier, fighting for them and his country, hoping for no other reward than their praise. And if again we are called upon to meet the enemy in battle, the thoughts of you and your heroic devotion to the sacred cause of our country, will nerve our hearts and arms to strike with tenfold vigor, and we trust with the assistance of God to drive his poluting footsteps from our soil and restore peace once more to our bleeding and unhappy country."

SIXTH ISSUE — APRIL 6, 1863

In spite of the desire of the government to issue more bonds and reduce paper money circulation, people continued to demand more currency, which resulted in further inflation. That the government was unable to stay the ever increasing production of the printing presses is vividly illustrated by the Act of March 23, 1863, which authorized this issue: The $5 to $100 notes could be issued in amounts not exceeding $50 million monthly; plus a total of $15 million of the 50 cents, $1 and $2 notes (for the entire issue).

The Confederacy had not yet been defeated at Gettysburg and Vicksburg when this issue first appeared, but the pressure of the war was making itself felt. With this issue all except the three lower values again carried the clause indicating that payment of the notes would be made "two years after the ratification of a treaty of peace."

The 50 cents, $1 and $2 notes have plain backs, while the higher denominations have ornate backs of the same type used on the issue of December 2, 1862. It will be noted that the $5 to $100 notes are overprinted with the month and year they were issued. The reason for this is that these notes could be funded into 6% bonds if done within 12 months of the first day of the month stamped on the notes. If not funded into bonds within that time limit, these notes were payable without interest two years after a treaty of peace. Actually, had the Confederacy survived, notes of this and earlier issues would have been worth less than that due to the provisions of the act authorizing the next issue of February 17, 1864.

The above illustration of the reverse of the $10 note is shown here to give an example of the ornate style of reverse used on the December 2, 1862 and April 6, 1863 issues.

Engraved by Archer & Daly

In 1861, John Archer of New York came to Richmond, Virginia where he formed a partnership with Joseph Daly for the production of Confederate postage stamps due to the uncertainty of getting stamps and plates from De La Rue & Co. of England through the blockade. The two main engravers were John Archer and (later) Frederick Halpin, both from the North. The 50 cents is the only paper money printed by this firm for the Confederacy, although they also produced several bonds in addition to postage stamps.

57. 50 cents— Profile head of Jefferson Davis, president of the Confederate States. This is the same design as used on the 10 cents postage stamp (Scott No. 9-12) and was engraved by Halpin. Printed signatures. Pink paper.

GOOD	VG	FINE	VF	XF	UNC.
$10	$20	$25	$30	$45	$75

1st and 2nd Series. 36 plate letter varieties (A to I), with and without flourishes above letter. The serial numbers were stamped in both large and small size. 1,831,517 notes.

The 50-cent note of this and the 1864 issue are the only regularly issued Confederate notes to bear printed signatures although there was a demand for printed signatures on higher values as well. This was hardly an unreasonable demand when we consider the amount of labor and time lost in signing two signatures to millions of pieces of paper money. The closest parallel that comes to mind is that of the Continental Currency of the Revolution, which fared no better although it was similarly hand signed. The idea of hand signing notes was to help prevent counterfeiting but since such a large number of persons was required to sign all of the notes, the mass of signatures merely became confusing.

Engraved by Keatinge & Ball

Except for the $500 note, all denominations were engraved by Keatinge & Ball and the designs are similar to the issue of December 2, 1862. Other firms helping to print the notes were B. Duncan, $10; J. T. Paterson & Co., $5, $10 and $20; Evans & Cogswell, $1, $2, $5, $10 and $20. Work on the higher denominations was never sublet.

The number of printing varieties of the April 6, 1863 issue is extensive as indicated by the descriptions following each note. Some of these varieties are rare but the majority are of similar value. As indicated elsewhere in this catalog, prices are for the more common kinds.

Prices of Rarities

Rare notes that are in strong demand tend to rise continuously in price. This is particularly true of the Montgomery issue and certain other notes.

58. $1— Bust of Clement C. Clay, Confederate senator. Plain back. Pink paper.

GOOD	VG	FINE	VF	XF	UNC.
$20	$35	$50	$80	$100	$175

1st and 2nd Series and without series. Over 110 plate letter (A to H) and printer's imprint varieties. 1,645,800 notes.

59. $2— Large "2" in center. Bust of Judah P. Benjamin, Confederate cabinet member, at right. Plain back. Pink paper.

GOOD	VG	FINE	VF	XF	UNC
$40	$75	$125	$275	$400	$700

1st and 2nd Series and without series. 32 plate letter (A to H) and printer's imprint varieties. 689,600 notes.

Important

Where more than one variety was issued of a note, the prices listed are for the more common kinds, not a rare minor variety. Where no value is indicated, the price is speculative due to such notes being rare in higher grades and seldom offered. Most of the illustrations in this catalog are either larger or smaller than the actual specimens.

60. $5— Capitol of the Confederate States (Virginia State Capitol, Richmond). Bust of C. G. Memminger, Confederate cabinet member, at lower right. Blue ornate reverse with denomination. Plain and watermarked paper (CSA Block, CSA block letters with wavy borderline, J Whatman 1862, Hodgkinson & Co. Wookey Hole Mill). J Whatman 1862 and Hodgkinson & Co. watermarked notes are scarcer.

GOOD	VG	FINE	VF	XF	UNC.
$15	$25	$35	$45	$75	$150

Overprinted at right with month of issue, April 1863 to February 1864. 1st, 2nd and 3rd Series and without series. More than 180 plate letter (A to H), printer's imprint and paper variety combinations. If date overprints and other minor varieties are included, the number is greatly increased. 7,745,600 notes.

61. $10— South Carolina State Capitol, Columbia. Bust of R. M. T. Hunter, Confederate cabinet member, at lower right. Blue ornate reverse with denomination. Plain and watermarked paper (CSA block letters with wavy borderline, CSA block, J Whatman 1862, Hodgkinson & Co. Wookey Hole Mill). J Whatman 1862 and Hodgkinson & Co. watermarks are very scarce. A very rare variety is known on paper watermarked J. Green & Son 1862.

GOOD	VG	FINE	VF	XF	UNC.
$20	$30	$40	$60	$100	$225

Overprinted at right with month and issue, April 1863 to February 1864. 1st, 2nd, 3rd, 4th and 5th Series and without series. Over 160 plate letter (A to H), imprint and paper variety combinations. If date overprints are included, the number is much higher. 7,420,800 notes. Beware of fake series numbers on certain notes of this issue.

62. $20— Tennessee State Capitol, Nashville. Bust of Alexander H. Stephens, vice-president of the Confederate States, at lower right. Blue ornate reverse with denomination. Plain and watermarked paper (CSA block, CSA block with wavy borderline, J Whatman 1862 and Hodgkinson & Co. Wookey Hole Mill). The J Whatman and Hodgkinson watermarks are very rare.

GOOD	VG	FINE	VF	XF	UNC.
$15	$25	$40	$100	$200	$300

Overprinted at right end with month of issue, April 1863 to October 1863. 1st, 2nd and 3rd Series and without series. Over 100 plate letter (A to H), printer's imprint and paper variety combinations. As usual, date overprints and minor varieties increase this number considerably. 4,428,000 notes.

63. $50— Bust of Jefferson Davis, president of the Confederate States. Printed in black and green. Green ornate reverse and denomination. Plain and watermarked paper (CSA block with wavy borderline). Also J Whatman 1862 (very rare).

GOOD	VG	FINE	VF	XF	UNC.
$50	$75	$100	$150	$160	$270

Overprinted at right end with month of issue, April 1863 to February 1864. Without series and 1st Series. More than 60 plate letter (WA to ZA), paper and other varieties. If date overprints are included, the number is larger. 2,324,000 notes.

64. $100— "Women of the South" as represented by Lucy H. Pickens. Two soldiers at lower left. Bust of George W. Randolph, Confederate cabinet member, at lower right. Green ornate reverse with denomination. Watermarked paper (CSA block letters with wavy borderline).

GOOD	VG	FINE	VF	XF	UNC.
$50	$90	$170	$225	$300	$400

Overprinted at right end with month of issue, April 1863 to January 1864. Without series and 1st Series. The "2nd Series" is a spurious overprint on genuine notes originally issued without overprint. Unwatermarked counterfeits also exist of this note. 12 plate letter varieties (A to D). There are also more than 70 date overprint varieties. 1,931,600 notes.

Above is the style of back used on notes of the February 17, 1864 issue.

SEVENTH ISSUE — FEBRUARY 17, 1864

Under the Act of February 17, 1864, a new issue of notes was authorized that was printed in unlimited quantities (probably about 1 billion dollars). All earlier notes were to be retired after being funded into bonds by certain dates after which any remaining notes were to be taxed out of existence. Apparently this converse effort to reduce circulation was not too successful judging by the number of earlier issues still in existence. By this time the value of the Confederate dollar was so low that it didn't matter much whether one redeemed the notes in equally inflated bonds or not. Circulating side by side, one issue was worth as much as the other.

The 1864 bonds given in exchange for redeemed notes were not immediately available from the printers while at later times the supply of bonds at a given depository might be insufficient to equal the quantity of notes to be exchanged. To meet this exigency Section 2 of this Act provided for certificates to be given in lieu of bonds. These Certificates of Deposit could later be exchanged for bonds or could be used as a form of money in payment of taxes. These certificates come in several varieties and read, "This will Certify That ____ has paid in at this office ____ Dollars, for which amount Registered Bonds, of the Confederate States of America, bearing interest from this date, at the rate of four per cent per annum, will be issued to him, under the 'Act to reduce the currency, and authorize a new issue of notes and bonds,' approved February 17, 1864, upon surrender of this Certificate at this office." Other certificates in fixed amounts such as $500 and $1000 state that "In pursuance of the authority (etc.)."

The $1 to $500 notes of this issue have a reddish-pink web background on the obverse. The 50 cents, $1, $2 and $500 notes have plain backs while the other values have blue backs. Except for the $10 and $500 notes the obverse designs are similar to the issue of April 6, 1863.

Raphael P. Thian, who compiled the "Register of Confederate Debt," was unable to obtain complete data for the 1864 issue. Accordingly, the figures given in this catalog, which are based on his records, are somewhat less than the actual amount believed to have been issued of these last notes of the Confederacy.

Engraved by Archer & Halpin

Originally Archer & Daly, the firm was reorganized under the names of the two engravers, John Archer and Frederick Halpin.

65.   50 cents— Profile head of Jefferson Davis, president of the Confederate States. (See No. 57.) Printed signatures. Plain back. Pink paper.

GOOD	VG	FINE	VF	XF	UNC.
$15	$20	$25	$30	$45	$75

1st and 2nd Series with a total of 18 plate letter (A to I) varieties. 1,047,212 notes (incomplete data).

Engraved by Keatinge & Ball

The only work sublet for this issue was to Evans & Cogswell who helped print the $1, $2, $5 and $10 notes. As with the preceding issue, the bulk of the work remained in the hands of Keatinge and Ball.

66. $1— Bust of Clement C. Clay, Confederate senator. However, at the time this note was being circulated he was a Confederate agent in Canada. Pink and black. Plain paper.

GOOD	VG	FINE	VF	XF	UNC.
$30	$45	$70	$100	$125	$175

Over 70 plate letter varieties (A to H), most of them minor. 598,400 notes (incomplete data).

67. $2— Large "2" in center. Bust of Judah P. Benjamin, Confederate cabinet member, at right. Pink and black. Plain paper.

GOOD	VG	FINE	VF	XF	UNC.
$25	$35	$75	$90	$100	$150

64 plate letter varieties (A to H), most of them minor. 822,392 notes (incomplete data).

68. $5— Capitol of the Confederate States (Virginia State Capitol, Richmond). Bust of C.G. Memminger, Confederate cabinet member, at lower right. Pink and black. Blue web reverse with denomination. Plain paper.

GOOD	VG	FINE	VF	XF	UNC.
$15	$25	$35	$50	$75	$100

Issued in Series 1 to 7 and without series for a total of 64 plate letter varieties (A to H). 5,525,264 notes (incomplete data). One of these notes was found in President Lincoln's wallet after his assassination.

69. $10— Field artillery. Bust of R. M. T. Hunter, Confederate cabinet member, at lower right. Pink and black. Blue web reverse with denomination. Plain paper.

GOOD	VG	FINE	VF	XF	UNC.
$15	$20	$25	$45	$60	$85

This is the most commonly available Confederate note today. Issued in Series 1 to 10 and without series. Over 120 plate letter varieties (A to H) plus many insignificant differences in plate letters. 9,135,920 notes (incomplete data).

The design is said to represent Braxton Bragg's artillery at the Battle of Buena Vista in 1847 during the War with Mexico. If correct, it is apparently based on a portion of a contemporary painting by Carl Nebel, except from a different angle. Bragg became a Confederate general during the Civil War.

70. $20— Tennessee State Capitol, Nashville. Bust of Alexander H. Stephens, vice president of the Confederate States, at lower right. Pink and black. Blue web reverse with denomination. Plain paper.

GOOD	VG	FINE	VF	XF	UNC.
$20	$25	$35	$50	$75	$90

Issued in 11 series and without series. More than 100 plate letter varieties (A to D), which include differences in flourishes above "Confederate States of America." 4,297,004 notes (incomplete data).

71. $50— Bust of Jefferson Davis, president of the Confederate States. Pink and black. Blue web reverse with denomination. Plain paper.

GOOD	VG	FINE	VF	XF	UNC.
$30	$40	$50	$60	$80	$120

Issued in Series 1 to 4 and without series. With and without flourish over "Con" of "Confederate," making a total of 36 plate letter varieties (WA to ZA). 1,671,444 notes (incomplete data).

72. $100— "Women of the South" as represented by Lucy H. Pickens. Two soldiers at lower left. Bust of George W. Randolph, Confederate cabinet member, at lower right. Pink and black. Blue web reverse with denomination. Plain paper.

GOOD	VG	FINE	VF	XF	UNC.
$35	$50	$75	$85	$100	$150

Series I and II and without series. 12 plate letter varieties (A, B, C, D of each). There are probably over 100 minor varieties due to differences in engraving and size of notes within frame line. Some have attributed the difference in size to paper shrinkage but this would hardly cause more than 1/8 inch difference while some notes may be as much as 5/16 inch shorter, others are sizes in-between, with less pronounced differences in width. Since the words "For Register" and "For Treasurer," etc. can be found spaced in many different ways, along with differences in dashes, it is obvious that the different sizes are not the result of paper shrinkage but were differently engraved. Similar differences have been found on the $100 notes of 1862 and 1863 (Nos. 56 and 64) but those of this issue are better known. 896,644 notes (incomplete data).

Smaller size counterfeit with plate letter D

There is also a $100 note popularly known as the "Havana counterfeit" that appears in D plate letter only and is approximately 1/4 inch smaller in both width and length. Specimens in new condition can be readily distinguished from genuine notes by the size, engraving differences, and hazy blue back. But used notes tend to take on a "real" look. When in doubt check these points: Genuine notes have two dots under the "th" of 17th in the date, the false note has one; genuine notes have a tiny "spear" sticking downward from Randolph's cravat against his shirt front; this spear does not appear on false notes. Mrs. Pickens' lips have a more puckered appearance. The false note is one of the more interesting counterfeits and is often included in type collections. It usually sells for about $35 in Fine to Very Fine condition and $75 when Uncirculated. (Counterfeits were also printed in Havana of the $50 (No. 71) and $500 (No. 73) but it is the $100 note that is the most famous. In fact, it was listed as a genuine note in Bradbeer's catalog.)

73. $500— Bust of Lieut. General T. J. ("Stonewall") Jackson at lower right. Confederate flag and seal atop war implements at left. Pink and black. (Not rare but its popularity with collectors has caused it to rise in price.)

GOOD	VG	FINE	VF	XF	UNC.
$150	$200	$325	$450	$600	$800

Shades of pink vary on notes of this denomination. Red notes are usually valued higher than those of lighter shades. The illustrated note shows a portion of the palmetto shield overprint at the upper right comer. Four varieties, plate letters A to D. 150,428 notes (incomplete data).

Notes of 1864 are occasionally found stamped in red with a portion of a shield bearing a palmetto tree at the corner of the notes. This was the seal of the Treasury Department. Specimens bearing this control mark are worth up to 25% more for $20 to $500 notes and 25% to 50% more for $1 to $10 notes. Double for 50 cents notes. A few 1863 notes were similarly stamped (apparently the control mark on corner of sheet, which is the reason it does not appear on all notes, was first used about the beginning of 1864 and its use on 1863 notes represents late printings of that issue). 1863 notes so stamped are worth double. Very likely this stamp marking was intended as a means of detecting theft of paper stock and notes, either by workmen (not an uncommon thing at that time) or in case of loss during shipment.

As for the colors of the 1864 notes, which vary from pale pink to deep red, this could have resulted from printing presses running low on ink or the inability of obtaining ink of consistent quality during the late days of the war and then only at intervals as indicated by serial number sequences. One thing that was consistent was the surprising ability of the Treasury to obtain dual signers of this and other notes to the last.

About Sizes

The sizes of Confederate States notes may vary slightly, due to differences when the sheets were cut apart, but most are approximately 3 to 3¼ inches by 7 to 7¼ inches in size except Nos. 43-46, which are 2¾ by 61/8 inches. The 50-cent notes (Nos. 57 and 65) are approximately 2¼ by 4¼ inches.

THE COMPLETE HISTORICAL SET OF CONFEDERATE NOTES OF
FEBRUARY 17th, 1864.
———— ...ALL CLEAN AND CRISP. ————

50 Cents Vignette of Davis			10
$1 head of C. C. Clay			15
$2	"	Benjamin	15
$5	"	Memminger, Capitol at Richmond	10
$10	"	Hunter, Artillery in Centre	10
$20	"	Stephens, Capitol at Nashville	15
$50	"	Davis	25
$100	"	Mrs. Davis	25
$500	"	"Stonewall" Jackson	75

A Discount on full sets. Orders promptly filled.

STEVENS & CO.,
DEALERS IN RARE COINS,
90 RANDOLPH ST., CHICAGO.

Some idea how Confederate currency has advanced in price may be gleaned from a dealer's advertisement of about 1900 that was printed on the back of the $1 note of 1862. The prices are in cents, not dollars. Don't order from it!

A circular distributed during the Civil War included the statement that "Paper should now bear a price in GOLD, or its equivalent in currency . . . the price of paper has barely kept pace with the depreciation of the currency. . . ." It took over a hundred years but nearly all Confederate notes have risen in price above their face value.

Uncut Sheets

A small number of Confederate notes are known in uncut sheets. A listing of these follow, arranged by catalog number.

19. $5, Sept. 2, 1861. Commerce seated. Printed by J.T. Paterson & Co. 8 notes in sheet. $2,500.00.

21. $20, Sept. 2, 1861. Sailing ship. Printed by Hoyer & Ludwig. 8 notes in sheet. $3,000.00.

30. $20, Sept. 2, 1861. Industry and large 20. Printed by B. Duncan. Known in two varieties, "First Series" and "2 Series." 10 notes in sheet. $3,500.00.

43. $1, June 2, 1862. Steam-sailing ship. Printed by B. Duncan. 10 notes in sheet. $5,000.00.

47. $10, Sept. 2, 1862. Ceres seated. Printed by Hoyer & Ludwig. 8 notes in sheet. $5,000.00.

58. $1, April 6, 1863. Clement C. Clay. Engraved by Keatinge & Ball. 8 notes in sheet. $4,000.00.

65. 50 cents, Feb. 17, 1864. Profile head of Jefferson Davis. Engraved by Archer & Halpin. 9 notes in sheet. $2,500.00.

68. $5, Feb. 17, 1864. Confederate States Capitol. Engraved by Keatinge & Ball. 8 notes in sheet. $1,200.00.

69. $10, Feb. 17, 1864. Field Artillery. Engraved by Keatinge & Ball. 8 notes in sheet. $1,000.00.
Same, obverse only. $500.00.
Same, reverse only. $400.00.

72. $100, Feb. 17, 1864. Lucy H. Pickens. Engraved by Keatinge & Ball. 4 notes in sheet. Rare. $7,500.00.

73. $500, Feb. 17, 1864. Stonewall Jackson. Engraved by Keatinge & Ball. 4 notes in sheet. This is the rarest sheet presently known.

Prices, where quoted, are for crisp sheets that have been folded due to their large size. Uncirculated sheets that have not been folded are worth 25% more.

It is entirely possible that other sheets may exist that have not as yet been reported, particularly of the 1864 issue when, due to the cutting apart of the Confederacy, it was not possible to deliver and issue all of the notes.

Errors on Confederate Notes

When we consider the scarcity of skilled engravers in the Confederate States and the multitude of plates that had to be prepared to print all of the Confederate notes, it is not surprising that errors occurred.

Most of these errors are insignificant but there are a number that collectors will find of more than average interest. A selection of these follow, numbered according to the catalog section of this reference. With the exception of No. 47, all are uncommon or scarce. Those of greater rarity are indicated.

No. 9 —"For" printed before and above "Treasr" (twice).

No. 10 —"For Treasr" printed twice.

No. 12 —"For Treasr" printed twice. (Very scarce)

No. 16 —$20 note on watermarked "TEN" paper. (Very scarce)

No. 21A —Inverted "XX."
Inverted small "D" above "A" in plate letters. (Rare)
"Treasr" misspelled "Teasr." (Rare)

No. 26 —Dated September 2, 1861 instead of June 2, 1862. (See catalog listing)

No. 28 —Plate letter F with engraver's first initial as "R" instead of "B."

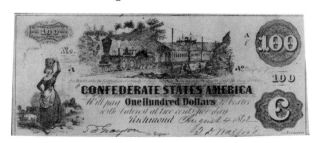

No. 29 —Second series. Plate number "5" at left, "I" at right. (Extremely Rare)

No. 30 —First series (Richmond). Plate letter "I" at left, "5" at right. (Very rare)

No. 33 —Plain paper or CSA block letters. With "Receivable" spelled "Receivable." (Rare)

No. 37 —"Of" before "the" omitted (on some notes of all three varieties of "X-X" shading). No flourish above "bearer." (Scarce to Very Rare)

No. 40A —Clouds completely missing above ship. (Rare)

No. 42 —"For Treasurer" at left and right. (Rare)

No. 45 —Second series. Plate letter "1" at left, "10" at right. (Very scarce)

No. 46 —Plate letter "I" at left. "10" at right. (Rare)

No. 47 —No notes authorized with September 2, 1862 date. Some notes with "month" instead of "months." (See catalog listing)

No. 52 —2nd Series. Plate letter "H" at left, "A" at right.
2nd Series. Plate letter "D" at left, "A" at right. (Very scarce)

No. 53 —3 Series. Two printers' names (instead of one) appear next to each other at left end. "Printed by Duncan Ptd. by Evans & Cogswell."
4th Series. As above.
3rd Series. "Ptd. by Evans & Cogswell. B. Dune" (partly removed from plate).
4 Series. Plate letter "C" at left, "G" at right. (Very rare)

No. 55 —"Between the" missing from Ratification of Treaty inscription.
Upper right side inscription "Ratification of a Treaty, etc." printed at both sides.

No. 60 —"St. Series" (no "1") on some plate E notes.
1st Series. Plate letter "A" at left, "D" at right.
1st Series. Plate letter "C" at left, "A" at right.
1st Series. Plate letter "E" at left, "A" at right.
1st Series. Plate letter "E" at left, none at right.

No. 61 —1st Series. Plain paper. Plate letter "A" at left, "C" at right.
2nd Series. Plain paper. Plate letter "H" on left side inverted.

No. 62 —1st Series. Plain paper. Plate letter "A" at left, "E" at right.

No. 63 —1st Series. Inverted green overprint. (Rare)

No. 68 —Series 7. Some notes exist with plain back. (Very scarce)

No. 69 —No series. One plate letter (G) only at left.
1st Series. Plate letter "B" at left, "A" at right.
3 Series. Plate letter "A" at left, "C" at right.
3 Series. Plate letter "C" at left, "A" at right.
3 Series. Plate letter "E" at left, "A" at right. (Very scarce)
(Bradbeer, Nos. 553-557 does not mention the series of the notes on which these plate letters appear so they have been assumed by many collectors and other catalogs to be the 10 Series.)

No. 70 —No series. Counter at upper left reads "Six months after . . ."
while the counter at upper right reads "Two years after . . ." (Very rare)

Notes with inverted backs are not included in this list. Such notes are very scarce or rare. Nor are those included that are printer's waste or trial impressions.

Please bear in mind that when a specific series is mentioned, most notes of that series are likely to be correct and not of the error variety. There are also clerical errors such as two different serial numbers. Still other "errors" exist that are counterfeits or alterations. Genuine notes with significant errors are generally more valuable than normally printed notes, particularly if they are in nice condition and the errors show clearly.

Errors on Notes of the Southern States

Errors were not limited to currency produced by the Confederate States. The currency of the individual states also included a number of important errors that are generally valued more highly than normal printings. Notes printed on the backs of other notes or forms are not errors but result from a scarcity of paper and were regularly issued. The numbers refer to the catalog listing.

AL-5 — "ONE" inverted.

FL-13 — "FIFTY" beneath the word "FLORIDA" is inverted. (Scarce)

GA-1 — Red portion of design is inverted.
Same, red overprint appears on back of note, not face. (Scarce)

GA-2 — Red overprint inverted.

GA-19 — Red overprint on back. (Very rare)

MO-9 — Overprint inverted. (Very rare)

MO-10 — Overprint inverted. (Very rare)

MS-6A — Inverted overprint. (Very rare)

MS-19 — "25 Cts" in red inverted. (Very rare)

NC-1 — "ONE DOLLAR" printed twice on back. (Rare)
Same, "ONE DOLLAR" in red inverted on back. (Scarce)

NC-2 — "ONE DOLLAR" inverted on back.
Same, "ONE DOLLAR" double printed on back. (Rare)
Same, "ONE DOLLAR" printed twice on back. (Rare)
Same, January spelled "Jonuary." (Very rare)

NC-4 — "TWO DOLLARS" on back inverted. (Rare)

NC-27 — Red "25 Cts" inverted. (Rare)

NC-35 — Red "TWENTY" inverted. (Very rare)

TX-14 — DUES is spelled "DEUS".

There are other errors in addition to those listed, some of which are mentioned in descriptions of Southern states notes in Part III. The above list is intended only as a sampling of the more important errors.

THE END OF CONFEDERATE CURRENCY

The Seventh Issue was the last but an Eighth Issue for $80 million to pay the Army was authorized by Congress at its last meeting on March 18, 1865. It was vetoed by President Davis who felt the 1864 issue was to replace older notes and reduce circulation, and to authorize another issue "would be accepted as a proof that there is no limit to the issue of Treasury notes . . ."

Even without this issue, about two billion dollars in Confederate currency of all issues was produced (including state, bank and local notes). The destruction of Columbia, S.C., Confederate printing headquarters in February 1865 did not entirely stop the deluge. Some equipment was saved and transferred further North but by then it was hardly worth the cost of printing.

Although there were attempts to make then so, Confederate "Bluebacks" were never legal tender. Worth 95 cents on the dollar in gold when first issued, Confederate currency dropped to 33 cents by 1863, and 1.6 cents by Appomattox (April 9, 1865). May 1, 1865, was the last active trading in Confederate notes at 1,200 for 1. It is of the highest order of patriotism when we observe that, except for speculators, most Southerners continued to accept this money to the last. (By way of comparison, the lowest point of the legal tender "Greenbacks" of the North was slightly over 35 cents on the dollar in gold, July 11, 1864. At the end of 1865, the value had risen to approximately 69 cents.)

Interestingly, unlike foreign countries that have experienced rampant inflation and issued postage stamps in high denominations, those of the Confederate States never exceeded 20 cents. A fee of an express company was often added, but the charge still failed to reflect the depreciation of the currency. Despite many hardships and disruptions, the postal service functioned reasonably well under Postmaster John H. Reagan after that which was provided by the Federal government ceased on June 1, 1861. In all there were nearly 9,000 post offices in the South. A rate of 5 cents for letters of ½ ounce was established that was increased to 10 cents on July 1, 1862. For letters going to or from the Trans-Mississippi Department, the rate was 40 cents.

In the end the South was not beaten by General Grant or Sherman — it was beaten by General Hard Times. Its primitive home industries could only partly replace the many necessities cut off by the blockade, and these with inferior goods. It was like a modern mechanized army having to run on kerosene instead of gasoline. The engine collapses on low-grade fuel.

We can only guess at the outcome had the Civil War been decided on the military field alone with a fully equipped army. That the Confederate army existed as long as it did (privates' pay was "frozen" at $8-$13 a month when cavalry boots alone were costing $500 in inflated currency by 1864) on slim rations and insufficient equipment can only attest to the devotion of these men to the Southern Cause. And, men that believe in such causes often perform so far "beyond the call of duty" as to be beyond human comprehension.

We will end on a note of irony: Most Confederate notes read that they will be redeemed six months or two years "after the ratification of a treaty of peace between the Confederate States and the United States of America." So, for those who held on to their Confederate money it is probably a good thing that collectors are paying such high prices for it, since there has been no treaty of peace yet!

Vignettes on Confederate Notes

Throughout the catalog section are references to the use of the same vignette on other notes, either before or after the Civil War. Some of these are transfers from original engravings, others are copies. An example of a "before" and "after" transfer is illustrated here in the work of the American Bank Note Co. The Navigation Seated vignette was used on $20 note No. 24 (see catalog description) printed by Southern Bank Note Co. (American Bank Note Company's New Orleans branch).

Pre-war use of central vignette.

Post-war use of vignette at right.

INDEX OF VIGNETTES

An interesting way to collect Confederate notes is by representative designs or vignettes. In fact, this may be the ideal way for collectors with limited budgets, since even a type set is now difficult to complete and can cost thousands of dollars.

Many notes have vignettes representing the same subject in one or more forms. As a convenience to collectors interested in the vignettes, the following list with short identifying data should be of value. The numbers refer to the catalog numbers of the notes on which the vignettes appear.

Two of the above men, R.M.T. Hunter and Alexander H. Stephens, together with Assistant Secretary of War, John C. Campbell, a former U.S. Supreme Court Justice, acting as peace commissioners from the Confederate States, met with President Lincoln and Secretary of War Edwin M. Stanton at Hampton Roads on February 3, 1865. They failed to secure a negotiated peace as Lincoln insisted on unconditional surrender. Davis thought of the meeting in terms of securing peace between "the two countries" whereas Lincoln viewed it as bringing "peace to the people of one common country."

CROSS-INDEX OF CATALOG NUMBERS

Since the first listing of Confederate currency appeared in the *American Journal of Numismatics* in 1867, there have been less than 20 important catalogs or studies of Confederate States currency. Most of these, while of historical value, are no longer used in cataloguing Confederate notes that, for many years, have relied on a catalog number for each type. As an aid to collectors, the author has prepared a cross-index of catalog numbers presently in use.

Raymond, Wayte. "The Standard Paper Money Catalogue," 1940. This catalog really was "standard" during the 1940s but has since been largely superseded by other works. The catalog numbers from the Confederate note portion are still sometimes encountered in older collections.

Chase, Philip H. "Confederate Treasury Notes," 1947. This catalog is distinguished by detailed research of printing varieties and counterfeit notes. The first digit of each type number identifies the year of issue, i.e. "1" for 1861, "2" for 1862, etc.

Bradbeer, William West. "Confederate and Southern State Currency," 1915 and later reprints. A separate number is given for each major variety and serial letter.

Criswell, Grover C., Jr. "Confederate and Southern State Currency," 1957-1996. Criswell brought the Bradbeer work up to date and has largely replaced it. In general, the Criswell numbers follow the Bradbeer numbers for individual varieties and these may be determined by referring to the column of Bradbeer numbers. Criswell has, however, recognized the importance of types and these numbers, which are given alongside each illustration in the catalog, are the type numbers listed here.

Krause Publications. *Standard Catalog of World Paper Money,* (Vol. 2, General Issues), 6th and subsequent editions (1990 and later), devoted to government issues of the entire world, include Confederate States paper money. Catalog numbers (KP) are given for the convenience of those who use this reference. The numbering system is largely a cross between the Slabaugh and Chase arrangement.

Slabaugh No.	Denomination and Description	Raymond No.	Chase No.	Bradbeer No.	Criswell No.	KP No.
Montgomery Issue, 1861						
1	$50 Three slaves in field	4	101	4	4	1
2	$100 Railroad train at station	3	102	3	3	2
3	$500 Cattle in brook	2	103	2	2	3
4	$1000 Calhoun and Jackson	1	104	1	1	4
Richmond Issue, 1861						
5	$50 Industry and Agriculture	6	105	6	6	5
6	$100 Railroad train	5	106	5	5	6
July 25, 1861 Issue						
7	$5 "Manouvrier" note	12	108	46-49	12	8
8	$5 Liberty and eagle	11	107	42-45	11	7
9	$10 Liberty, eagle and flag	10	109	34-41	10	9
10	$20 Sailing ship	9	110	23-33	9	10
11	$50 George Washington	8	111	14-22	8	11
12	$100 Ceres and Proserpine	7	112	7-13	7	12
13	$20 Female Riding Deer	—	B-110	—	XXI	—
September 2, 1861 Issue						
14	$5 "Indian princess"	32	118	271	35	18
15	$10 Liberty, shield and eagle	30	126	221-229	27	26
16	$20 Commerce, Ceres, Navigation	19	130	99-100	17	30

Slabaugh No.	Denomination and Description	Raymond No.	Chase No.	Bradbeer No.	Criswell No.	KP No.
17	$50 Moneta with treasure chest	14	135	59-78	14	35
18	$100 Slaves loading cotton	13	138	50-58	13	38
19	$5 Commerce and cotton bale	37	119	272-283	36	19
20	$10 Ceres and Commerce	27	127	230-236	28	27
21	$20 Sailing ship	20	131	101-136	18	31
22	$5 Seated women	31	114	243-245	31	14
23	$10 Indian family	25	121	150-152	22	21
24	$20 Navigation beside globe	21	132	137-138	19	32
25	$50 Train	15	136	79	15	36
26	$2 Confederacy striking down Union	38	113	286	38	13
27	$5 Sailor and cotton bales	34	120	284-285	37	20
28	$10 Slave picking cotton	22	128	237	29	28
29	$10 Sweet potato dinner	23	129	238-242	30	29
30	$20 Industry seated behind 20	17	133	139-143	20	33
31	$5 Blacksmith	33	115	246-249	32	15
32	$5 CG. Memminger, green	36	117	250-261	33	16
33	$5 C.G. Memminger, black	35	116	262-270	34	17
34	$10 Wagon load of cotton bales	26	122	153-155	23	22
35	$10 R. M. T. Hunter and child	24	123	156-167	24	23
36	$10 Hope with Anchor	28	124	168-172	25	24
37	$10 Hope with Anchor. X-X in red	29	125	173-220	26	25
38	$20 Alexander H. Stephens	18	134	144-149	21	34
39	$50 Jefferson Davis	16	137	80-98	16	37

1862 Interest Notes

40	$100 Train, straight steam	40	201	287-297	39	43
41	$100 Train, diffused steam	41	201D	298-309	40	44
42	$100 Three slaves in field	39	202	310-333	41	45

June 2, 1862 Issue

43	$1 Steam-sailing ship	44	203	339-341	44	39
44	$1 Same, green overprint	45	204	342	45	40
45	$2 Confederacy striking down Union	42	205	334-337	42	41
46	$2 Same, green overprint	43	206	338	43	42

Dated September 2, 1862

47	$10 Ceres reclining on cotton bale	46	207	343-344	46	46
48	$10 Ceres seated ("Essay note")	-	208	346	48	47
49	$20 Liberty with shield ("Essay note")	-	209	345	47	48

December 2, 1862 Issue

50	$1 C.C. Clay	53	210	397-401	55	49
51	$2 Judah R Benjamin	52	211	391-396	54	50
52	$5 Confederate States Capitol	51	212	379-390	53	51
53	$10 South Carolina Capitol	50	213	369-378	52	52
54	$20 Tennessee Capitol	49	214	363-368	51	53
55	$50 Jefferson Davis	48	215	350-362	50	54
56	$100 Lucy H.Pickens	47	216	347-349	49	55

April 6, 1863 Issue

57	500 Jefferson Davis	61	301	485-488	63	56
58	$1 C.C. Clay	60	302	474-484	62	57
59	$2 Judah R Benjamin	59	303	470-473	61	58
60	$5 Confederate States Capitol	58	304	448-469	60	59
61	$10 South Carolina Capitol	57	305	429-447	59	60
62	$20 Tennessee Capitol	56	306	418-428	58	61
63	$50 Jefferson Davis	55	307	405-417	57	62
64	$100 Lucy H. Pickens	54	308	402-404	56	63

February 17, 1864 Issue

65	500 Jefferson Davis	70	401	578-579	72	64
66	$1 C.C. Clay	69	402	572-577	71	65
67	$2 Judah P. Benjamin	68	403	566-571	70	66
68	$5 Confederate States Capitol	67	404	558-565	69	67
69	$10 Field Artillery	66	405	540-557	68	68
70	$20 Tennessee Capitol	65	406	504-539	67	69
71	$50 Jefferson Davis	64	407	495-503	66	70
72	$100 Lucy H. Pickens	63	408	490-494	65	71-72
73	$500 Stonewall Jackson	62	409	489	64	73

Part II — Historical Data

THE TRANS-MISSISSIPPI NOTES

During the Civil War, both the North and the South divided the military theaters into departments. For example, the Confederacy had the Department of Northern Virginia and the Department of North Carolina and Southern Virginia, among others. Our concern here is the Trans-Mississippi Department that was created on May 26, 1862. It included Arkansas, Missouri, Western Louisiana, Texas and the Indian Territory. As the largest department in the Confederacy, it was a major supplier of agricultural products and goods for the East, especially those that arrived from Europe via Mexico.

One would think that such an important part of the Confederacy would have been coddled but throughout the war the transfer of goods was almost entirely West to East. What the Trans-Mississippi Department needed more than anything else was Confederate currency of which there was more than an ample supply in the East. But seemingly it required personal remonstrations before the Treasury in Richmond would send it to the West, even before communications were disrupted by the closing of the Mississippi River by Union troops in the summer of 1863. Consequently, the payrolls of the soldiers and payments to suppliers of goods were almost always in arrears and this resulted in a great deal of general dissatisfaction plus the difficulty of maintaining the army at full strength. In short, the Trans-Mississippi Department lacked enough money to meet its needs.

General E. Kirby Smith had become commander of the Trans-Mississippi Department on March 7, 1863 and until nearly the end of the war he was still pleading with Richmond to supply more currency to the western half of the Confederacy. In February 1865, he reported that the department owed over $50 million. A semi-independent branch of the Treasury Department was established at Marshall, Texas by an Act of January 27, 1864. P. W. Gray was appointed the agent with power "to discharge any duty or function on the other side of the Mississippi which he, the said Secretary (Memminger), is competent to discharge."

This was all very well except that the Trans-Mississippi Department lacked the facilities to produce engraved currency of the same type that was being printed by the Confederate government in the East. Accordingly, when repeated demands for more currency from the East failed to bring more than a portion of that required, Kirby Smith ordered the earlier notes on hand to be reissued. The Act of March 23, 1863 had included provisions for retiring notes dated prior to its adoption to be funded into bonds, etc. To circumvent that and to identify the reissued notes, the Trans-Mississippi Department stamped them with red or black circular or straight-line handstamps. Depending upon the type, these overprints increase the value of the notes (to collectors) up to 50% more for circular overprints in red dated February 1864, 75% more for March 1864; double for black; double for straight-line overprints. Other varieties also exist.

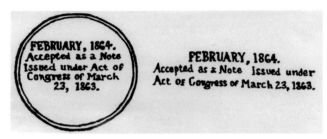

Worse was to come. The Act of February 17, 1864, which authorized a new issue of Confederate notes bearing that date, also included provisions that would tax earlier non-interest bearing notes out of existence. That is if they were not funded into bonds by "the first day of April 1864, east of the Mississippi River, and the first day of July 1864, west of the Mississippi River," beginning with a tax of 33.33% plus 10% per month thereafter. The West was given only a three-month grace period, even though nowhere near enough of the February 17, 1864 notes were forthcoming to replace the earlier issues. And, General Smith refused to use earlier notes after that to pay the soldiers because he did not feel it was right, after having sometimes waited for months to be paid, to receive notes that would soon be worth only two-thirds of face value.

This measure brought forth additional numismatic items. Exchange Certificates were issued from the Confederate States Depository Office as a receipt to show that older notes had been deposited for which new notes would be issued equal to two-thirds of their value. (These Trans-Mississippi certificates are rare.) At the same time the office recognized that it might be a long time before new currency was received since the certificates further state that they would be exchanged "when this office shall be supplied with funds for this purpose, upon surrender of this certificate." It almost sounds "tongue-in-cheek." Interestingly, the illustrated specimen was for a deposit by the Post Office Department that also had its headquarters for the Trans-Mississippi Department located in Marshall, Texas. If another government department couldn't obtain new notes, what chance had the soldiers? Local currency issued by a number of merchants about that time in Texas also carried the message that it was redeemable in Confederate States Treasury Notes but would be reduced to two-thirds of its face value after July 1, 1864.

Kirby Smith was one of the South's finest generals who may have thwarted Grant's campaign to gain control of the Mississippi River if he had received money to buy supplies and pay his soldiers. His forces were the last Confederate army in the field when they surrendered on May 26, 1865, a month after General Lee's surrender at Appomattox. President Davis, in his effort to escape, had hoped to reach the Trans-Mississippi Department via Mexico and continue the war from there.

It should be mentioned, however, that Brigadier General Stand Watie of the Cherokee Nation, which had allied itself with the Confederates, and who conducted a guerrilla campaign against Union forces during the last days of the war, did not surrender until June 23, 1865. Brigadier General Joseph Shelby never did surrender. Instead, he took a small force to Mexico. Unable to accomplish anything from there, he returned two years later to Missouri where he was a popular hero.

Exceeding the ground forces in length of "postwar" service was the commander of the Confederate cruiser, Shenandoah, who was at sea when the war ended and did not learn until August that the Confederate States was no more. Prior to that, the ship had been actively destroying vessels of U.S. whalers in the Northern Pacific near the Arctic Circle. Not until November 6, 1865, did Capt. James I. Waddell, CSN, surrender, and then not to the United States but to British authorities.

THE ENIGMATICAL ISSUES

Through the research of Sydney C. Kerksis and Douglas B. Ball, it has been determined that the $10 note, No. 47, which bears no printer's name, was the work of Hoyer & Ludwig. As mentioned elsewhere in this catalog, Hoyer & Ludwig did not wish to make the move from Richmond, Va., to Columbia, S.C., where the currency printers were being relocated, and accordingly sold out to J.T. Paterson in May 1862. Paterson obtained the Hoyer & Ludwig contracts for Confederate notes and continued to print notes for a time using vignettes and transfers obtained with the purchase. Hoyer & Ludwig retained a part of their equipment, expecting to engage in job printing work in Richmond, but officially their production of Confederate currency ended when they sold that portion of their business to Paterson. (However, they continued to produce the crude Virginia $1 Treasury Notes they had previously printed with May 15, 1862 date and later dates of July 21, and October 21, 1862 as well as Virginia bank notes and local scrip.)

Apparently Ludwig had an urge to print Confederate currency again so he wrote Secretary of the Treasury Memminger in August 1862 about the possibility of printing more notes for the Confederacy. He made the price so low it could hardly be refused and Memminger accepted. In other words, after assuring Paterson that Hoyer & Ludwig's contracts were his and that the Treasury would not again renew work with Hoyer & Ludwig (after their refusal to move to Columbia) even if printing was resumed in Richmond, the Secretary secretly broke the agreement. But Paterson somehow learned of Hoyer & Ludwig's proposition, and he was boiling. As a result, Memminger asked Hoyer & Ludwig to leave their name off the $10 note he had requested from them. Ludwig was vain enough to want recognition, though, and he added his name in tiny letters beneath the cotton bale in the center vignette.

While we know what happened that led to the production of an "illegitimate" $10 note (No. 47), the background of the so-called Essay Notes (Nos. 48 and 49) has never been conclusively determined. A number of theories have been projected that have supporting arguments for their acceptance but all have certain flaws, including my own (both published and unpublished). I respect the opinions of my colleagues, but until someone comes forward who can prove that an ancestor was responsible for their production, we may never know their exact source.

A number of things can be ascertained by studying Nos. 48 and 49 but there still remains some very puzzling questions. First of all, it is obvious that the two notes are laid out in a style similar to the $10 note that was actually issued (No. 47). This points to Hoyer & Ludwig as the source, as espoused by Sidney B. Kerksis in the March 1951 issue of *The Numismatist*. In previous editions of this catalog, I offered the possibility that the source might instead be Paterson, who had good reason to feel short-changed and who may have insisted on showing what he could do. There is still another possibility, assuming that the designs originated with the Confederate printers, and that is Blanton Duncan. The quality of his work was on about the same level as Hoyer & Ludwig and Paterson, but what points to him as a possibility is the different type of paper used for these notes. Duncan hoarded much needed paper of various kinds, including some that really belonged to others. It was found and seized under orders of Joseph D. Pope, Chief Clerk of the Columbia Treasury Note Bureau, but all that had been hidden may not have been located.

There is, of course, the possibility that both of these notes (Nos. 48 and 49) are bogus issues prepared in the North. Douglas B. Ball has frequently propounded this as fact since he first discussed them in the August 1966 issue of *The Numismatist*. He offers as support a letter from a Confederate soldier in Tennessee who wrote that he was sending a $20 note of September 2, 1862 to the Confederate Treasury for exchange because it had been damaged by washing, which ruined its appearance and made it appear to be a counterfeit. However, the soldier also states that he thinks "it is a good bill from my knowledge of it." It is simply too bad that other contemporary material about these two notes has never shown up. A single letter can hardly be considered overwhelming proof inasmuch as the soldier apparently had considerable faith in the genuineness of the $20 note to have forwarded it to the Treasury. How many doubtful U.S. notes have you been brave enough to send to the Secret Service?

Ball rightly states, though, that any true essay note presented for approval in the normal manner would entail no more than a couple examples of each. I offer the possibility that these two notes were originally essay notes of which the impressions have been lost, and that the specimens presently available represent subsequent printings by unknown persons. Let us assume, for example, that Hoyer & Ludwig actually presented three designs to Treasury Secretary Memminger for approval from which he selected the $10 note (No. 47). In that case, the plates for the other two notes may have been put away for possible future use but some workman got a hold of them and surreptitiously printed a small quantity. Or, perhaps the plates "disappeared" (stolen) and Hoyer & Ludwig (or another printer if they weren't the source) would hardly have wanted that known if they were to receive any future business from the Confederate government. (Manouvrier, who produced the $5 note, No. 7, received no further government contracts due to carelessness.)

Unfortunately, like other projections relative to the origin of these notes, all have flaws because we are hampered by what we do not know. A major problem with the two unaccepted designs, regardless of whether they are of Confederate or Northern origin, is the misspelled printer's name, Keatings & Ball, Columbus, S.C., which appears on the notes. If we knew the answer to this question, it would go a long way toward solving the mystery of these notes. For, we may ask, why should the two notes (Nos. 48 and 49) bear any imprint at all? The $10 (No. 47), which was engraved in the same overall style, carried no printer's name (other than Ludwig's last name hidden in the design). It logically follows that if these two notes were originally Confederate essays submitted at or near the same time as the accepted $10 note, that they would likewise have lacked the printer's name or at the very least would not have included the erroneous imprint found on existing notes. The same holds true if the $10 (No. 47) was used as a master design in the North to produce bogus notes. Why add an imprint when it wasn't on the original, and an incorrect one at that?

If the imprint was subsequently added in the South (and I have no proof that it was), it may indicate that Paterson was the source of these two notes, based on the assumption that the Columbus, S.C. error in the printer's address may have resulted from confusion by a Georgia engraver who was thinking of Columbus, Georgia. (Paterson had moved men and equipment to Augusta, Georgia.) The error in the printer's name is more easily explained by the fact that the printers sometimes partook of too much strong drink or simply because the engraver was under considerable stress while clandestinely making the addition to the plates. We know that the notes shouldn't have carried the name of Keatinge & Ball at all since they do not resemble their work, but this may have been an attempt to cover up the source.

The signatures on the two notes also present problems, but it is known that consideration was being given about that time to having them printed instead of handwritten. Having such a large number of signatures caused confusion and largely defeated their value as a counterfeit deterrent. The U.S. government, which at first hand-signed Demand Notes, had begun using printed signatures and this certainly wasn't unknown to the Confederate Government since some "green backs" trickled South. If essays originally existed of these two notes, they may or may not have included signatures. If they did bear the signatures of J.M. Miller and P.B. Hooe, which appear on existing notes, they were obviously selected at random to illustrate how they would look in printed form. It is hardly likely that regularly issued notes would have carried the names of two clerks rather than those of Robert Tyler and E.C. Elmore as subsequently appeared on the 50 cents notes, the only denomination to bear printed signatures. On the other hand, if these notes are bogus, the engraver simply copied this particular combination of signatures from another Confederate note.

The central vignette on the $10 note (No. 48) is a common one of which transfers existed in both the North and the South. If an essay of this design was presented to Memminger, he was probably aware that this vignette had been widely used and chose the other $10 design instead. The $20 (No. 49), on the other hand, bears a vignette that I have been unable to locate on any bank note except a $5 note of the Dubuque, Marion & Western Rail Road Company of Iowa, dated June 15, 1861 and a 25 cents note of R.C. Paine's Banking House, January 1, 1861. Both notes were engraved by Edward Mendel of Chicago, who was capable of producing original work but who also copied the work of others and may have knowingly or unknowingly printed counterfeits. Normally, his work bears his imprint, but at least a couple notes do not, including a $3 note of 1861 issued by the City of New Orleans. It closely resembles a note of the same denomination produced by the American Bank Note Co. The use of the design on the $20 note, therefore, raises a question: Since this was apparently a recent and as yet a little used vignette, had one been delivered to the Southern Bank Note Co. (the New Orleans branch of the American Bank Note Co.) where it would have been found in their effects after they were shipped to Richmond? If so, this could indicate a Southern source for the $20 note. Or, did Mendel produce these notes under the impression, after having engraved notes for New Orleans, that he was dealing with a Confederate agent? In the past, bank note printers have not been overly scrupulous about the legitimacy of those ordering bank notes-more important was the matter of payment. Money up front would have solved that question and should these two notes be a Northern production, then a very likely source (but not the distributor) would be Mendel. He may or may not have added the printer's name.

In offering several scenarios how these notes may have come about, you are free to draw your own conclusions as you should have the right to do. One thing is certain — the two notes (Nos. 48 and 49) were never regular issues of the Confederate States. Like the Female Riding Deer Note (No. 13), they need not be collected as a part of a type set of Confederate currency unless one wishes. I have included the three notes in this catalog because all are known to have seen some circulation during the Civil War. Unlike counterfeits of other notes, all are of distinctive designs.

We may also be certain that the arguments over these notes have not caused the value of them to drop; on the contrary, they seem to emulate the 1804 dollar that collectors know is a restrike made after the date on the coin. Still, it continues to escalate in price. If these are really bogus or counterfeit notes, they surely rank among the most valuable of this genre.

THE CHEMICOGRAPHIC BACKS

It will be noted that the style of reverse used on the 1864 notes is not nearly so intricate as that used on the 1862 and 1863 series. It was not intended thus. The 1864 series was to replace earlier notes and, obviously, they would have been difficult to distinguish if the backs had been of the same type as previous notes, since the obverses were very similar.

Elaborate backs were prepared for the 1864 issue but never used. These are the Chemicographic (chemico = chemically prepared; graphic — printing) plates ordered in 1863 from S. Straker & Sons of London, England. The name is actually a trade name of Straker's for a process of making electrotype plates, and each plate states that it is Chemicographed by S. Straker & Sons, London, England.

There were made 200 "pairs" of plates of the $5, 200 of the $10, 125 of the $20, 80 of the $50, 51 of the $100 and 28 of the $500. A pair consisted of a surface plate for the "surface" or second and final impression and a machine engraved ground plate for the background or first impression. The copper plates were silver plated for use with colored inks. Apparently in an effort to combat counterfeiting, the Confederacy planned to use two-color printing in such a way it would be difficult to imitate. The $5 to $500 plates illustrated are the Chemicographic backs for surface printing. The $5 and $10 machine engraved plates have long been a mystery as they bear no manufacturer's name. They were rescued along with the other plates, and it appears that these must be the plates for background printing on the front of the notes. When the 1864 issue is compared with the 1862 and 1863 issues of similar design, it will be noted that a reddish pink web background has been added. Apparently, when these plates failed to arrive, Keatinge & Ball hurried and added a background of their own design to each note.

The plates were shipped during January to March, 1864 to Nassau in the West Indies and from there were to be sent to Wilmington, North Carolina. By that time, though, only one out of two blockade runners were getting through (compared to 9 out of 10 early in the war) and the plates seem to have been captured by the North. They were later sold for scrap metal, but some were by chance rescued from melting by a Charles Chaplin (see *American Journal of Numismatics*, July 1877).

It seems, however, since Mr. Chaplin loaned only the $5 and $10 background plates and $5 to $50 surface plates to the *American Journal of Numismatics* for illustration, that he did not obtain the $100 and $500 surface plates or the higher denominations of the background plates. Since the $100 and $500 surface plates exist, this indicates that some of the plates may have arrived safely or were captured on the high seas by a different U.S. ship. Thus they did not find their way into the same lot that Mr. Chaplin saw. The plates had been snipped from England to Nassau in different shipments to reduce chance of loss. It is not unlikely that the crates containing the plates were also sent on separate blockade runners to Wilmington, N.C., the only open port. It appears, though, that even if one shipment did get through, that the plates were either captured by U.S. forces while making the overland journey from Wilmington, N.C., to Columbia, S.C. (the printing center), or if they did arrive, there weren't enough plates to be of practical use.

Most plates are gone. None of the $20 to $500 ground plates are known to have survived. Perhaps the higher denominations had already been melted before Mr. Chaplin discovered the plates. Or perhaps, since the ground plates would not have been so easily distinguished, he may not have noticed the different denominations. If he did, since he likely had to pay the same price for each, he may not have considered the plainer background plates to be worth the cost.

Of the surface plates, a complete set now reposes in the Smithsonian Institution through the courtesy of Philip H. Chase, Confederate currency researcher. At one time only the $5 to $50 were known of the surface plates. From what he has written, it appears that the $100 and $500 plates he formerly owned were discovered hidden in the home of a Northern Civil War veteran about 1950. This set is supposed to be unique, but I have good reason to believe another set exists. About 1940, a complete set of $5 to $500 plates was discovered and I had the opportunity to purchase it. While I do not now own the set, I feel certain that it is not the set in the Smithsonian. The background history does not match. More recently, a partial set was discovered in Georgia that included the plate for the $500 note. Of course, the odds are against it, but actually out of the 28 possible complete sets there could be several sets in existence. There are at least a few of the lower denominations in existence, though, since more of these were made and it is understandable that more were likely to escape destruction. More of the lower denominations were needed and printed than higher denominations. Four or eight plates were used at a time and they wore out after awhile, so it is not difficult to see why the Confederate Treasury needed so many plates.

Impressions exist of the Chemicographic plates, printed in black and colors. Some were prepared in the 19th century but those occasionally available now are usually modern printings produced from the set of plates formerly owned by Mr. Chase.

This explains why the 1864 issue has comparatively simple backs. When the Chemicographic backs couldn't be used, Keatinge & Ball had to hurry in preparing a substitute. By the time the loss was apparent, the 1864 obverses were ready for printing.

However, since the $500 Chemicographic plate indicates that denomination was already planned, why wasn't a new back prepared for it as well? As the highest denomination of the 1864 issue, it should have been the first to receive this added deterrent against counterfeiting.

While on the subject of plates, this is as good a place as any to say that some of the plates and printing stones regularly used for printing Confederate notes also exist. Most were lost or destroyed but a few of those buried at the end of the war have since been found.

REDEMPTION OF CONFEDERATE CURRENCY

Due to the large amount of Confederate currency that has survived, one might gain the impression that the Confederate States made no attempt to redeem its notes. On the contrary, the government was well aware of the dangers of an inflationary surplus of currency (an exception was the Trans-Mississippi Department where there was not enough). For this reason, a majority of the notes were interest bearing or indicate that they were fundable into Confederate bonds, both being measures intended to remove them from general circulation once they had served their initial purpose of paying for goods or the army. However, extraordinary measures were sometimes used to encourage the purchase of bonds (see section on Trans-Mississippi Notes).

Notes that were used to purchase bonds or were redeemed have, to a certain extent, survived with cancellation marks in various forms. Although some simply bear a handwritten inscription indicating that they have been cancelled or are stamped to that effect, most of the redeemed notes are cut cancelled.

Stamped Cancellation

Hole Cancellation

On this and the previous page are illustrations of typical cancellations used on Confederate notes, part of which originally appeared in an introductory article on this subject by L. Miles Raisig. Although these cancellations disfigure the notes more or less, thereby reducing their value to collectors, it is not advisable to repair or reconstruct them. These cancellations are a part of the Confederate currency story. They indicate the good intentions of the Confederate Treasury, even though circumstances beyond its control made impossible the full redemption of these notes "two years after the ratification of a treaty of peace between the Confederate States and the United States."

Cross and "X" cut cancellations (at top).
Half moon and triangular cut cancellations (at bottom).

COUNTERFEIT AND ALTERED NOTES

I think it can be safely said that either counterfeits or facsimiles exist of all Confederate Treasury notes. In making this statement I do not wish to imply that Confederate notes were especially susceptible to counterfeiting; rather it was partly a symptom of the times. The years 1836 to 1896 have been called the Golden Age of Counterfeiting in the United States. Prior to the Civil War, every banker and merchant had either a book listing the known counterfeits or subscribed to one of the bank note reporter magazines. Newspapers also carried reports. Obviously, this means there was a lot of counterfeiting going on when the country could support not one, but many different bank note reporters and counterfeit detectors. This was the day of state banks and a multitude of different bank notes. Each bank issued its own kind, and no one could hope to know them all, especially notes from distant banks.

When the Civil War came, the United States government began issuing its own paper money. The Confederacy did also with the result that this competition reduced the number of state bank issues that, in the United States, were shortly taxed out of existence. The counterfeiters turned their talents to U.S. and Confederate notes.

Since lengthy descriptions and illustrations are necessary to identify the various counterfeits, a detailed listing of known Confederate counterfeits is impractical in this catalog. No sure-fire method that will detect all counterfeits can be given in a few sentences but these suggestions may be of some help:

The work of National Bank Note Co., Southern Bank Note Co., Keatinge & Ball, and Archer & Daly (Halpin) is generally superior. Notes bearing the imprints of these firms that seem rather crude (assuming the appearance is not caused by considerable wear) are likely to be counterfeits or facsimiles. The work of Hoyer & Ludwig, J. Manouvrier, J. T. Paterson and B. Duncan is not as good. Thus, a note that may appear somewhat crude to the uninitiated could very well be genuine. Doubtful notes should be compared with notes of the same plate variety that are known to be genuine. Wrong type of paper, printed signatures (except on the 50-cent notes and $10 and $20 "essays") and wrong shade of color are points to check (counterfeiters had difficulties in getting proper materials, too). Close examination for engraving differences is necessary on the better counterfeits.

One of the best known counterfeits, which is widely collected, appeared near the end of the war. This is the so-called "Havana counterfeit" that is believed to have been produced in Cuba and smuggled into the Confederacy. More information and an illustration of this note may be found at the listing for No. 72 in the catalog section.

Counterfeits that were detected by Confederate officials were marked or stamped "Counterfeit." Such markings add interest and value to the note.

Unlike counterfeits, which duplicate existing notes as closely as possible and are printed to enter circulation as "real" money, there is no profit to altering genuine notes unless it is to "raise" the denomination. A notable exception applies particularly to the alteration of Confederate notes since there were so many engraving differences that resulted in the numerous varieties sought by collectors. Skillful engravers have been able to create new varieties by the addition of swirls, plate letters, or other differences and, where existing varieties are seldom encountered, create more of them by altering examples of a more common variety of the same note.

A prime example of this kind of alteration may be found on the illustrated $5 note of September 2, 1861 (No. 19), which purports to be of the Third Series. Raphael Thian, in his Register of the Confederate Debt, indicated that 2,189 sheets of 18,312 notes were printed of the Third Series. Since this is not many by Confederate standards, locating a genuine example of the Third Series is exceptionally difficult, unlike the first series. Not only is the First Series readily available, it bears no indication of the series. Solution: take a First Series note, add the information that it is from the Third Series and presto, a rarity has been created. It's a successful deception if one does not realize that genuine notes of the Third Series have low serial numbers or that Thian's compilation shows the signature combinations to be wrong.

Thian's listing of signature combinations in Confederate Treasury records is practically always a reliable means of detecting alterations. However, it is not impossible that a few exceptions may exist. It appears that security was often sacrificed at the printing plants due to the urgency to produce huge quantities of currency. One of the English printers stated after the war that "One form of laxness which cost the Confederates a large amount of their paper notes was their carelessness in handling the unsigned notes in the offices. The printers were allowed to take these notes in any quantities they liked while at work and one of the men got in the habit of carrying off five or ten sheets of ten, twenty of fifty dollar notes every day. Of course, it was necessary for him to commit forgery in signing them, but there were so many different signatures on the notes that it was not easy to detect a spurious one, and this enterprising individual had taken some $300,000 of notes before he was found out. Then he was promptly sentenced to be shot but this was in 1865, when Sherman was close at hand, and the sentence was never executed. After that, however, detectives were set to watch the men at work, and a strict accounting was kept.

"When the Confederacy began to get into desperate financial straits it adopted a curious shift to pay the printers, and instead of giving them its own notes, it allowed them to print notes bearing their own name and redeemable in Confederate bills . . ." The source of this statement was apparently referring to the notes of 500, $1 and $2 issued by Keatinge & Ball, one of which is pictured.

BOGUS NOTES

The Female Riding Deer Note

Bogus notes are fantasy notes of types that were never issued by the authorities mentioned on the notes. Of these the most famous is the Female Riding Deer note (No. 13). Its interest has caused it to be collected by many collectors of Confederate States paper money even though it is a bogus note and was never issued by the Confederate States. An element of doubt and mystery as to its source has caused its genuineness to be argued by collectors since the close of the Civil War. For this reason, this note will be discussed at length.

While it appears that this note was known in the South during the Civil War, this can be easily explained by the fact that many counterfeit and facsimile notes were being passed, a large number of them having been made in the North and brought into the South by soldiers and others to purchase goods (mainly cotton) and undermine the currency. A Confederate senator said that Upham's facsimiles "had done more to injure the Confederate cause than General McClellan and his army."

Records of the Confederate Treasury do not mention the Female Riding Deer note as having been issued by the Confederacy. We do not know who was the original source of this note. Using the design itself as a basis the author has spent considerable time in trying to track it down. While additional information has been unearthed, it still is not possible to say definitely that any particular person was the first to print this note.

The central design of the note is actually that of the Greek goddess Artemis (or Roman Diana) with her silver bow and arrows and riding a stag. But as few if any knew the figure by this name while this and other notes bearing similar designs were in circulation, or since, but has rather been described as "a female riding a deer," let it continue by this name.

A similar vignette was used on the following notes: G.W. Holt, New Orleans, January 1, 1862. $1.00, "plain" style, with values in circles; $1.00, $2.00 and $3.00, larger denomination figures not in circles and with the box at right end containing dog and safe vignette. Blue with red overprint. Printed by Clark & Brisbie.

County of Monroe, Madisonville, Tenn., January 5, 1863, $1 in two types, both similar but one has Indian chief at left with bow and tomahawk (illustrated), while the other has an Indian princess with hand to forehead (a design copied from a Rawdon, Wright, Hatch & Edson engraving). Black with red overprint on ruled tablet paper. Printed by Haws & Dunkerly, Knoxville.

Haws and Dunkerly apparently liked the Female Riding Deer vignette since they also printed a $5 note of 1863 for Cocke County and a 50 cents note of 1862 for the county of Blount, Marysville. Another printer, H. Barry, produced $1 and $2 notes for the County of Blount in 1862 that used the same vignette.

It is even known from Nebraska Territory where it appeared on a $2 note of November 5, 1857, issued by the Brownville Hotel Company, Brownville. Printed by Furnas & Langdon Print, Brownville, N.T.

Still another Midwestern example is a $3.00 note of Butcher, Dailey & Co., Camanche, Iowa, which is likewise from the 1850s. Some idea of how widely this vignette was distributed is indicated by its appearance on an 1864 stock certificate of the Ruba Gold & Silver Mining Co. of Reese River District, Lander County, Nev.

But the major use of the design was in Virginia where the following notes bearing a female riding deer vignette of this type made their appearance:

John T. Hicks, Culpeper, C. H., Va., October 1861. 10 cents, 15 cents, 20 cents. Johnston, Pr., Lynchburg.

P. Duffy & T. H. Renick, February 28, 1862. 200, 25 cents issued from Frankford, Va. and 75 cents issued from Lynchburg, Va. Virginian Pr., Lynchburg.

Jos. H. Houseworth, Orange Court-House, Va. February 16, 1862. 25 cents. Virginian Pr., Lynchburg.

Stewart & Kasey, Stewardsville, Va. February 15, 1862, 5 cents, 200. Virginian Pr. Lynchburg. (Illustrated.)

Lynchburg Savings Bank, Lynchburg, Va. Dec., 1861. 10 cents, $1.50. No imprint. The Peoples Savings Bank, Richmond, Va. September 3, 1861. 25 cents, 37½ cents, 50 cents, $1.00. No imprint.

While I doubt if this is a complete list of locally printed notes and scrip using the female riding deer design, it is sufficient to show that various printers had this particular cut in stock and could have made up the original of the Confederate States Female Riding Deer note. But who? Illustrated is a facsimile of the regularly issued $10 note of July 25, 1861, showing Liberty seated with flag and eagle. This note was the work of S. C. Upham of Philadelphia and it will be noted that there is a very close similarity to the $20 Female Riding Deer note. The same signatures, and similar style of center denomination counter; especially note that the top of the "R" of Richmond is missing on both notes; although it is complete on the genuine notes.

Does this mean that Upham originated the Female Riding Deer note? Although I originally thought not, based on Upham's statement that "none of the designs of the notes were original with me," in an 1874 letter to Dr. William Lee (an early Confederate currency historian), I am now not so sure, as further study of Mr. Upham's work indicates that either because of a hazy memory or because he desired to present a "good appearance" about his work to Dr. Lee, he wasn't quite accurate about a few things.

For example, Upham states to Dr. Lee that he put his name and address "on the margins of each and every note." This simply isn't true. It has been generally assumed that notes recognized as Upham's work that lack his imprint had it clipped off. Certainly this was the case in many instances, but after it came to Upham's attention, he apparently also supplied, on request, notes without his imprint. I have examined various specimens of his notes that have wide blank borders that couldn't possibly have his imprint cut off. A further indication of this is that later he arranged to supply notes, if desired, on a bond paper and without signatures. Thus, the buyer could hand sign them in the same manner as genuine Confederate notes. Naturally, such notes were intended to take South, since printed signatures were quite satisfactory for anyone merely wanting one of the reproductions as a souvenir.

Comparing again the lettering on the illustrated $10 note (No. 9) and the Female Riding Deer note (No. 13) and their obvious similarity, let us consider something that seems to smash his statement of not originating any of the designs. In the list of known Upham facsimiles is a note of the type of No. 9 ($10) but altered and overprinted in red for $20 using the same denomination counters as appears on the $20 Female Riding Deer note. In other words, a transitional design that shows the development of the Female Riding Deer note. But there is one surprising difference: unlike Upham's copies of other Confederate notes, the name of the original printer is omitted on the $20 note (No. 13). Was this an oversight or was Upham copying a note actually received from the South that did not bear the printer's name and of which the originals are now unknown?

While I do not wish to conclusively say that Upham originated the Confederate $20 Female Riding Deer note, he was certainly one of the first to produce it. Assuming that he did develop the design, it would appear that it resulted from someone sending North one of the locally printed notes bearing the female riding deer and Upham later substituted this on his $20 note. For, while Upham may have been technically correct in saying that none of the designs were original with him, he omitted saying anything about mixing his copied vignettes. In any event, Upham was certainly capable of originating or altering a design since he had printed a number of original patriotic covers (envelopes) beginning in 1861.

However, the female riding deer vignette did not originate with Upham since it is an ordinary printer's cut of that period. It is probably from a drawing inspired by a similar engraved vignette on a bank note. A Southern note for $1.00 with this vignette was issued by the Banking House of Cray, MacMurdo & Co., New Orleans. In the North it seems peculiar to Massachusetts where it was issued by the Western Bank, Springfield, $10; Leicester Bank, Leicester, $5; and Rollstone Bank, Fitch-burg, $2. Such an engraving also appeared on checks of the Farmers Bank of Kentucky that were engraved before the war by Rawdon, Wright, Hatch & Edson, Cincinnati. There are quite a few engraved vignettes on bank notes that have their counterparts in cheaper "cuts" for letterpress work. Some are excellent reproductions (often used on checks of the time), others are crude such as the copied vignettes used on State of Missouri notes printed by D. Weil during the Civil War.

The Indian smoking at lower left is probably a stock cut used by printers at that time for tobacco tags or advertisements. The blank space on the front of the barrel contained a tobacco name, "Old Virginia." This brand of tobacco was sold by P. Whitlock, but as far as known, other than making use of a similar cut on which the barrel is blank, it has no connection with the Female Riding Deer note.

It is generally considered that the "originals" have a plain back, with red and black face. At least this variety was the earliest reported. It also exists similarly in orange plus later printings in red, orange and green with different types of backs. The notes with printed backs utilize three basic designs with different borders for a total of seven types. Within the borders appear a pair of "X-X" denominations or TWENTY DOLLARS similar to those used on the front of the notes, either alone or in combination with a vignette showing a wagon load of cotton being pulled by mules. The wagon vignette is a crude copy of a similar design used on a $5 note of the Miners and Manufacturers Bank, Knoxville, Tenn., the same state where private scrip was printed with the Female Riding Deer vignette. Interestingly, Tennessee was one of the routes used to send fakes to the South so the printed backs may be earlier than believed. These printings are letterpress work on which the black ink design was printed separately from the colored part.

Assuming that Upham or others produced a number of these notes during the Civil War in the manner stated as a means of making money, what about the notes produced since? I believe here it can be reasonably assumed that at least a part of the notes were made by R. Toney of Richmond, Ind., for Al E. Bonsall of the same city, as it has been reported that Bonsall and Toney were seen printing the notes (with printed back) years ago. When H. D. Allen wrote his series of articles on Confederate currency in *The Numismatist* in 1917, Bonsall wrote him that he received a specimen of the Female Riding Deer note "while soldiering up the Shenandoah Valley, Virginia." Since many notes bearing the female riding deer design were printed in Lynchburg, Virginia, this is not unlikely. The question is, was the note one of the local issues or was it a note purporting to be of the Confederate States? If the latter, it is possible that Lynchburg was the source of the "original" note. A spurious $20 note showing a different type of female riding deer (to the left) is known from the Bank of Pittsylvania in nearby Chatham. The notorious "Merchants Bank" fakes of the type known with many different addresses throughout the United States are also known from Lynchburg.

While it is only natural that Bonsall (who also bought and sold numismatic items) would prefer the notes to appear genuine to help sales, it is not unlikely that his first specimen did come from the Civil War and that, after his discovering it to be bogus, gave him the idea of reproducing some himself. For, it is also known that this was a source for the Ohio River Bank notes, an illustration of which shows the similarity of the colored background as used on the Female Riding Deer note. The Ohio River Bank notes are also bogus (every river has a "bank"). This Indiana source probably also made notes of the States of Indiana State Stock Bank at Logansport (typeset with same denomination "oyster shell" counters as used on Ohio River Bank's notes, not the genuine engraved notes). Since too many notes could not be placed on the market without arousing undue suspicion, this deterrent to quantity sales was apparently made up by these state bank issues and by making new varieties of the Female Riding Deer notes. At one time (late 19th century) they sold rather high — $10 or more when Confederate notes were still cheap — apparently this was before the later printings relieved their scarcity.

Further proof that at least a part of the later printing with a back design have an Indiana origin is the fact that I have a specimen printed on Kashmir bond paper. This paper was distributed by the old Indiana Paper Company of Indianapolis (not the successor firm organized in 1945). Neither this firm nor this brand of paper was in existence during the Civil War. It also appears on other bond papers. Ordinarily, the Female Riding Deer notes appear on a plain paper. As a general printer, Toney likely had on hand various bonds and other papers that were readily available in the Indiana area, of which Kashmir bond was one, the watermark being the property of the previous Indiana Paper Company. Whether the printers ran short of paper on a press run one time or whether a small quantity of the bond paper got mixed in by accident is not known, but the Kashmir bond paper has pinpointed one source of these notes as Indiana.

Since the producers of the aforementioned notes are no longer active, a photographic reproduction has been made in recent years from an earlier note that had been folded and the fold shows as a white line in the printed reproduction. Interestingly, the illustrated example has a number of differences in the design. For example, the shape of the "2" in 20 differs. And, since the Upham facsimile also differs from other printings, it means that there are at least three versions of the face of this note.

Other Bogus Notes

There are other bogus Confederate notes although none are as famous as the Female Riding Deer notes. Some of these notes are only partially bogus. How can that be? As may be seen by the accompanying illustrations, there are a number of fake backs that were added to already printed Confederate notes to create new varieties. A close study of these backs will show that they were printed over designs already appearing on the notes, such as the interest-paid markings on the $100 notes of 1862. In fact, some of these bogus backs are known to have been overprinted on counterfeit notes, which offers additional proof of their doubtful nature. Other than those that were intended for use as stage money, the usual target of bogus notes has been the collector's pocketbook. We know that we shouldn't, but they are hard to resist.

The following bogus backs are known to me:

Figure 1 — $100 ornate back, "3rd Series," in green on the $100 interest-bearing note (train design), No. 40.

Figure 2 — $100 "Confederate States of America" with "One Hundred Dollars" in center with "C" and "100" at sides within a field made up of decorative border type. Green. Found on Nos. 40, 41, 42 interest-bearing notes.

Figure 3 — "One Hundred Dollars" with "C" and "100" above, within decorative border; rayed sun in corners. Said to have been produced by R. C. Dietrich in green, red or tan (orange). Printed on back of train-type interest-bearing notes. $1000 printed on back of Nos. 18 and 19.

Figure 4 — "One Thousand Dollas" in center of a decorative back. Green. Used to represent greenbacks on the stage. Has been found on notes Nos. 9, 10, 18, 21, 40, 41, 42, 67.

Solid green scroll back (no denomination) on back of $10 note, No. 69. For use as stage money about 1900.

Solid green back on $20 note, No. 21.

These notes with bogus backs made up to about 1900 generally sell for approximately $75 to $100 or more when in nice condition.

There are still other bogus notes printed prior to World War I that bear designs never used by the Confederacy. These notes sometimes had advertising printed on the backs, which means that they can be classified as both bogus and advertising notes.

One of these notes is in the denomination of $100, dated February 17, 1864, and is similar to the regularly issued note of that date except that the vignettes have been changed. In the center is a standing youth. Printed signatures. Plate letter D.

A note that claims to be a Confederate facsimile (but isn't) shows us how General Robert E. Lee may have looked had he ever appeared on the paper money of the South. Based on a $50 note of September 2, 1861, which first carried the portrait of President Jefferson Davis (No. 39), this note has been seen with a plain back and also with late 19th century advertising. At the left side appear the initials G.H.T.

Still another note is one of somewhat smaller size in the denomination of $10, printed in black and pale green, which depicts a sickly-looking locomotive as the central vignette with Justice and the head of an Indian at the sides. This note, which is dated September 2nd, 1861, also comes with an advertisement on the back and may have been intended for that purpose only although the design is one that was never used by the Confederacy.

Bogus Confederate notes are not entirely a thing of the past. Recent bogus notes are in $10,000 and $100,000 denominations dated 1861 and made up from reproductions of No. 4 and 12 with added zeros and fake back. The Confederacy never issued paper money in these denominations. The $1000 (No. 4) note has also been reproduced with the $100 Chemicographic back altered to $1000. All of these are pink and black with blue backs. Some bear advertisements.

Still others include the $100 note of 1864 (No. 72) with a $100,000 denomination and the $500 note of Stonewall Jackson (No. 73) with a $1,000,000 denomination. All of these have printed backs and are intended as souvenirs. But apparently they still fool some people. I once had a woman write to me demanding that I send her $1,000,000 for the note she had, under the impression that since I wrote this catalog of Confederate currency, that in some way I represented the defunct Confederate Treasury. I don't think she ever accepted my explanation.

About Prices

Genuine Confederate and Southern states currency in exceptionally choice condition may command a higher price than indicated by the valuations. General economic changes or the popularity of certain notes may also affect prices.

CONTEMPORARY FACSIMILE NOTES

Unlike counterfeits that are intended by the maker to deceive and be used as money, facsimiles are reproductions made primarily as souvenirs or to be used for advertising purposes. In the United States, a large number of these facsimile notes have incorporated reproductions of various Confederate notes of which the most famous and desirable are those printed by Samuel C. Upham of Philadelphia, Pa., during the Civil War. How did this happen and which notes were reproduced?

Think back to 1861. It was a time when patriotism filled the air, both North and South. Entrepreneurs hurried to capitalize on it by offering the public various badges, ribbons and paper items printed in red, white and blue or filled with patriotic messages. If you don't want to go back that far, try World War II for the same effect. "Remember Pearl Harbor" emblems in various forms were soon on the market, followed by many others, and they weren't being sold to help the government other than keeping morale high.

Enthusiasm dwindled as the Civil War wore on and with it the demand for patriotic items as souvenirs. But that doesn't mean a lack of business. Wars have generally been profitable to those who supply the needs of armies, or even for such things as coffins after the battle of Gettysburg. Then there were those entrepreneurs who devised their own business based on the real or imagined needs of the public, although one doesn't really require a war for that.

Samuel Upham was one of these entrepreneurs who was already operating a combination drugstore, perfumery and stationery shop when the war began. Not an originator, he was quick to grasp the sales potential of items introduced by others. While Upham is best known for his facsimile Confederate notes, these were not his first effort to capitalize on the Civil War. Nor was he the only one in Philadelphia who concentrated on what collectors now call printed ephemera. A number of printers and engravers (especially of wood cuts) were located near his store. From one of the engravers, E. Rogers (132 S. 3rd St.), Upham purchased rights to a card that showed the head of a jackass transformed into the head of Jefferson Davis. Heads up, Davis is going to war, while reversed it shows his drooping, later appearance. Subsequently, Upham used the design on stationery that he advertised on a large business card as the "Jeff. Davis letter sheet" June 30, 1861. Upham's letter sheets were priced at $1 for 100, $8 per 1,000. Envelopes bearing the same design were 50 cents per 100, $4 per 1,000. His business card stated that "Should you wish to engage in the sale of them, which I advise you to do, as I know by experience that they will sell rapidly, please address all orders to S.C. Upham, 310 Chestnut Street, Philadelphia. N.B. Having purchased the above copyright, I alone have the power of appointing agents. Anyone selling without my authority will be prosecuted." Nevertheless, others did produce patriotic envelopes copying this design. (Upham also used the vignette on a circular that urged the public to "Try Upham's Cream Soda" sold in his drugstore.)

The illustrated patriotic envelope, bearing the imprint of S.C. Upham, depicts General Winfield Scott, head of the U.S. Army, being urged to attack a 7-headed hydra of Southern states. The design was possibly a reference to Scott's "Anaconda Plan" of defeating the South through blockade. Since seven states had seceded by February 1861, and Scott retired at the end of October, it stands to reason that this was one of the first patriotic envelopes produced by Upham during the spring or summer of that year. In other words, the envelopes came first and from there it was only a small step for Upham to recognize that other items such as Confederate currency facsimiles might similarly be in demand by a war conscious population.

Upham was soon selling other patriotic envelopes that bear his imprint. I have examined or am aware of more than 30 kinds and based on their style, I believe they were produced for him by James Magee, an envelope maker located at 316 Chestnut Street, who was a major seller of patriotic envelopes under his own name. Magee may have also provided some of the small envelopes to carry postage stamps that were used as a substitute for small change during the coin shortage early in the war. Upham had some printed, bearing his name, which he offered as part of his stationery line. However, I do not believe that Magee was connected with Upham's subsequent facsimiles of Confederate currency since it's not unlikely that his own envelope designs were engraved by others.

Gen. Scott killing the Secession Hydra.

S. C. Upham, 310 Chestnut St.

☜MEMENTOS OF THE REBELLION.

CONFEDERATE NOTES
AND
SHINPLASTERS.

THE undersigned has just published perfect FAC-SIMILES of the following "Confederate States of America" *Notes and Shinplasters*, which will be found curious as well as interesting mementos of the Rebellion.

$10 Confederate Note, issued at Richmond, Va
$5   "   "   "   "   "
10 Cent Shinplaster, issued by the Bank of Tennessee.
15   "   "   "   "   Corporation of Winchester, Va.
5   "   "   "   "   "   "   "
15   "   "   "   "   "   Charlestown, "
5   "   "   "   "   "   Richmond,   "

☞RETAIL PRICE, 5 CENTS EACH.
☞TRADE SUPPLIED AT $2 per 100, or $15 per 1000.

ADDRESS,
S. C. UPHAM,
No. 403 CHESTNUT STREET, PHILADELPHIA, PA.

March, 1862.

NOTICES OF THE PRESS.

☞SAMUEL C. UPHAM, of Philadelphia, advertises that he will sell Confederate notes at easy prices. We at first thought that he had taken some of them for a very bad debt, but it appears he has executed fac-similes of them which he disposes of as mementos. The rates offered by MR. UPHAM are very moderate, and yet we assure all who are anxious to speculate, that his lithographed notes are worth just as much as those issued by Jeff. Davis.—*Louisville Journal.*

CONFEDERATE NOTES.—MR. S. C. UPHAM, 403 Chestnut Street, has published fac-similes of the $5 and $10 Confederate notes issued in Richmond, which will be curiosities ere long, when the rebellion is crushed. MR. UPHAM'S notes are as valuable, we dare say, as the originals.—*Philad'a Press.*

Mr. S. C. UPHAM, No. 403 Chestnut Street, Philadelphia, publishes fac-similes of the Confederate State notes, which are quite interesting to the curious.—*N. Y. Tribune.*

Confederate Bank Notes, of the denomination of FIVE and TEN Dollars each, have been issued by S. C. Upham, No. 403 Chestnut Street, and are sold by him at the most remarkable discount on record. The engraving is fully equal to that of the originals, and the notes are perfect fac-similes of those prepared at Richmond. — *Philadelphia Inquirer.*

Confederate Money.—Mr. S. C. Upham, 403 Chestnut Street, has got out excellent fac-similes of the $5 and $10 notes of the "Confederate States of America," which he sells at prices even cheaper than they bring in Richmond and Memphis. They are curious and interesting, and will become more so as time advances.—*Phila. Evening Bulletin.*

This is the first of Upham's circulars or handbills that he used to advertise his facsimiles. It is dated March 1862, when he began offering them. The same month he inserted a classified advertisement in newspapers that read: "Confederate notes in the denominations of $5 and $10 for sale at UPHAM'S, 403 CHESTNUT STREET, Philadelpia. Ten $5 and ten $10 Confederate notes sent postpaid to any address on receipt of $1. Trade supplied at $2 per 100, or $15 per 1000. Send your orders at once." This ad contains no mention that the notes are facsimiles.

MEMENTOS OF THE REBELLION.

REBEL NOTES, SHINPLASTERS AND POSTAGE STAMPS.

THE undersigned has just published perfect FAC-SIMILES of the following Rebel Notes, Shinplasters and Postage Stamps, which will be found curious as well as interesting mementos of the Rebellion.

$10 Confederate Note, issued at Richmond, Va.
$5 " " " " "
10 Cent Shinplaster, issued by the Bank of Tennessee.
15 " " " " Corporation of Winchester, Va. "
5 " " " " " " "
15 " " " " " Charlestown, "
5 " " " " " Richmond, "
25 " " " " " Camden, N. C. "
50 " " " " " Mech's Savings Ass'n, Savannah, Ga.

10 Cent Confederate States of America Postage Stamp.
5 " " " " " "
5 " Postage Stamp, issued by Postmaster at New Orleans.

RETAIL PRICE OF THE NOTES AND SHINPLASTERS, FIVE CENTS EACH.
" " " " POSTAGE STAMPS, THREE CENTS EACH.

Agents supplied with the NOTES and SHINPLASTERS, at $2 per 100, or $15 per thousand.
" " " POSTAGE STAMPS, at $1 per 100, or $7 50 per thousand.

One each of the above *Notes, Shinplasters* and *Postage Stamps,* sent post-paid to any address, on the receipt of FIFTY cents.

QUICK SALES AND LARGE PROFITS.

Upwards of $80,000 of the *Notes, Shinplasters* and *Postage Stamps* have been sold during the past four weeks, and the cry is still for more. Orders by MAIL and EXPRESS promptly filled.

Address, **S. C. UPHAM,**

May, 1862. No. 403 CHESTNUT STREET, PHILADELPHIA, PA.

NOTICES OF THE PRESS.

REBELDOM HIGHLY INDIGNANT.—'YANKEE TRICK.' The rebel papers contain the following:
"PHILADELPHIA CONFEDERATE BONDS.—Detective Goodrich, of the rebel Treasury Department, has exhibited to the editor of the Richmond *Dispatch* what he terms 'the last and greatest piece of Yankee scoundrelism, and an infernal means to discredit the currency of the Southern Confederacy.' 'It consists,' says the *Dispatch,* 'in well executed counterfeits of our five dollar Confederate notes, struck off in Philadelphia, where the news-boys are selling them at five cents a piece. This note is well calculated to deceive, and in nearly every particular is a fac-simile of the original. We caution persons receiving this money to be exceedingly careful, as there is no means of knowing to what extent they have been circulated.'

"The 'Yankee Scoundrel' who has counterfeited these *Valuable* notes is Mr. S. C. Upham, 403 Chestnut Street. He has issued fac-similes of seven kinds of rebel shinplasters and two denominations of their notes. He has also issued exact copies of rebel postage stamps of three kinds, the five and ten cent stamps issued by the Confederate Government, and the five cent stamp got up by J. S. Riddell, the postmaster at New Orleans, and bearing his name. Mr. Upham sells these fac-similes very cheap, but they certainly bring as much as the originals are worth."—*Philadelphia Bulletin.*

SAMUEL C. UPHAM, of Philadelphia, advertises that he will sell Confederate notes at easy prices. We at first thought that he had taken some of them for a very bad debt, but it appears he has executed fac-similes of them which he disposes of as mementos. The rates offered by MR. UPHAM are very moderate, and yet we assure all who are anxious to speculate, that his lithographed notes are worth just as much as those issued by Jeff. Davis.—*Louisville Journal.*

Confederate Bank Notes, of the denomination of FIVE and TEN Dollars each, have been issued by S. C. Upham, No. 403 Chestnut Street, and are sold by him at the most remarkable discount on record. The engraving is fully equal to that of the originals, and the notes are perfect fac-similes of those prepared at Richmond. — *Philadelphia Inquirer.*

CONFEDERATE NOTES.—Mr. S. C. UPHAM, 403 Chestnut Street, has published fac-similes of the $5 and $10 Confederate Notes, issued in Richmond, which will be curiosities ere long, when the rebellion is crushed. MR. UPHAM'S notes are as valuable, we dare say, as the originals.—*Philadelphia Press.*

MR. S. C. UPHAM, No. 403 Chestnut Street, Philadelphia, publishes fac-similes of the Confederate State notes, which are quite interesting to the curious.—*N. Y. Tribune.*

Confederate Money.—Mr. S. C. Upham, 403 Chestnut Street, has got out excellent fac-similes of the $5 and $10 notes of the Confederate States of America," which he sells at prices even cheaper than they bring in Richmond and Memphis. They are curious and interesting, and will become more so as time advances.—*Phila. Evening Bulletin.*

The broadside illustrated above is presumably Upham's second circular, dated May 1862. The number of Confederate notes offered is still limited to the two kinds printed from the newspaper electrotypes obtained by Upham but the "shinplasters" have been augmented by two additional notes that give some idea of the sequence in which they were produced. Plus, there are three postage stamps. We also learn that "upwards of 80,000" have been sold. For some reason, the Mechanics Savings and Bank of Tennessee note (with Adrian Sharp name) are printed on the back of this advertisement.

HALF PRICE! HALF PRICE!!

CONFEDERATE NOTES AND SHINPLASTERS

SELLING AT

ONE-HALF FORMER PRICES.

FOURTEEN DIFFERENT

REBEL NOTES, SHINPLASTERS AND POSTAGE STAMPS,

Perfect FAC-SIMILES of the originals, (printed in red, green and black ink,) sold by the 100 or 1,000 at the following reduced rates:—

50 cents per 100, or $4 per 1,000. One each of the fourteen different kinds sent post-paid to any address, on receipt of 25 cents.

All orders by Mail or Express, promptly executed.

Address,

S. C. UPHAM, 403 Chestnut St. Philadelphia, Pa.

500,000 SOLD THE PAST THREE MONTHS.

CARD TO THE PUBLIC.

As an individual in New York and a "shyster" in this city, lacking the brains to originate an idea or the liberality to pay for a respectable drawing or engraving, have recently gotten up "shocking bad" copies of several of my FAC-SIMILE REBEL NOTES and SHINPLASTERS, which they are endeavoring to foist upon the public, I have this day reduced the price of my FAC-SIMILE Notes, Shinplasters and Postage Stamps to 50 cents per 100 or $4 per 1,000, and shall be happy to receive and fill orders in large or small quantities at the above rates.

N. B.—BEWARE OF BASE IMITATIONS! Each and every FAC-SIMILE issued by me bears my imprint.

S. C. UPHAM,

Philad'a, May 30, 1862. No. 403 Chestnut St.

NOTICES OF THE PRESS.

"REBELDOM HIGHLY INDIGNANT.—'Yankee Trick.' The rebel papers contain the following:

"PHILADELPHIA CONFEDERATE BONDS.—Detective Goodrich, of the rebel Treasury Department, has exhibited to the editor of the Richmond *Dispatch* what he terms 'the last and grossest piece of Yankee scoundrelism, and an infernal means to discredit the currency of the Southern Confederacy.' 'It consists,' says the *Dispatch*, 'in well executed counterfeits of our five dollar Confederate notes, struck off in Philadelphia, where the news-boys are selling them at five cents a piece. This note is well calculated to deceive, and in nearly every particular is a fac-simile of the original. We caution persons receiving this money to be exceedingly careful, as there is no means of knowing to what extent they have been circulated.'

"The 'Yankee Scoundrel' who has counterfeited these *Valuable* notes is Mr. S. C. Upham, 403 Chestnut Street. He has issued fac-similes of seven kinds of rebel shinplasters and two denominations of their notes. He has also issued exact copies of rebel postage stamps of three kinds, the five and ten cent stamps issued by the Confederate Government, and the five cent stamp got up by J. S. Riddell, the postmaster at New Orleans, and bearing his name. Mr. Upham sells these fac-similes very cheap, but they certainly bring as much as the originals are worth."—*Philadelphia Evening Bulletin.*

SAMUEL C. UPHAM, of Philadelphia, advertises that he will sell Confederate notes at easy prices. We at first thought that he had taken some of them for a very bad debt, but it appears he has executed fac-similes of them which he disposes of as mementos. The rates offered by Mr. Upham are very moderate, and yet we assure all who are anxious to speculate, that his lithographed notes are worth just as much as those issued by Jeff. Davis.—*Louisville Journal.*

Confederate Bank Notes, of the denomination of Five and Ten Dollars each, have been issued by S. C. Upham, No. 403 Chestnut Street, and are sold by him at the most remarkable discount on record. The engraving is fully equal to that of the originals, and the notes are perfect fac-similes of those prepared at Richmond.—*Philadelphia Inquirer.*

CONFEDERATE NOTES.—Mr. S. C. Upham, 403 Chestnut Street, has published fac-similes of the $5 and $10 Confederate Notes, issued in Richmond, which will be curiosities ere long, when the rebellion is crushed. Mr. Upham's notes are as valuable, we dare say, as the originals.—*Philadelphia Press.*

Mr. S. C. Upham, No. 403 Chestnut Street, Philadelphia, publishes fac-similes of the Confederate State notes, which are quite interesting to the curious.—*N. Y. Tribune.*

Confederate Money.—Mr. S. C. Upham, 403 Chestnut Street, has got out excellent fac-similes of the $5 and $10 notes of the "Confederate States of America," which he sells at prices even cheaper than they bring in Richmond and Memphis. They are curious and interesting, and will become more so as time advances.—*Phila. Evening Bulletin.*

(left margin, vertical) N. B.—If you order by the 100, send 18 cents in addition to the price of each 100, to PRE-PAY postage.

(right margin, vertical) The $5 and $10 Notes, on Bank Note Paper, at $3 per 100, or $20 per 1,000.

Upham's circular illustrated above is a surprise. Dated May 30, 1862, it states that "500,000 sold in the past months." Unfortunately we do not know the number of notes since stamps are apparently included in the quantity. Nevertheless, it is obvious from the price reduction that the market was becoming satiated, not only by his own production but also through the competitors he mentions. Note his statement "Beware of base imitations! Each and every facsimile issued by me carries my imprint."

The story of how Upham began producing facsimiles of Confederate notes is rather well known, but I will recount it briefly. We are fortunate that Dr. William Lee, an early researcher of Confederate currency, wrote to Upham in 1874 for information on the production of facsimiles. (It is regrettable, however, that he did not obtain a complete list and more details about his production.) Upham did inform Lee that his incentive was the great demand in his store for the *Philadelphia Inquirer* newspaper dated February 24, 1862. Upon being told that it contained a reproduction of a $5 note (No. 22), the first seen in Philadelphia, Upham hurried to the *Inquirer's* office where he was able to purchase an electrotype of the note from which he initially had 3,000 copies printed that sold like "hot cakes" at 1 cent each. A cent sounds insignificant today but it had greater purchasing power in 1862. The entire newspaper, containing the reproduction, cost 2 cents.

Upham stated that the next note that he reproduced with his imprint was a $10 note (No. 9), which was printed from an electrotype obtained from *Leslie's Illustrated Newspaper* where it had appeared in the issue of January 11, 1862. Other notes were to follow that included Southern bank, city and county issues. Oddly, no state issues were reproduced although they should have been more easily found than the local issues. Just how many kinds in all were reproduced is uncertain.

When Upham replied to Lee, he gave a figure of 28 kinds of currency and 15 kinds of Confederate postage stamps that he stated were produced between March 12, 1862, and August 1, 1863, to a total of 1,564,050 pieces. While that number may be correct, we don't know the breakdown between the notes and the stamps nor does the number agree with any of his known advertisements. Three of his handbills (see illustrations) give much lower numbers while a fourth (not illustrated) states that he has "published FAC-SIMILES of thirty-five different Rebel Notes and Postage Stamps, which will be found curious as well as interesting novelties of the Rebellion." On this circular the price is 50 cents per 100 or $5 per 1,000. Unlike the other offerings, this one also offers $1, $2, $5, $10, $50 and $100 notes, printed from the same plates on bank note and bond paper, with the numbers left blank to be filled by the purchaser, at $1.50 per 100, or $10 per 1000. As a part of a special notice, Upham requests that "persons ordering the notes will please either state whether they want those from new or old plates; and if from the new plates, whether WITH or WITHOUT signatures." This mention of "old" and "new" plates may be the explanation of why his imprint at the bottom of his facsimiles appear in two styles, roman (upright) and italic (slanted) type. It may have been his way of easily distinguishing the plates, although there appears to be no difference between the two other than the possibility that the "old" plates were becoming worn.

The foregoing circular, which may have been distributed only to dealers, raises the question whether the $1 or $2 notes are Confederate States notes (Nos. 43, 45) or whether they are local issues from Virginia (see list that follows). Another question arises from Upham's statement that the notes were printed on bank note and bond paper. I have examined quite a number of Upham facsimiles and I don't recall any on bond paper. Perhaps his definition differed from that used today. On the other hand, this handbill does explain the existence of notes bearing handwritten signatures or serial numbers (not printed) that do not bear his imprint despite any denials that he never produced them without his name and address at the bottom. Apparently Upham learned that certain buyers of his notes were trimming off his statement at the bottom and he offered to save them the work. (Since the price for "blank" notes is higher, Upham apparently felt that such kinds were likely to be used for nefarious purposes, such as taking them South to buy cotton, and for that reason he ought to share a little in the profit. They wouldn't have cost any more to print than those with the numbers, signatures and his advertisement.)

Upham's addresses and business emphasis changed over the years. On his patriotic envelopes, his address was 310 Chestnut Street but by the time his facsimile notes appeared he had relocated to 403 Chestnut Street. And, on a Centennial token of 1876, his business is simply given as being a perfumer, although the drugstore continued to be operated. At that time he was located at 25 S. Eighth Street, which indicates that Upham was aware that the business center of Philadelphia was moving westward. Upham died in 1885 at the age of 66 and one may infer from the inventory of his estate that the stationery portion of his business had been discontinued since only drugstore and perfumery articles were listed. However, there is mention of electrotype plates, which, if they were not illustrations for his store advertisements, may have been for his Confederate facsimiles. Should that be correct, it is a good guess that they were the plates of some of the local issues and that he had been unable to sell them. Even during the Civil War, one has to wonder whether there was much demand for local issues such as the reproductions of a 5-cent note of C.R. Bricken or the 25-cent note of County of Camden that had no vignettes. If Upham sold the plates for his notes to others after he ceased production, the buyers undoubtedly preferred those that reproduced issues of the Confederacy.

Facsimiles that can positively be identified as having been reproduced by Upham bear an inscription on the bottom, "Fac-Simile Confederate note.-Sold wholesale-and retail, by S.C. Upham, 403 Chestnut Street, Philadelphia." The imprint is in small caps or italic type. Notes are found with both styles of imprint. Although many were printed, they are no longer common as many had Upham's address clipped off. Still others have been destroyed over the years. Some, if not all, were available without Upham's imprint and these notes were taken South where they entered circulation as counterfeits. Thus, unlike most facsimiles, they had a secondary use as money. Due to their close association with the Civil War, these notes are now an historical item that command $75 to $100 in Fine condition for the Confederate notes with Upham's advertisement intact. In Uncirculated condition they are worth $250. Those listed as scarce or rare are worth more. Bank and local issues printed by Upham have a value of $35-$50 in Fine and $75 or more in Uncirculated with Upham's imprint intact. Notes without his imprint and those in lower grades are worth less. All of these facsimiles are printed in black on white paper unless otherwise stated.

A Listing of Upham Facsimile Notes

Confederate Treasury Notes. Numbers refer to catalog.

9. Printed signatures and serial No. 10,447. This note was illustrated in *Harper's Popular Encyclopedia of United States History,* by Benson J. Lossing, New York, 1893, as a genuine Confederate note. Also without printed signatures and numbers. The printer's name incorrectly appears as Noyer & Ludwig on this note.

— Transitional printing by Upham (not a note issued by the Confederacy). Type of No. 9, but instead of the usual $10, it has value XX and with a red overprint like on the $20 Female Riding Deer note (No. 13). Very rare, probably never went beyond the sample stage.

13. Printed signatures and serial No. 6430. Upham may or may not be responsible for some of these notes without his imprint, signatures or serial numbers. Red and black. Rare with Upham's imprint on note. Interestingly, Upham's circulars do not list a $20 note.

17. Printed signatures and serial No. 3408. Also without printed numbers.

18. The rear wagon wheel on the left shows 10 spokes instead of seven, as on the genuine note. Serial No. 15,049. Printed signatures, Also without printed signatures and numbers.

21. Printed signatures and serial No. 40,389. Hoyer & Ludwig. Scarce.

22. This was the first facsimile issued by Upham. Printed signatures and serial number 364. Also without printed numbers. Red and black.

23. Printed signatures and serial number 3312. Also without printed signatures. Printed in red and black. A very scarce variety includes the name of Adrian Sharp at the lower edge.

24. Printed signatures and serial number 4316. Also without printed numbers. Printed in red and black.

32. Printed signatures and serial number 8644. Also without printed signatures and serial numbers. Printed in green and black.

Local bank, city and county issues. Excepting the $1 and $2 Corporation of Richmond notes, which indicate they are "Confederate," Upham's inscription on these issues is changed to read "Fac Simile Rebel Shinplaster."

5¢ No. 4, Exchange Block, Richmond, Va. September 3, 1861. Printed in blue or black. Printed signature of C.R. Bricken.

50¢ Mechanics Savings and Loan Association, Savannah, Ga. October 25, 1861. Serial No. 155. Printed signatures.

10¢ Bank of Tennessee, Nashville. December 1st, 1861. Imitation of a note originally printed by J. Manouvrier, picturing train and Mexican coins. Printed signatures. There are two plate varieties. The name of Adrian Sharp will be found on one variety (scarce) at lower right edge.

5¢ Corporation of Winchester, Virginia. October 4th, 1861. Serial No. 150. Printed signatures. Tan paper. Also with VIRGINIA spelled VIRGINLA (Upham printing?)

15¢ Corporation of Winchester, Virginia. June 24, 1861. Printed facsimile signatures, date, and serial No. 2708. Printed in red.

15¢ As above, with same serial number but many differences in style of type. No CG at left of small beehive at bottom of note. Upham?

15¢ Corporation of Winchester, Virginia. January 15, 1862. Printed in blue.

$1 Corporation of Winchester, Virginia. Nov 23d, 1861.

25¢ The City of Richmond, Virginia. April 14, 1862. Serial No. K3970. Printed signatures. Scarce.

$1 The Corporation of Richmond, Virginia. 19th April 1861. Printed signatures and serial No. C3451. Printer's and engraver's names (Hoyer & Ludwig) missing from bottom of note as was on original. Green, black. (This missing imprint may be the same thing that occurred on the Female Riding Deer note if there was an original.)

$1 Also noted with printed serial number C2767 that appears identical except Pres, is spelled Pras. Upham?

$2 Corporation of Richmond, Virginia. April 19, 1861. Serial No. F9502. The final "2" in the serial number resembles a "3". Printed signatures. Printed in red and black. Scarce.

15¢ The Corporation of Charlestown, Virginia. January 1, 1862. Serial No. 576. Printed signatures. White or light blue paper.

15¢ As above but printing error. The CRPORATION of Charlestown. Scarce.

15¢ As above, correct spelling and same serial number but the words "The Corporation of Charlestown" are not wide enough to reach beneath No. and G. at the sides and the denomination is of thicker type. Upham"

$2 Madison County, Virginia. September 2, 1861. Serial No. 298. Unlike most notes, Upham had this printed in a combination of colors on light tan paper, Basic design is in dark blue, signatures in black, serial number and vertical signature of secretary in red.

25¢ County of Camden, North Carolina. This note has Carolina spelled CAROLNA (missing "I"). Very deceptive. Printed in green with signatures, date (September 9th, 1861) and serial number (No. 71) in black in a fine script that appears to be "real" and not printed. Plate letter Z. With or without Upham's imprint at bottom of note. Thin, light tan paper.

25¢ As above, but with heavier obviously printed signatures, and different floral decorative design at ends of note. No plate letter, serial No. 71. (Upham printing?) No inscription indication that it is a facsimile.

Excepting varieties of the Winchester, Richmond, Charlestown and Camden notes, which may not be Upham's, all are known with his inscription at the bottom. Not including the transitional printing between types 9 and 13, this list includes 23 major types out of the 28 Upham said he printed. Other facsimiles may be Upham's, but that have not been seen with his imprint include types 19, 27, 30, 37 (solid "X"), 39, 42, 43 (Plate No. 10) and 45 (Plate No. 10). It is possible that part or all of these additional notes were among his productions since as late as the October 18, 1862, issue of *Harper's Weekly*, Upham advertised "Thirty-five different rebel notes, shinplasters and postage stamps sent postpaid, on receipt of fifty cents,"

I am under the impression that certain notes designated as "Upham" in lists published elsewhere do not actually bear his imprint but are described as such based on their appearance. This will certainly cause confusion to collectors and researchers of the future who are searching for notes bearing Upham's advertisement at the bottom of the notes. I have not listed any facsimile Confederate notes that do not bear his edge inscription, although some of them may be Upham's. There are, however, a number of other Confederate notes that have edge inscriptions indicating that they are facsimiles. Most of them closely resemble Upham's copies and may have been produced from his plates after he ceased production. They are listed here as an aid to collectors. All of these notes, plus the Upham facsimiles listed previously, I either own or have personally examined and collectors may be assured that they exist.

Other Confederate Facsimiles with Edge Inscriptions

These notes appear to be printed from the same plates as Upham's, but do not bear his name. Other facsimiles exist that are apparently contemporary to the Civil War, but I have listed only those that include the word "Facsimile." Numbers refer to the catalog section of this book.

Inscription at left side in Roman type: Fac-Simile Confederate note.
    Nos. 9, 17, 18, 23, 24, 32, 42 (Plate No. 10), 44, 45 (Plate No. 10).
    Generally without printed numbers. No. 23 with or without New Orleans at lower left.

Inscription at left side in italic type: Fac-Simile Confederate Note.
    Nos. 9, 17, 18, 21, 23, 24, 32, 40, 41, 43 (Plate No. 10).

Inscription at both left and right sides in Italic type: Fac Simile Confederate Note.
    No. 40 (Very scarce.)

Inscription at right side in Roman type: Fac-Simile Confederate Note.
    No. 42 (Very scarce with imprint on right side.)

Inscription at right side in italic type: Fac-Simile Confederate Note. No. 42 (Very scarce.)

Inscription at bottom in Roman type: Fac-simile Confederate Note.
    No. 30, 32, 36, 37 (Solid "X").

Inscription at bottom in italic type: Fac Simile Rebel Note. (Very scarce version.)
    No. 27 (excellent work, appears superior to Upham's), 30, 32, 37 (Solid "X,"
    no signatures or serial number), 39

Inscription at bottom on italic type: Fac Simile Confederate Note. No. 21.

Inscription at left side in italic type: Fac-simile of Rebel Note. (Very scarce.)
  No. 19, Second Series. Printed signatures, no serial number.

Inscription at bottom in capitals: Fac Simile of a Treasury Note, lately issued by the
  Confederate Government, Richmond, Va. No. 9, 22, (Upham's first imprint?)

Inscription at left side: Fac-Simile Rebel Shinplaster. (Very scarce version.)
  $1, Corporation of Winchester, November 23d, 1861.

It should be noted that this list does not include variants in style of the edge inscriptions. For example, some have dashes at one or both sides of the inscription although most do not. Does this indicate more than one printer or different press runs by the same printer? The answer to that is yet to be determined. Also to be determined is the printer or printers who produced the facsimiles for Upham and who engraved them after he obtained the first two electrotypes from newspapers. We know the engraver of two notes, the Bank of Tennessee 10-cent note and the Confederate $10 (No. 23), since both of these may be found with the name of Adrian Sharp at the lower edge. Apparently, Upham did not like this competition with his name and it was removed from later printings. Adrian Sharp, by the way, was not an individual. It was the firm name of William Adrian and Joseph E. Sharp, wood engravers at 138 S. 3rd St., Philadelphia.

Whether Upham was sufficiently irritated at Adrian Sharp to discontinue having them handle his engraving after including the name on two of his facsimiles is unknown. If that should have happened, there were a number of other engravers in Philadelphia, among whom was E. Rogers (123 S. 3rd) from whom Upham had earlier obtained the jackass engraving used on his envelopes and lettersheets. As for printers, there were many in Upham's area, notably James B. Chandler, 308 Chestnut, and James Gibbons, S.W. 4th & Chestnut.

However, as a part of my continued research of the Upham story, it is possible that I have found the answer to what happened to Upham's production of facsimile notes. As far as I can determine, Upham sold his business at 403 Chestnut Street to John J. Kromer and relocated at 1320 S. 5th Street before moving to 25 S. 8th Street in 1865. Whether Kromer obtained the rights to the facsimile notes, I am not certain, but since he obtained the rights to Upham's Hair Dye, it is not unlikely. Not only that, since Kromer was located in an area of Philadelphia where there were many printers, he may have added additional facsimiles of his own. Elsewhere I have indicated Upham's possessive attitude toward stationery and other designs he owned and an apparent desire to protect his name. This, coupled with Kromer's desire to eliminate Upham's name on the hair dye, tends to indicate that any subsequent production of Upham's facsimiles would not bear his name. In the accompanying list there are a number of facsimiles that appear to be identical to those sold by Upham but the edge inscription does not indicate the source. Whether Kromer was a source is an intriguing question but the illustrated example that has his advertisement on the back shows that he was familiar with them. While I would like to be able to conclusively say that Kromer was the source for facsimiles after Upham ended sales in August 1863, one or more printers on their own may not have wanted to let this opportunity pass.

As for other printers of facsimile notes, Upham states in his circular of May 30, 1862, that "an individual in New York and a 'shyster' in this city" were producing "shocking bad" copies. According to Upham's letter to Dr. Lee, the New York source was Haney & Hilton, but he does not identify the Philadelphia source. Very likely he was referring to John Storey who was the source of a facsimile 5 cents note dated January 1862 from Dunnington & Cockrell, Dumfries, Va. While it is true that this is a poorly printed note on cheap tan paper, as far as known it is not a copy of any produced by Upham. Rather, it appears that Storey, who was a tobacconist located at 216 N. 10th St., having seen Upham's success, decided to likewise expand his business.

While it is true that the notes offered by John Storey were "shocking bad," those of Haney & Hilton were equal or superior to the facsimiles sold by Upham. This competition and a decline in sales probably contributed to Upham's decision to cease production in August 1863, particularly if Kromer made him an offer that was too good to refuse. Both Winthrop E. Hilton and S.C. Upham advertised in *Harper's Weekly* during 1862 and 1863. The quality of Hilton's work apparently forced Upham to reduce the price of his facsimiles but without effect.. Those seeking facsimiles, which were really counterfeits that they wished to use in the South, very likely preferred Hilton's notes.

Throughout the ages, there have been many people who have been willing to make friends with the devil if it served their needs. Christopher G. Memminger, the Confederate Secretary of the Treasury, must have been aware that some high quality counterfeits were entering the South but did not wish to cause panic by making it public knowledge. Why not have one of the Confederate agents in New York City or Canada contact Hilton and see whether he might not be enticed to work instead for the South? The Confederacy paid its English engravers in gold, why not someone in the North? Since Hilton openly advertised facsimiles, "exactly like the genuine," which were a detriment to the Confederate government, he would likely be above suspicion. This scenario may sound unbelievable, but the Civil War contains many examples of double agents, codes and intrigues used by both sides to undermine each other. Moreover, it should be recalled that Memminger had previously broken an agreement with Hoyer & Ludwig and J.T. Paterson (see Enigmatical Issues). Perhaps this time he would secure a really good engraver.

In any case, it is known that in December 1863, a letter from New York to a Confederate agent in Canada was intercepted that led to Hilton's arrest. It was written in code but, after being deciphered, it read "Say to Memminger that Hilton will have the machine all finished and dies ready for shipping by the first of January. The engraving of the plates is superb." Unfortunately for Hilton, both the North and the South often used a secret code called the "Vigenere Tableau." Once the key letter is figured out, translation is easy.

There must be some truth in this matter. While I tend to downgrade newspaper sensationalism, it was reported that Hilton did normal printing work in his shop by day and had other men producing Confederate notes at night under a contract for $50 million of them that were being smuggled into the Confederate States. It was further reported that when he never received the promised payment in gold, he continued to have Confederate notes printed on his own. The story doesn't quite agree with his advertising, due to conflict of dates, but the newspaper indicated that he was arrested and locked up in Fort Lafayette.

If this occurred, Hilton was apparently able to convince the government that by counterfeiting the Confederate currency, he was really aiding the North since by 1866 he was again in the business of imitations — this time by printing and advertising Hilton's Ten Cent Books, which capitalized on the popularity of Beadle's Dime Novels.

MODERN FACSIMILES

Facsimiles of Confederate notes and other currency did not end with the Civil War although those of that period, being contemporary, are of the greatest interest. Those printed since the Civil War have been used primarily for advertising purposes and for that reason generally bear advertising printed on the backs. (See the chapter on Facsimile Advertising Notes). However, one will occasionally find a facsimile printed between the end of the Civil War and the 1950s that came from a printer's stock without advertising being added. Rather than attempt to list such exceptions, this chapter will deal with modern reproductions that do not bear advertising (although they may have been used for that purpose in the form of premiums) and that have frequently caused problems between dealers, collectors and finders. The finders often provide a good story along with the notes to the effect that they were found in their great grandmother's Civil War trunk or the attic of an old house, although the facsimiles aren't that old.

One of the most widely distributed groups of Confederate facsimiles were those packaged in Cheerios breakfast cereal in 1954-55. They consist of the 1864 notes ($1-$500, Nos. 68-73) and the $1,000 notes of 1861 (No. 4). The backs are plain except for the words "Reprinted in U.S.A. 1954" at the lower edge but this is often erased by those attempting to sell them.

Another problem set was distributed by Whitman Publishing Company during the 1960s that includes $1 to $50 reproductions of 1864, plus a $100 note of 1862 (No. 42A). However, these can be readily distinguished by a style of blue back not used on the genuine notes and the word "Facsimile" in small letters at the lower left side. These notes were initially printed on white stock but are more commonly found on paper that appears yellowed. Likewise, individual specimens are more often seen than complete sets in descriptive envelopes. Still another group of reproductions was produced by Gilbert Humphrys in 1953 that contains no indication that they are facsimiles. Like other kinds, they can be distinguished by their printed signatures with the possible exception of the 50 cents note of 1863 (No. 57), which may be confusing. It bears serial No. 104508.

Other recent issues include a set of Confederate facsimiles (approximately 5½" by 2½") with pink and black fronts and black, blue and white backs that were distributed in 1964 by A.B.C. Chewing Gum, Ltd, of England. There are supposed to be 15 kinds in the denominations of $1 to $1000 selected from the 1861, 1862 and 1864 issues but there may have been more since the set appears to be the same as the one of 17 kinds issued earlier by the Topps Company in the United States. One of the most aggravating of the modern issues are those produced on a parchment-like paper that has been artificially aged to give it a yellowish-brown appearance. Besides a number of Confederate and Southern states issues, these reproductions include what is perhaps the most famous of all modern facsimiles — the $1,000 note of the Bank of the United States, bearing serial No. 8894, and dated 1840. Although not related to the Confederacy, it is worthy of mention due to its frequent appearance. Fortunately, a good many of these yellowish-brown notes, which are printed in black, have advertising added to the backs that should readily make them identifiable as reproductions even to the uninitiated.

ADVERTISING ON CONFEDERATE NOTES

Few things attract attention like money. And attention is what you want if you are advertising. One way to get people to give an advertisement more than a casual glance is to print it on a bank note. Naturally, printing ads on "real" money that is currently in circulation would be the most attention-getting; but that would most likely be too expensive, besides being against the law. On the other hand, paper money that has lost its value and is no longer in circulation has been an ideal advertising medium for many years. However, most examples today utilize reproductions (see elsewhere in this catalog for information on facsimile notes).

The use of actual money on which to print ads saw its greatest use after the Civil War when large quantities of Confederate notes were available at a very low price. However, the practice did not originate then. Ads in the form of paper money were used in the United States as far back as the 1830s, if not earlier. Although ads were sometimes printed on the notes of various banks that were no longer in business ("broken banks") or that were no longer redeemable, the majority of the pre-Civil War advertising notes were specially printed designs that resembled currency. This is also true of the late 19th century (and since) but a number of enterprising individuals and firms printed their ads on the paper money of the Confederate and Southern states, which could be obtained after the war about as cheaply as having an original design made up in bank note style.

There are hundreds of advertising notes but those printed on Confederate currency are among the most desirable if not always the most interesting. Generally, the ads are printed on the backs of the notes, either horizontally or vertically. Some of the advertisements are more common than others although all have risen greatly in price during recent years as the collecting of advertising notes has become popular. Advertisements printed on genuine Confederate notes that are in Fine to Very Fine condition now sell for $50 or more with $75 to $150 becoming the usual price. Exceptionally nice or seldom-seen examples may be worth $100 and up. Should the note on which the advertisement appears be a rare variety, the value may increase even further.

Below is a listing in roughly alphabetical order of advertisements appearing on "real" notes. The description usually includes only the large lettering or main wording of the ads. Additional information has been added where applicable. The numbers following each advertisement are the catalog numbers of notes on which they have been found. These ads may have also appeared on other notes, including those of Southern states issues. This is not a complete list of advertisements or the notes on which they may be found. Collectors are invited to submit additions to the author or publisher.

The Great Broad Gauge, Atlantic & Great Western Route, between the East and the West. 19, 22, 30, 35, 52, 53, 55, 63.

C.H. Bechtel, New York City. (Ad for albums of Confederate notes. Bechtel published a catalog of Confederate currency as early as 1877 and was one of the first dealers in Confederate notes.) 68.

Bee Line Ticket Office, Cor. 5th and Chestnut Streets, (Laclede Hotel,) St. Louis, Mo. (Long inscription, front and back, advertising this railroad route.) Missouri Defense Bond, $1, $3, $4.50.

Bellevue Livery, First Class Rigs at Reasonable Rates. Traveling men Accommodated at All Times. J. P. Mann, Proprietor, Bellevue, Iowa. 71.

Virginia Homes (Very long inscription about farms), A. O. Bliss, Ashland, Va. 69, 71.

Happy New Year's Greetings 1-1-1899. H. H. Brown, Securities Dealer and Loan Office. 42.

Relics of the War, Childrey, the Druggist, dealer in old Coins, Stamps and Relics, 1722 Main St., Richmond, Va. 42. Also on North Carolina $2 note, 1861.

Write to J. H. Childrey, 1722 Main St., Richmond, Va. for Confederate Money, Stamps, Bonds, Coins, &c. 22, 40, 41, 42.

Columbus Textile Mfg., 1905, 72.

A Relic of the Southern Confederacy. This is a genuine note that was used in the South during the war. Accept it with the compliments of H. Choate, dealer in dry goods, Winona, Minn. 69.

Confederate poem on back, Souvenir of the Grand Commandery of Georgia, Louisville, 1901, 71 and 1907, 69. (Also noted from their convention in San Francisco, 1904, and may exist for other years. 68, 70).

Confederate Veteran's Reunion, Charleston, S.C. May, 1899, in blue on face of note. Confederate poem on back. 68.

Confederate poem as reprinted from the Augusta, Ga. Daily Press of March 26, 1866. 69.

Confederate poem on back exists in various types of printings without advertising. 42, 67 (scarce), 68, 70, 71. (A copy of this poem appears on page 137.) One source was Francis Bannerman Sons, New York, a dealer in military relics.

25th Confederate Reunion. 69.

Dixon & Murphy, Coal Merchants, Savannah, Ga. Confederate poem on back. 71.

Southern Hepatic Pills, G. W. Deems, Goldsboro, N.C. 70.

Famous Clothing, Toledo. 68.

Ford's Hotel, Richmond, Va. (Long inscription.) Board only $2.50 Per Day. 61, 69, 70.

Ford's Hotel, Richmond, Va. (Ex Powatton House) 69.

Ford's Hotel, Richmond, Va. Situated in the Heart of the City (etc.) 69, 70.

Rare coins, paper money: Gold bought and sold. Dennis Forgue, Hillside, Illinois. (Outline picture of 1794 dollar.) Printed on back of State of Alabama fractional notes. (About 1960.)

Compliments of the General Railroad Ticket Office, No. 4 Kimball House, Atlanta, Ga. 1881. 72. (See also R. D. Mann.)

General Railroad Ticket Office, 4 Kimball House, Atlanta, Ga. (View of train.) Pullman sleeping car office, European steamship ticket office, R.D. Mann, Agent. On back of State of Georgia 25 cents and 50 cents notes, 1863.

Kenton Grimwood & Co., Lumber, Providence, R.I. 60.

When in Chicago Buy Gunther's Candy and be Happy. 69. (1870s.)

The best Route from the North and West to Florida and the South is via Atlanta, Ga. Don't forget the Kennesaw Route. The North Georgia Fair will open in Atlanta October 21, 1878 and continue six days. 69, 70, 72.

Kromer's Hair Dye, Philadelphia. 27, 32, 39, 40, 41 (varieties).

Imported Cigars at Low Prices, Walter C. Leary The Direct Importer, Lower Ferry St., Ottawa, Ontario. (Canada). 70. (Also overprinted on Kennesaw Route ad.)

Yours Truly, R. D. Mann, General Ticket Agent, Always at Home, No. 4 Kimball House, Atlanta, Ga. 71.

R.D. Mann, Agent, Atlantic & Western Railroad, Atlanta, Ga. 71, 72.

Redeemable at Last, at the General R.R. and Steamship Ticket Office No. 4, Kimball House, Atlanta, Ga. R. D. Mann, Agt. (Inscription about steamship tickets.) On backs of Georgia, $3 and $4 notes 1864. (R. D. Mann and the General Railroad Ticket Office at Atlanta, Ga., used other ads in addition to those listed. The ads are also known on 67, 68, 70, 71, 72.)

From the General Rail Road-and-Steamship Ticket Office, No. 4 Kimball House, Atlanta, Ga. R.D. Mann, Agent. (Printed vertically with pointing hands at sides.) 69.

Compliments of Ann & Johnson, General Railroad Ticket Agents, 4 Kimball House, Atlanta, Ga. Branch offices International Cotton Exposition Building (etc.) 70.

A.B. Mayer, 1014 to 1022 N. 12th St., St. Louis, Mo. Wanted! Dry buffalo bones (etc.). Cartoon of two men in center. Bone black, fertilizers, &c. Printed on back of Missouri Defense Bond $1, $3, $4 and $4.50 notes.

John E. Morse, Dealer in U.S. Coins and Medals, Paper Money (etc.), Hadley, Mass. Outline picture of Brasher Doubloon. 57, 65.

John E. Morse, 12 Middle Street, Hadley, Massachusetts. I buy, sell and exchange paper money of all kinds. Am a collector and dealer. (Etc.) Photographic illustration of Confederate $500 note of 1864. Printed on State of Georgia $5 note of January 15, 1862. Others? (Morse was active during the first three decades of the 20th century.)

The Old Book Store, Atlanta, Ga. Confederate poem, 69.

"Secret Service." 68, 69, 70. Only these two words appear on this note. This is the name of a stage play during the early 1900s and was used to advertise it. Written by William Gillette, its subject was the Civil War and the setting was Richmond.

Sewell's Lunch Room and Ale Vaults at Sewell's Point, 250 Broadway, New York. 22.

Smoke "Confederate!" Best 5c Cigar At Exchange News Depot. Under Exchange Hotel. on back of State of Alabama $50 note, AL-8.

Stevens & Co., Dealer in Rare Coins, 90 Randolph St., Chicago (Lists sale prices of February 17, 1864 Confederate notes, "All clean and crisp," at 10 cents for the 50 cents note to 75 cents for the $500 note. Apparently from about 1900-1910 when Stevens was a major Chicago coin dealer.) 43. See illustration on page 71.

Virginia Exposition, Richmond, October 3rd to November 21st, 1888. On back on State of Virginia $1 note.

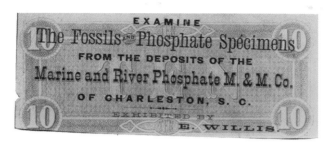

Examine the Fossils and Phosphate Specimens from the deposits of the Marine and River Phosphate. M. & M. Co. of Charleston, S.C. — Exhibited by E. Willis. 68, 69, 70.

Yarboro' House, Raleigh, N.C. Has good sample rooms of first floor for mercantile travellers. 70.

Yarboro' House, Raleigh, N.C. As preceding but with corrected inscription: Has good sample rooms on first floor for mercantile travelers. 69, 70, 71.

FACSIMILE ADVERTISING NOTES

When Confederate notes were still plentiful and readily available at a low price, they were frequently used by those who liked to present their advertising on the backs of bank notes. (A selection of genuine Confederate notes on which advertising was printed will be found elsewhere in this catalog.) Eventually, though, both the supply and cost made it impractical to print ads on the original notes. This problem was solved by producing facsimiles. Some of these facsimiles actually date from the late 19th century since not everyone had access to a supply of the "real thing." But a majority of them are from the early 1900s from which time they continued to be available to advertisers for a good many years. These pre-World War II issues can usually be identified by the word facsimile, which is hyphenated. The most common type is a $10 note depicting field artillery and bearing the serial number 49981. It is an imitation of type No. 69 in this catalog and may be found with many different ads on the back.

These and other older facsimiles have, in recent years, escalated in price far more than they should be worth. Admittedly, many bear fascinating advertising such as those that list prices for various goods at a fraction of their cost today. Also, one must bear in mind that these were originally giveaways that were often printed on cheap paper; most have long since been discarded, thereby contributing to their rarity. Of the facsimiles from the early 1900s, one of the most common and best known bears the advertisement of Dr. Morse's Indian Root Pills on the back. Because the value of these earlier advertising notes varies widely, they are too difficult to price, due to the numerous kinds that have been issued. Depending upon the interest of the ad, condition and attractiveness of the note, prices of $50 or more for earlier kinds are not uncommon. This is a collecting area in which there is an increasing interest, and prices are on the rise.

Facsimiles of paper money for advertising purposes are not a thing of the past. It is true that during World War II, when there was a paper shortage, that advertising by this means virtually ceased. By the 1950s, there was a revival (see "Modern Facsimiles" for additional data), but the majority of the advertising notes issued since that time have been given out at coin and paper money shows or conventions. Generally, these bear an ad on the back for the show or that of a dealer in numismatic material. Only part of these are reproductions of Confederate notes; many are reproductions of obsolete bank notes. These recent issues have very little value but as the years go by, they may rise in price like those of pre-World War II vintage.

Among the more interesting examples that have already gained a premium is a set used to advertise Southern Comfort liqueur. These notes are in various denominations of Confederate currency, printed in pink and black. The backs bear the firm's advertising that includes the statement that "The Confederate bill, on opposite side, is an authentic reproduction of money often used in purchasing Southern Comfort in those times." I can't find anything in reference works to support that statement but it "sounds good." These notes are 6" x 2-1/8" in size.

A $10 note of approximate actual size, similar to the one pictured in this chapter, but complete with the original back, was reproduced in 1983-84 by the Wookey Hole Mill, Somerset, England. This firm supplied some of the paper used to print Confederate currency during the Civil War and on the bottom of the back is the statement that this note is "reproduced on hand made paper made at the Wookey Hole Mill, Somerset." According to a circular included with the note, this example on heavy paper was made in the same manner as the 19th century, using pure cotton imported from North Carolina. As such, it is one of the more historical recent reproductions.

This old advertising note was not likely to fool anyone when opened, but when appropriately folded so that only the "10" portion showed, it resembled one end of a $10 Confederate note of the 1862, 1863 and 1864 series that pictures R. M. T. Hunter.

"WHEN THIS CRUEL WAR IS OVER"

The title of this chapter is taken from a Civil War song of the same name that refers to the hardships of the war. But the hardships did not end with Appomattox, particularly in the South, where the former members of the Confederate States were treated like an occupied country and not like the return of the prodigal son to the Union. The Reconstruction Era contains too many affronts to people of the South to be enumerated here and in any case the details are best learned from a book devoted to that period. Other than giving a general overview, the subject of this work is primarily Confederate currency and related ephemera that is treasured by collectors.

Nevertheless, let us single out a couple examples of postwar hardship. Obviously, many landowners and others were left nearly destitute when Confederate currency could no longer be redeemed. And, on top of this, Federal agents came South to seize cotton that had survived the war, on the grounds that it was the property of the Confederate Government (that received part of its tax payments in kind rather than money). The U.S. government did obtain money from the sale of this cotton but corrupt agents obtained more. The logical answer to this deprivation would seem to be that of growing more cotton to replace what was lost, but that became another nightmare when the U.S. government placed an unfair tax on cotton. It was unfair because a similar tax was not placed on Northern crops. Property was frequently seized for the amount of tax claimed to be due, a condition that still applies today, but which for Southern families after the Civil War was especially onerous due to their lack of money. Oftentimes this resulted in the loss of a home or land that had been held by a family for generations.

There has been so much romanticization of Southern life that one might believe the South came out of the war virtually unscathed outside of the route of Sherman's March. On the contrary, in this bloodiest of America's conflicts, the South lost nearly one out of every five white males of military age compared to one out of 16 in the North. The total number killed on both sides was over 600,000 men. These losses were deeply felt and soon Decoration Day (now Memorial Day) was being observed in both the North and the South.

Unlike soldiers who fought for the North, who were granted a disability pension in 1862 that was expanded in 1890 to cover all Union veterans, the soldier of the South did not receive one, nor did his widow. Even worse, the U.S. government stopped the pensions of Confederates who had been veterans of previous wars. During the war, money for the support of Southern families, who had members in the army, often depended upon county assistance. This situation continued for many years afterward as the individual states and others helped with the purchase of artificial limbs for the wounded and aid to the widows.

It wasn't too many years ago that the veterans of the Civil War were talking over the days when "we drank from the same canteen." Time enhances the memory of bravery under fire and dims the hard times and lack of jobs to which the veterans returned, whether they were from the North or from the South. After the Civil War, many Northern veterans joined the Grand Army of the Republic (G.A.R.). In the South there was a similar fraternal organization of the United Confederate Veterans (U.C.V.). Both the G.A.R. and U.C.V. included wives, sons and daughters among their auxiliaries. They met annually each year at state and national levels. In 1938, a joint reunion of the Blue and the Gray was held at Gettysburg on the 75th anniversary of the battle. The last meeting of the G.A.R. was held in 1949, followed by the final meeting of the U.C.V. in 1951. By that time the number of surviving veterans attending the meetings of either group could be counted on one hand.

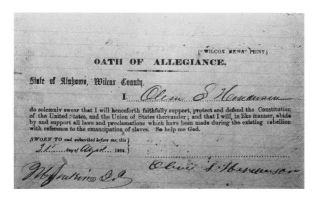

Not all of the Confederate veterans remained in the United States at the end of the war. Those who did were required to take an Oath of Allegiance to the United States before they could regain their citizenship. Some of the more prominent leaders never did regain it. Others, like Secretary of State Judah P. Benjamin, left the country and established new roots elsewhere. "South of the border" was favored and among the important Confederate colonies was one in Brazil. It should also be noted that people in the South who did not join the rebellion, particularly in the border states such as Tennessee, but who suffered damages from the war, had to fill out long forms and offer sworn proof to the United States government in order to obtain redress for their losses. This procedure required years of waiting and even then less than 10% of the claimed losses was ever paid.

The U.S. government did much better on its claims of loss. During the war, the Confederates had ships built in England, the most famous of which was the Alabama, the Confederate raider under the command of Raphael Semmes, which captured or destroyed nearly 70 U.S. merchant ships. The United States had warned the British government, which had Confederate sympathies, against permitting the ship to leave port. After the war the U.S. government demanded compensation for its shipping losses, charging negligence and violation of neutrality. The matter was finally settled by arbitration at Geneva, Switzerland that resulted in a payment of $15,500,000 by Great Britain. In commemoration, a small number of facsimiles of the payment was given to those who participated in the settlement.

Today, one may gain a clearer concept of what the Civil War was like by visiting battlefields. There one can follow, by their own reading or listening to a guide, where the opposing forces were situated and the outcome as they charged each other. In the East, Antietam, Fredericksburg and Gettysburg are among the best known battlefields open to the public. Gettysburg has become quite commercialized, but if you like a profusion of cannons and monuments, it is the place to see. The largest and most imposing is the monument of the State of Pennsylvania, which is understandable since it was here that this great battle was fought. Of the 200 monuments placed by the South, the one erected by the State of Virginia is as heart-touching as any. The base of this monument, which has a group of Confederate soldiers in the foreground, bears the inscription "Virginia to Her Sons at Gettysburg" and is surmounted by an equestrian figure of General Robert E. Lee. There is also another monument of special importance to the South that commemorates the "High Water Mark of the Confederacy." It is placed at the farthest advance of Pickett's Charge.

Equally imposing monuments may be found in Montgomery, Ala., and Richmond, Va., among other southern cities. A memorial of interest to Confederate and Civil War aficionados is not located at a battlefield but is sculptured on the side of Stone Mountain near Atlanta, Ga. (See enlarged illustration of the commemorative stamp issued upon completion of the memorial in 1970.) Here, one may see President Davis, General Lee and Jackson still riding to battle. And, if you would like to see a live "battle," small-scale reenactments are held from time to time at Civil War battlefields. For information on these events, the battlefields and their museums, it is recommended that a travel handbook be consulted.

Returning again to Confederate currency, you may be aware that the U.S. government has from time to time tried to reduce the amount of paper that is being continuously accumulated in Washington. The problem is deciding what needs to be saved of current and older documents. There is also the question of redundancy. After the Civil War, a large quantity of Confederate currency was taken from Richmond to Washington where it was used in connection with Confederate Treasury records by Raphael P. Thian to compile his "Register of the Confederate Debt." Although Thian and others procured a considerable number of the better notes, apparently there were still many of the more common kinds on hand nearly 50 years after the war. During the time Franklin MacVeagh was Secretary of the Treasury (1909-1913), letters were sent to G.A.R. posts, colleges and others deemed suitable, which included a selection of approximately a dozen Confederate notes in worn condition. Apparently these represented the dregs of the remaining supply and the government wanted to be rid of them.

However, the Treasury Department failed to completely dispose of its hoard of Confederate notes and they remained there until the mid-1930s before being transferred to the newly completed National Archives building. Again, bureaucracy played a part, and it wasn't until 1998 that the hoard arrived at the Smithsonian Institution that was the intended destination. In all, the hoard contains about half a million notes, mainly of 1862 and 1863 issues, but some of 1864. The reason for the preponderance of 1862 and 1863 notes is because they were being taxed out of existence and replaced by the 1864 issue. (See introduction to the Seventh Issue and chapter on Trans-Mississippi notes.) The 1864 notes should have been used to pay soldiers and meet other needs in the final days of the Civil War but by that time it probably mattered little. In June 1865, Major S.A. Jones wrote an eulogy on the back of a Confederate note that tells the story. It appears at the end of Part II.

TREASURY DEPARTMENT

WASHINGTON

October 15, 1912.

H. C. McKinley Commander.

M. C. Lowry Post No. 214, G. A. R.,

Myersdale, Pa.

Gentlemen:

Believing that your Post will be interested in receiving specimens of notes issued by the Confederate States of America, for exhibition purposes in the Post headquarters, I take pleasure in sending you an assortment of the same.

These notes came into the possession of the Union Army about the close of the Civil War, and were turned over by the War Department to the Treasury of the United States in the year 1867.

The Treasury Department has no complete series of the notes, and in presenting such specimens as are now in its custody the Department feels assured that proper disposition will be made for their safe keeping so as to render them of permanent value to your Grand Army Post as historical relics.

Very truly yours,

Franklin MacVeagh

Secretary.

Courtesy Leonard W. Engle

THE SOUTH RESTORED

The Civil War did not exactly end with the surrender of General Lee at Appomattox in April 1865, or with the end of hostilities in the West a month later. Unlike the Confederate government, which recognized the existence of the United States on its currency, the U.S. government played a two-faced game during and after the war. President Lincoln did not recognize the right of the Southern states to secede and when he called for troops in 1861, they were to put down an insurrection. Later, the South was described as "states in rebellion." They were not officially admitted as being a part of a separate nation. It would seem, then, that they had always been and still remained a part of the United States when the war ended. But no, each had to be readmitted to the Union. Readmission was not immediate but occurred over a period of years. When Grant ran for president in 1868, residents of Mississippi, Texas and Virginia could not vote in the election because those states had not yet been readmitted. In Florida, the electors were appointed by the legislature. Government documents from that period describe them as "insurrectionary districts." (See illustration below.)

President Johnson, who succeeded Lincoln after he was assassinated, wanted to be "reasonable" toward the South as he felt Lincoln would have been. By July 1865, he had named governors in each of the states that comprised the Confederacy. On April 2, 1866, Johnson proclaimed the insurrection at an end in all of the Southern states except Texas, where, on August 20, peace was likewise declared to have been restored.

Unfortunately for the South, radical Republicans had gained sufficient power in Congress to take control of the "reconstruction." When the 39th Congress convened on December 4, 1865, the members from the Southern states, where the president had reestablished federal administration, would not be seated. Admittedly, the South had sent men who had served in Congress before the war and former Confederate officers, but who else could they send who had knowledge of government? Congress felt insulted and the House voted the same day to establish a Joint Committee on Reconstruction under the chairmanship of Thaddeus Stevens, one of the most vindictive of the radicals who insisted that the South should be regarded as a "conquered province."

Consequently, the readmission of the states under Johnson's plan was voided. Instead, Congress passed three Reconstruction Acts and six Enforcement Acts over Johnson's veto and decided itself when the Southern states were ready for readmission. The first Reconstruction Act of March 2, 1867, divided the South into five military districts. Thus, the South was placed in the unusual position of being under military occupation by fellow Americans.

Each state was required to prepare a new constitution that recognized the end of slavery and gave full citizenship rights to everyone except disenfranchised Confederates. It also required the 13th and 14th Amendments to the Constitution be approved. The 13th Amendment abolished slavery, the 14th concerned citizenship rights while the 15th Amendment of 1870 that was subsequently adopted, required that race be no bar to voting rights. At that time only eight states in the North met that requirement.

The South tried to circumvent the intent of these amendments through illegal and restrictive Black Codes. Such actions risked delaying readmission of a state to the Union, which coincided with the acceptance of its representatives in Congress. As a consequence, Georgia, the last state to be readmitted, did not have its members seated until July 15, 1870. Interestingly, the Supreme Court, as early as 1876, began gutting portions of the 14th and 15th Amendments, not as a favor to the South but because the court's decisions tend to reflect political leanings and the tenor of the times. The result was a "separate but equal" policy in both the North and the South. It was not until the 1960s that these decisions were reversed.

To a considerable extent, Reconstruction represented a political strategy by the radical Republicans to gain control of the Southern vote through registration of the former slave population and through the establishment of "carpetbag" governments. Although these governments did help rebuild the country, it was at such bloated cost that the states fell deeply in debt. The resulting antagonism turned the former Confederacy into a "solid South" bastion that voted Democratic for nearly 100 years.

A near casualty of Reconstruction by Congress was President Johnson himself. Having passed reconstruction measures over Johnson's veto, the Radicals were still not satisfied. Leaving nothing to chance, a Court of Impeachment was convened in the Senate during March 1868. When the hearings on 11 articles were abandoned on May 26, the President had been acquitted by one vote.

Troops were still being maintained in the South more than a decade after the Civil War. That was soon to end as politics again played a part. In the presidential election of November 1876, Samuel J. Tilden was the Democratic candidate while Rutherford B. Hayes was the Republican candidate. Tilden received 4,300,590 votes to 4,036,298 for Hayes but neither had the 185 electorial votes that were then needed to win. Tilden had 184 and Hayes had 165. A vote from Oregon was in dispute but the primary area of contention was the Southern votes of Florida, Louisiana and South Carolina, which had "carpetbag" governments supported by Federal troops.

Who was to be inaugurated president on March 5, 1877? (The normal date of March 4 was on Sunday.) Congress was deadlocked over the matter as the inaugural date was fast approaching. Finally, on January 29, 1877, it set up an Electorial Commission of 15 members of which five were from the House, five from the Senate and five from the Supreme Court. Seven of the members were Democrats and seven were Republicans with the fifteenth member being the non-partisan Judge David Davis of Illinois. At the last moment, however, Judge Davis was elected to the Senate by the Illinois legislature and was replaced by Judge Joseph P. Bradley who cast his ballot for Hayes. Excitement was high over the outcome and since space was limited in the House of Representatives, special tickets were printed to view the proceedings.

The political aspect of Hayes' election is known as the "Compromise of 1877." Before the vote, there had been maneuvers among congressmen and party officials to end the deadlock. The gist of it was that in return for accepting Hayes, the South would receive federal support for internal improvements, including railroads, and the naming of a Southerner as Postmaster General, the cabinet member with the most patronage jobs. Most importantly, Federal troops would be removed from the South.

Hayes immediately appointed (March 5) David M. Key of Tennessee as Postmaster General and the last Federal troops were removed (from New Orleans) on April 24. With their removal the "carpetbag" governments were soon replaced in those states where they still held power. It cannot be claimed that it was a perfect ending, but to the South it meant the restoration of "home rule" and that was more important from a long-term standpoint than the election of a president who might be in office for only four years.

The Confederate Note

Representing nothing on God's earth now,
And naught in the waters below it -
As the pledge of a nation that passed away,
Keep it dear friend and show it —
Show it to those that will lend an ear
To the tale that this trifle will tell;
Of liberty born of a patriot's dream,
Of a storm-cradled nation that fell.

Too poor to possess the precious ores,
And too much of a stranger to borrow,
We issued to-day our "promise to pay"
And hoped to redeem on the morrow.
The days rolled on and weeks became years,
But our coffers were empty still,
Coin was so scarce the Treasury quaked
If a dollar should drop in the till.

But the faith that was in us was strong indeed,
Though our poverty well we discerned,
And this little check represented the pay
That our suffering veterans earned.
They knew it had hardly a value in gold,
Yet as gold our soldiers received it.
It gazed in our eyes with a promise to pay
And every true soldier believed it.

But our boys thought little of price or pay
Or of bills that were over due -
We knew if it bought our bread to-day
'Twas the best our poor country could do.
Keep it, it tells all our history over
From the birth of the dream to its last,
Modest and born of the Angel Hope
Like our hope of success, It passed

The above poem, attributed to Major A.L. Jonas, CSA, was written on the back of a Confederate note, at the end of the Civil War and has been reprinted many times since.

Part III — Catalog
SOUTHERN STATES

Paper Money of the Southern States

When South Carolina seceded on December 20, 1860, there was expectation that the state might be followed by the other 14 states that were considered to be a part of the South. That did not happen; by the time the Confederate States was being organized at Montgomery, Ala., during early February 1861, seven states had seceded. More were to join but not the border states of Delaware, Maryland, Kentucky and Missouri. While not brought to public vote, Kentucky and Missouri did pass Ordinances of Secession and were represented in the Confederate Congress. Moreover, Missouri is among the states that issued currency.

The question of secession in most states was decided by delegates to conventions held for that purpose rather than by the public at large. Otherwise, they may have failed since many people hoped that a compromise could be found. President Lincoln's election and call for troops after the fall of Fort Sumter on April 14, 1861, was a deciding factor for many. That action also decided the question in the North where, conversely, there were people sympathetic to the South.

Once the Confederate States was established, its currency circulated widely throughout the South during the Civil War. Yet there never seemed to be enough. Nearly all of the individual states took advantage of their "States' Rights" to issue their own currency. Believing that many readers of past editions of this catalog may also have an interest in the paper money of the Southern states, the author has included a listing of these issues in this edition.

Since this is a type catalog, descriptions of minor varieties are not included nor are plate letters, printing colors or papers unless there should be more than one. The more significant will be mentioned. Even assembling all but rare types represents a challenge. The notes are printed in various sizes but other than the lowest denominations, all are similar in size to the larger Confederate notes. All are printed in black on plain or white paper unless otherwise stated. Notes that are dated after the Civil War may or may not be included in a collection devoted to the wartime issues, since they were generally printed for postwar "carpetbag" governments or resulted from huge wartime debts.

Confederate States' notes are more widely collected than the issues of the individual Southern states, and this is reflected in the valuations. In fact, some of the more common issues are available from dealers at prices of $10-$15 in Uncirculated condition, which means that examples that are only Good or Very Good have very little value. At the other extreme are State notes listed as Rare or Very Rare without any valuation. This is to be regretted but such notes are so seldom offered for sale that it is not practical to establish a prevalent price. Collectors should be aware, however, that rare State notes are not likely to be valued as highly as Confederate States' notes of similar rarity. Generally, depending on the note, Rare and Very Rare State notes will command a price ranging from a couple hundred dollars to several thousand dollars.

ALABAMA

Alabama entered the Union as the 22nd State in 1819. Previously it had been a part of Georgia and Mississippi. There remained a great deal of divisiveness in Alabama between Union and Secession factions at the time of Lincoln's election as U.S. President in 1860, but an ordinance of Secession was adopted at Montgomery on January 11, 1861, when 61 delegates voted for secession and 39 against. Alabama thus became the fourth state to leave the Union and was a major center of activity until after Virginia seceded in April. Until then, the state capital at Montgomery served as the capital of the Confederate States and was the site where delegates from the Lower South met on February 4, 1861, to establish the Confederacy. Coincidentally, this was the same day that an abortive peace conference opened at Washington, D.C.

After the Civil War, Alabama passed the 13th Amendment to the U.S. Constitution (Abolishment of slavery) but not before amending it in turn: "Be it further resolved, that this amendment to the Constitution of the United States is adopted by the Legislature of Alabama, with the understanding that it does not confer upon Congress the power to legislate upon the political status of freedmen in this State." Alabama was readmitted to the Union on July 13, 1868.

Important

Where more than one variety was issued of a note, the prices listed are for the more common kinds, not a rare minor variety. Where no value is indicated, the price is speculative due to such notes being rare in higher grades and seldom offered. Most of the illustrations in this catalog are either larger or smaller than the actual specimens.

Issue of January 1, 1863

Alabama did not begin to issue its own paper money until 1863. All notes were is-sued from the capital at Montgomery, Ala., and state that "The State of Alabama will pay (xxxx) to bearer in Confederate States Treasury Notes when presented at the State Treasury in sums of Twenty Dollars and upwards." In other words, this paper money would be redeemed in paper money, except a different type. The notes of this first issue bear the printed signature of John Gill Shorter (1818-72) who was governor of the state from August 1861, until December 1863. Each note bears a serial number and is hand numbered. Except as indicated, the notes are not printed on the back. All were engraved and printed by the branch of J.T. Paterson & Co., Augusta, Ga.

AL-1.   5 cents— Cotton balls. Black. First Series with large or small serial letters, A to U.

GOOD	VG	FINE	VF	XF	UNC.
$5	$12	$20	$30	$40	$50

AL-2.   10 cents— Map and tree within oval. (The map and tree were the first arms of Ala-bama.) Black. First Series with large or small serial letters, A to U.

GOOD	VG	FINE	VF	XF	UNC.
$5	$15	$20	$25	$30	$35

AL-3. 25 cents— Wagonload of cotton. Map and tree at upper left. Woman's portrait at lower right. Black with 25 cts in red. No series (actually First), 2nd Series (large and small letters) and 3rd Series. All with serial letters, A to O.

GOOD	VG	FINE	VF	XF	UNC.
$5	$10	$15	$20	$25	$35

AL-4. 50 cents— Map and tree within oval. Black with 50 cts in blue. (A scarce variety is also known in green.) No series and 2nd Series (large and small letters), A to O. The 2nd series is worth double.

GOOD	VG	FINE	VF	XF	UNC.
$5	$10	$15	$20	$25	$30

AL-5. $1— Portrait of Governor Shorter at left. State capitol at center. Map and tree at lower right. Black with ONE in green. 1st and 2nd Series, both with large and small letters, A to M. The 2nd series is worth double.

GOOD	VG	FINE	VF	XF	UNC.
$5	$15	$125	$30	$35	$40

The 1863 series was primarily of fractional notes, which were intended as a substitute for U.S. coins that had disappeared from circulation at the beginning of the war and had not been replaced by similar denominations of the Confederate government. While the lowest denomination of 5 cents may still have been equivalent to the prewar cent, after the Confederate loss at Gettysburg during the summer of that year, Southern currency inflated rapidly. One consequence was the 1864 series in higher denominations.

Issue of January 1, 1864

Engraved by W. Keenan & Co., Lith. &
Printed by J.T. Paterson & Co., Augusta, Ga.

The inscription on the notes of this issue state that they are "Redeemable in Confederate Treasury Notes or in Five Per Cent Coupon Bonds of the State, at the option of the State." At the end of the war, this option no longer mattered but while in effect the notes were receivable in payment of all taxes and public dues. Each note bears the handwritten signatures of the Comptroller and Treasurer, plus a handwritten serial number.

AL-6. $5— Overseer watching slaves at work. Liberty standing at lower left, map and tree at lower right. The overseer design was used on a number of bank notes, both North and South, and comes in altered versions. Interestingly, instead of using the appropriate cotton picking version, the scene is the variety that depicts wheat harvesting. Black. FIVE in green. Serial letters A to F.

GOOD	VG	FINE	VF	XF	UNC.
$20	$75	$75	$110	$135	$175

AL-7. $10— Portrait of Governor Thomas H. Watts (1819-92) between cotton bolls. Map and tree at lower right. Watts had been defeated by Shorter in the election of 1861. During 1862-63, he was Attorney General of the Confederate States. Although Shorter was a distinguished governor, he became unpopular after he was blamed for permitting the State's defenses to be breached by Union troops. Additionally, he was forced to increase taxes and institute a military draft. As a result, Watts won the election of 1863 and became governor on December 1 of that year, serving until the end of the war. The portrait on these notes is a good likeness of the governor. Printed in black with TEN in green. Serial letters A to F.

GOOD	VG	FINE	VF	XF	UNC.
$25	$35	$75	$100	$150	$200

AL-8. $50— Portrait of Governor Thomas H. Watts at center, similar to the $10 note but with a background of shipping, flags and military equipment at the sides. Indian at lower left. Map and tree at lower right. Printed in black with an ornate green back. Serial letters A to S.

GOOD	VG	FINE	VF	XF	UNC.
$40	$75	$125	$175	$225	$350

AL-9. $100— Indian family at center, map and tree at lower left, maiden at lower right. Black with ornate green back. Serial letters A to H.

GOOD	VG	FINE	VF	XF	UNC.
$60	$110	$165	$210	$275	$425

For some reason, no $20 denomination was issued, but another $50 note of the same design as No. AL-8 was released with the date of February 17, 1864, which coincides with the last dated issue of the Confederate States. This note was also lithographed and printed by J.T. Paterson & Co., as previously. See below.

AL-10. $50— Same type as AL-8, except orange overprint and differences of inscription. Very rare.

ARIZONA TERRITORY

The Confederate States was aware of the desirability of extending itself to the Pacific. President Jefferson Davis was familiar with the Southwest, having served in the war with Mexico (1846-47). As U.S. Secretary of War under President Franklin Pierce (1853-57), he had favored the Gadsen Purchase and a southern route for a transcontinental railroad. This area that became the Territory of New Mexico was a part of the Compromise of 1850 and included the future states of Arizona and New Mexico. As a part of the agreement that delayed the outbreak of the Civil War for another decade, California was admitted to the Union as a free state, while the territory in the Southwest was allowed to organize without restrictions on slavery.

Although Southern sympathizers caused some disruption and supported a "Pacific Republic" in California during 1860-61, the State Legislature denounced secession and remained strongly in favor of the Union. The Confederates were more successful in the Territory of New Mexico, where Lt. Col. John R. Baylor's troops took Fort Bliss and Fort Fillmore before declaring the Confederate Territory of Arizona on August 1. (In other words, the present State of New Mexico was considered to be a part of the Territory of Arizona.)

In December 1861, a larger Confederate army defeated the Union forces at the Battle of Valverde, and its apparent control of the area led the Confederate Congress to officially create the Territory of Arizona on January 24, 1862. The town of Mesilla became the capital, and a Representative was seated in the Confederate Congress at Richmond. However, the Confederates were defeated in a major battle at Glorieta Pass on March 28, 1862; by summer, the Territory of Arizona was no longer in Confederate hands, although it continued to be represented in Congress. No Confederate or State currency was issued but some rare private scrip exists that was redeemable in Confederate currency. After the area was recovered by the United States, it was divided (1863) into two territories, Arizona and New Mexico.

About Prices

Genuine Confederate and Southern states currency in exceptionally choice condition may command a higher price than indicated by the valuations. General economic changes or the popularity of certain notes may also affect prices.

ARKANSAS

Arkansas was at first a part of the Louisiana Territory that had been purchased from France in 1803. In 1812, Arkansas was made a part of the Missouri Territory where it remained until 1819 when a separate territory was established. By 1836, Arkansas had reached the required 50,000 population and was admitted to the Union as the 25th state. Although Arkansas was a slave state with a quarter of its 435,000 population in 1860 composed of slaves, there was much opposition to seceding from the Union. Wealthy lowland cotton plantation owners (who held the most political power) were able to have their way against the smaller farmers; on May 6, 1861, Arkansas became the 9th state to join the Confederacy.

However, after the Battle of Pea Ridge, March 7-8, 1862, Union forces gained control of much of Arkansas. Henry Massey Rector was governor, 1860-62, and afterward Harris Flanagin was Confederate governor until the end of the war, but the last meeting of the General Assembly of the Confederates was held on October 2, 1864. After Little Rock fell to Union forces in September 1863, the Confederate government of Arkansas moved to Washington in the Southwestern portion of the State. Since April 1864, the State also had a Union governor, Isaac Murphy, who had been the only delegate out of 70 to resist political pressure and cast a vote against secession in 1861. Despite his loyalty to the Union, he was not retained in office when Arkansas was readmitted on June 22, 1868.

Although only a part of Arkansas was under Confederate control during most of the Civil War, the State has one of the more extensive series of currency and one that includes many minor varieties, most of which are primarily due to the same types being printed in different colors or have changes in the inscription relative to their backing or redemption. Valuations are for the more common types.

Act of May 28, 1861

Redeemable Five years after 1st July, 1861

These notes bear the inscription "Arkansas War Bond," but since they are in low denominations and had no interest-bearing coupons, they were accepted as currency.

AK-1. $1— Standing typesetter (printer) in oval at left. Very rare.

AK-2. $2— Same type as above. Very rare.

AK-3. $3— Same type as above. Very rare.

AK-4. Stamped denominations of $5, $10 or $20. State arms at upper center. Usually hand dated September 16, 1861.

GOOD	VG	FINE	VF	XF	UNC.
$35	$40	$50	$75	$100	$150

Arkansas Treasury Warrants

Authorized by Acts of November 14 and 18, 1861
Written dates of 1861-1863

Inscription reads "Arkansas Treasury Warrant. On War Bond."

AK-5. $1— Indian maiden standing at left. White paper. Rare.

AK-5A. $1— As above. Blue paper.

GOOD	VG	FINE	VF	XF	UNC.
$150	$175	$325	$380	$450	$500

AK-6. $2— As above. White paper. Very rare.

AK-6A. $2— As above. Blue paper. Very rare.

AK-7. $3— As above. White paper. Very rare.

AK-7A. $3— As above. Blue paper. Very rare.

AK-8. $5— As above. Whitefs paper. Very rare.

AK-8A. $5— As above. Blue paper. Very rare.

AK-9. $10— As above. White paper. Very rare.

AK-9A. $10— As above. Blue paper. Very rare.

AK-10.   Written denomination. As above. White paper.

GOOD	VG	FINE	VF	XF	UNC.
$175	$250	$350	$425	$500	$600

AK-10A.   Written denomination. As above. Blue paper. Very rare.

Inscription reads "Arkansas Treasury Warrant. On Auditor's Warrant."

AK-11. $1— Indian maiden standing at left. Blue paper. Very rare.

AK-12. $2— As above. Blue paper. Very rare.

AK-13. $3— As above. Blue paper. Very rare.

AK-14. $5— As above. White paper. Very rare.

AK-14A. $5— As above. Blue paper. Very rare.

AK-15.   Written denomination. As above. White paper.

GOOD	VG	FINE	VF	XF	UNC.
$175	$225	$325	$400	$425	$500

AK-15A. Written denomination. As above. Blue paper. Very rare.

Inscription reads "Arkansas Treasury Warrant. On War Bond."

AK-16. $1— Indian warrior standing at left. White paper.

GOOD	VG	FINE	VF	XF	UNC.
$150	$225	$300	$375	$425	$500

AK-16A. $1— As above. Blue paper.

GOOD	VG	FINE	VF	XF	UNC.
$150	$225	$300	$375	$425	$500

AK-17. $2— As above. White paper.

GOOD	VG	FINE	VF	XF	UNC.
$200	$350	$425	$575	$725	$950

AK-17A. $2— As above. Blue paper. Very rare.

AK-18. $3— As above. White paper. Very rare.

AK-18A. $3— As above. Blue paper. (?)

AK-19. $5— As above. White paper.

AK-19A. $5— As above. Blue paper. Very rare.

AK-20. $10— As above. White paper. Very rare.

AK-20A. $10— As above. Blue paper. Very rare.

AK-21. Written denomination. White paper. Very rare.

AK-21A. Written denomination. Blue paper. Very rare.

Inscription reads "Arkansas Treasury Warrant. On Auditor's Warrant."

AK-22. $1— Indian warrior standing at left. Blue paper.

GOOD	VG	FINE	VF	XF	UNC.
$250	$525	$850	$1100	$1600	---

AK-23. $5— As above. Blue paper.

GOOD	VG	FINE	VF	XF	UNC.
$200	$350	$525	$700	$850	---

AK-24. $10— As above. White paper.

GOOD	VG	FINE	VF	XF	UNC.
$300	$625	$1100	$1600	$2600	---

AK-25. Written denomination. White paper. Very rare. AK-25A. Written denomination. Blue paper. Very rare.

Inscription reads "Arkansas Treasury Warrant. On War Bond."

AK-26. $1— Bust of maiden in hat at left. White paper.

GOOD	VG	FINE	VF	XF	UNC.
$150	$235	$300	$425	$525	$725

AK-27. Written denomination. Bust of maiden in hat at left. State seal at center. White paper.

GOOD	VG	FINE	VF	XF	UNC.
$100	$175	$250	$325	$475	$625

Inscription reads "Arkansas Treasury Warrant. On Auditor's Warrant."

AK-28. $1— Bust of maiden in hat at left. White paper. Very rare.

AK-29. Written denomination. Bust of maiden in hat at left. State seal at center. White paper. Very rare.

The most complicated group of Arkansas Treasury Warrants are those that resemble conventional bank notes with a portrait in the center of each. As a group, there may be over 300 varieties in all. Varieties include white or blue paper printed in green, red or blue. The printer's name may be omitted or given as J.D. Butler, Print. Lit. Rock. or Print. Little Rock. Some notes indicate at the sides of the center portrait that they are based on War Bonds, while others are on Auditor's Warrant. Still other varieties result from the inclusion, alteration or removal of the words "with Interest at Eight per centum per annum." Only the basic types will be listed. All have handwritten dates and signatures.

AK-30. $1— Jefferson Davis at center, Arkansas arms at left. Plate letter A.

GOOD	VG	FINE	VF	XF	UNC.
$50	$100	$150	$200	$250	$325

AK-31. $2— As above. Plate letter B.

GOOD	VG	FINE	VF	XF	UNC.
$75	$150	$175	$230	$275	$325

AK-32. $3— As above. Plate letter C.

GOOD	VG	FINE	VF	XF	UNC.
$100	$140	$175	$225	$300	$400

AK-33. $5— Governor or H.M. Rector at center. Slave carrying cotton at left. Plate letter D.

GOOD	VG	FINE	VF	XF	UNC.
$35	$70	$100	$125	$150	$200

AK-34. $10— Samuel Adams at center who was Acting Governor in 1844 and State Treasurer 1845-49. Slave carrying cotton at left. Plate letter D.

GOOD	VG	FINE	VF	XF	UNC.
$100	$150	$250	$500	$550	$600

Notes listed AK-30 to AK-34 are occasionally found printed on the back of a bill of exchange or with the back overprint inverted, but they are in the same price range.

Issues During The Reconstruction

Printed by National Bank Note Co. New York
Authorized by Act of March 16, 1871
Written dates of 1871 to 1875
Payable with interest at 5% per annum

AK-35. $1— Farmer with scythe at center, basket of corn at left, cotton boll at right. Black and green with ornate brown back. Very rare.

AK-36. $5— Three children at center ("The Young Students"), hunter and dog at left, mother and child at right. Black and brown with ornate back. Very rare.

AK-37. $10— Wagonload of cotton at center, Liberty standing at left. Black and brown with ornate brown back. Issued notes are very rare. Prices are for hole-canceled notes.

GOOD	VG	FINE	VF	XF	UNC.
$250	$500	$700	$900	$1250	—

AK-37A. $10— As above except black and green printing. Very rare.

During the Reconstruction period of 1868-74, the State debt increased over $9 million, largely due to railroad and levee schemes. Treasurer's Certificates of $1 and $10 (both typeset) were issued under the Act of January 20, 1875, but by that time the Reconstruction government had ended.

Prices of Rarities
Rare notes that are in strong demand tend to rise continuously in price. This is particularly true of the Montgomery issue and certain other notes.

DELAWARE

Delaware was considered to be a slave and border state, due to its proximity with Maryland, but by the time of the Civil War, the number of slaves had dwindled to about 2,000. Nearly 20,000 others had become free men. The State Legislature unanimously rejected secession on January 3, 1861. Subsequently, both sides obtained soldiers from Delaware, but the majority joined the Union forces. Nevertheless, the Federal Government took no chances, and its repressive measures were the cause of some resentment in a State that had never favored secession.

Delaware was associated with the Civil War in another way. There were more than 150 war prisons in the North and South but only the more infamous such as Andersonville (Ga.) and Libby Prison (Va.) are well known. In the North, Fort Delaware, located on the small swampy Pea Patch Island in the Delaware River, was among the most dreaded by captured Confederate soldiers.

FLORIDA

Since Florida expected to be isolated if it did not join the other Southern states, the convention deciding the question voted, 62 to 7, on January 10, 1861, to secede, stating that "all hopes of preserving the Union upon terms consistent with the safety and honor of the slave-holding States (has been) fully dissipated." Although the ordinance also described the State's withdrawal to be that of "a sovereign and independent nation," it did not follow that course and Governor John Milton of Florida was commended highly by President Davis for the aid given to the Confederate Government. This was especially true after the fall of Vicksburg (1863) reduced shipments from Texas and Florida became a primary source of beef and other food.

Issue of October 10, 1861
Printed by Hoyer & Ludwig, Richmond, Va.

FL-I. $1— Portrait of George Washington at lower left, Tellus seated at right. Date handwritten except 186_.

GOOD	VG	FINE	VF	XF	UNC.
$75	$90	$100	$225	$300	$500

FL-1A. $1— As above but with ONE added above Tellus at upper edge.

GOOD	VG	FINE	VF	XF	UNC.
$75	$135	$125	$250	$365	$575

FL-2. $2— As above except denomination. Date handwritten except 186_.

GOOD	VG	FINE	VF	XF	UNC.
$75	$125	$165	$225	$375	$525

FL-2A. $2— As above but with TWO added above Tellus at upper edge.

GOOD	VG	FINE	VF	XF	UNC.
$75	$135	$175	$250	$375	$575

FL-3. $3— As above except denomination. Date handwritten except 186_.

GOOD	VG	FINE	VF	XF	UNC.
$75	$135	$160	$225	$325	$525

FL-3A. $3— As above but with THREE added above Tellus at upper edge.

GOOD	VG	FINE	VF	XF	UNC.
$75	$135	$170	$250	$375	$575

FL-4. $5— Ceres seated at center. Printed date of October 10, 1861.

GOOD	VG	FINE	VF	XF	UNC.
$75	$125	$200	$250	$325	$525

FL-5. $10—As above.

GOOD	VG	FINE	VF	XF	UNC.
$100	$135	$165	$200	$365	$525

FL-6. $20— As above.

GOOD	VG	FINE	VF	XF	UNC.
$75	$125	$150	$225	$300	$400

FL-7. $50— As above. "50" and "L" in diagonal positions.

GOOD	VG	FINE	VF	XF	UNC.
$125	$200	$250	$275	$300	$450

FL-8. $50— As above except both "50" at upper corners and both "L" at lower corners.

GOOD	VG	FINE	VF	XF	UNC.
$110	$160	$200	$260	$300	$425

FL-9. $100— As above. "100" and "C" in diagonal positions.

GOOD	VG	FINE	VF	XF	UNC.
$100	$140	$170	$200	$250	$400

Important

Where more than one variety was issued of a note, the prices listed are for the more common kinds, not a rare minor variety. Where no value is indicated, the price is speculative due to such notes being rare in higher grades and seldom offered. Most of the illustrations in this catalog are either larger or smaller than the actual specimens.

Issue of January 1, 1862
Printed by Hoyer & Ludwig, Richmond, Va.

FL-10. $5— Ceres seated between Commerce and Navigation at center. Slave carrying cotton at left.

GOOD	VG	FINE	VF	XF	UNC.
$50	$100	$125	$200	$350	$550

FL-11 $10—As above.

GOOD	VG	FINE	VF	XF	UNC.
$50	$100	$165	$250	$350	$450

FL-12. $20— As above.

GOOD	VG	FINE	VF	XF	UNC.
$80	$135	$150	$225	$325	$450

FL-13. $50— As above.

GOOD	VG	FINE	VF	XF	UNC.
$135	$200	$250	$325	$425	$550

FL-14. $100— As above.

GOOD	VG	FINE	VF	XF	UNC.
$150	$200	$250	$350	$425	$550

About Prices

Genuine Confederate and Southern states currency in exceptionally choice condition may command a higher price than indicated by the valuations. General economic changes or the popularity of certain notes may also affect prices.

Fractional Notes

All are dated Feb'y. 2nd, 1863

No printer's name or serial numbers. Fractional notes were issued to meet the need for low denominations. All of these notes and those through FL-30 have the Public Lands of the State pledged for their redemption.

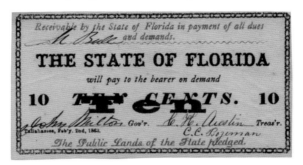

FL-15. 10 cents— Typeset. Black, red and blue with spaces for signatures of the Governor and Treasurer. The most common varieties are printed on unwatermarked paper. Scarcer are those printed on the backs of Florida notes or bonds with the scarcest being printed on paper watermarked W.T. & Co.

GOOD	VG	FINE	VF	XF	UNC.
$15	$25	$25	$50	$60	$70

FL-15A. 10 cents— As above. With one signature space, For Treasurer. Papers are the same as preceding except for very rare examples printed on paper watermarked FIVE and TEN.

GOOD	VG	FINE	VF	XF	UNC.
$15	$25	$25	$50	$60	$70

FL-16. 25 cents— Typeset. Black, red and blue. Similar to FL-15. Same papers.

GOOD	VG	FINE	VF	XF	UNC.
$15	$25	$25	$50	$60	$70

FL-16A. 25 cents— As above. Similar to FL-15A. Same papers except FIVE has not been noted and the TEN watermark, while scarce, is not a rarity.

GOOD	VG	FINE	VF	XF	UNC.
$25	$40	$50	$75	$100	$125

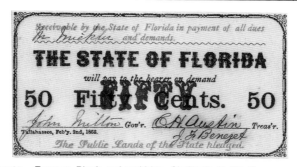

FL-17. 50 cents— Typeset. Black, red and blue. Similar to FL-15. Same papers

GOOD	VG	FINE	VF	XF	UNC.
$15	$25	$30	$40	$55	$70

FL-17A. 50 cents— As above. Same papers as FL-16A.

GOOD	VG	FINE	VF	XF	UNC.
$25	$40	$50	$70	$100	$125

Issue of March 1, 1863
Printed by Keatinge & Ball, Columbia, S.C.

FL-18. $1— Slaves harvesting cotton at center, child and State arms at left. Black with red overprint.

GOOD	VG	FINE	VF	XF	UNC.
$50	$100	$150	$200	$250	$500

FL-19. $2— Train at center, Ceres and State arms at left, Indian maiden at right. Black with red overprint.

GOOD	VG	FINE	VF	XF	UNC.
$80	$100	$235	$250	$275	$600

FL-20. $3— Sailing ship at center, State arms at upper left, Hope at right. Black with red overprint.

GOOD	VG	FINE	VF	XF	UNC.
$15	$25	$30	$225	$345	$450

FL-21. $5— Moneta seated at center, Indian standing at left, State arms at right. Black with red overprint. See FL-26 (1864) for illustration.

GOOD	VG	FINE	VF	XF	UNC.
$70	$120	$200	$275	$350	$550

FL-22. $10— Ceres seated at center, ship and State arms at left, slave with cotton at right. Black with red overprint.

GOOD	VG	FINE	VF	XF	UNC.
$70	$120	$200	$275	$350	$550

Issue of 1864

Printed by Keatinge & Ball, Columbia, S.C.

FL-23. $1 — Same type as FL-18 except date of Jany 1st, 1864.

GOOD	VG	FINE	VF	XF	UNC.
$80	$140	$200	$250	$350	$475

FL-24. $2— Same type as FL-19 except date of Jany 1st, 1864.

GOOD	VG	FINE	VF	XF	UNC.
$80	$140	$200	$250	$375	$475

FL-25. $3— Same type as FL-20 except date of Jany 1st, 1864.

GOOD	VG	FINE	VF	XF	UNC.
$80	$140	$200	$275	$425	$575

FL-26. $5— Same type as FL-21 except date of March 1, 1864.

GOOD	VG	FINE	VF	XF	UNC.
$50	$100	$150	$200	$300	$375

FL-27. $10— Same type as FL-22 except date of March 1, 1864.

GOOD	VG	FINE	VF	XF	UNC.
$70	$120	$200	$300	$400	$650

All of the above notes are printed in black with red overprint and watermarked W.T. & Co. Unwatermarked notes of FL-23 to FL-25 are very rare. Both watermarked and unwatermarked papers are approximately the same value for FL-26 and FL-27.

Important

Where more than one variety was issued of a note, the prices listed are for the more common kinds, not a rare minor variety. Where no value is indicated, the price is speculative due to such notes being rare in higher grades and seldom offered. Most of the illustrations in this catalog are either larger or smaller than the actual specimens.

Issue of January 1, 1865

No printer's name

The preceding notes generally bear the signatures of C.H. Austin, Treasurer, and John Milton, Governor. It would have been a lot of work had the Governor signed all of them personally. Abraham K. Allison held office as Governor for a brief period in 1865, and his signature together with C.H. Austin, who continued as Treasurer, appears on this issue of January 1, 1865. All of these notes are printed on the backs of Florida notes, due to the scarcity of paper. The high denominations resulted from inflation near the end of the war.

FL-28. $50— Typeset with ship at upper center. Very scarce.

GOOD	VG	FINE	VF	XF	UNC.
$600	$1200	$2000	$3000	$4500	$6000

FL-29. $100— As above. Very scarce.

GOOD	VG	FINE	VF	XF	UNC.
$1000	$2000	$3000	$4000	$5500	$8000

FL-30. $500— As above. Very Rare.

About Sizes

The sizes of Confederate States notes may vary slightly, due to differences when the sheets were cut apart, but most are approximately 3 to 3¼ inches by 7 to 7¼ inches in size except Nos. 43-46, which are 2¾ by 61/8 inches. The 50-cent notes (Nos. 57 and 65) are approximately 2¼ by 4¼ inches.

Postwar Issues

Printed by Peter Bowes, New Orleans

FL-31. $1— Portrait of Washington at upper left. Date of 186_. Very rare.

FL-32. $20— Seated woman with marble bust and shields at center. Woman's portrait at upper right. Date of 186_. Very rare. Other denominations?

Printed by National Bank Note Co., New York, March 1, 1870

FL-33. $1— Farmer with scythe at left. Ceres at right, Black with green overprint. Ornate green back. Plate letters A to D. Signed by Harrison Reed, who was Governor between 1868 and 1873. Very scarce.

GOOD	VG	FINE	VF	XF	UNC.
$2500	$4000	$6000	---	---	---

Any higher denominations that may exist are very rare.

About Prices

Genuine Confederate and Southern states currency in exceptionally choice condition may command a higher price than indicated by the valuations. General economic changes or the popularity of certain notes may also affect prices.

GEORGIA

The secession of Georgia solidified the Lower South from the eastern shores of North Carolina to the waters of the Mississippi. Although Georgia was the fifth state to secede, the secession was accomplished only by a lot of propaganda and by bullying the state's leaders, especially through the efforts of Robert Toombs, a popular Confederate firebrand. The final vote on the Ordinance of Secession was 208 in favor and 89 against. Alexander Stephens pressed for compromise with the North but, failing to prevent secession, he stated that he would go with the state. Having done so, he afterward became Vice President of the Confederacy.

As noted elsewhere in this catalog, the Constitution of the Confederate States emphasized state's rights. Perhaps no one took this emphasis more seriously than governor Joseph E. Brown (1821-94), who had become Governor in 1857 and served until the end of the war. He was a great believer in state sovereignty, placing the interests of Georgia above those of the Confederate States. As a result, he was often at odds with President Davis, to the extent that he would sometimes condemn certain Confederate policies while adopting the same for Georgia. Toward the end of the war, there was talk that Georgia might secede from the Confederacy; General Sherman, hearing this, offered to meet with Stephens and Brown, promising to order his troops to remain on the roads during their march through Georgia and not destroy the countryside. However, Governor Brown decided that it would not be honorable to accept.

Georgia had the most slaves of any Southern state, over 460,000 out of a population of about 1,060,000. Governor Brown would never consider arming the slaves, but many were ordered to work on fortifications. Arms were forbidden to be removed from the state since his priority was the defense of Georgia, even though large numbers of soldiers were supplied to the Confederacy. It was for things like this that Governor Brown was both condemned and praised. After the war, he recommended that the state submit to Reconstruction, which ended in 1870. As for Brown, he became Chief Justice of the State Supreme Court in 1868 and in 1880 became a U.S. Senator, serving until 1891.

Upper portion of impressment form printed on lined record paper. (Size reduced)

Act of December 5, 1861

Printed by Howell, Engr., Savannah and Douglas Engr., N. Orleans

These first notes were dated January 15, 1862, and state that they are "receivable in payment of all dues to the State and to the Western & Atlantic Rail Road" that was owned by Georgia. They also exhibit more confidence than other Confederate issues by indicating the notes were redeemable in "Eight per cent State Bonds or Specie Six months after a Treaty of Peace or when the Banks of Savannah and Augusta resume Specie payment if before that time." The band at the center of these notes, which enclose the spelled-out denomination, is printed in red. Notes with misplaced or inverted red overprints are errors and worth double or more as are those with two black state seals stamped at left instead of one.

GA-1. $5— James Oglethorpe, founder of Georgia, facing left.

GOOD	VG	FINE	VF	XF	UNC.
$10	$15	$20	$25	$35	$45

GA-2. $10— Ceres standing at center.

GOOD	VG	FINE	VF	XF	UNC.
$15	$20	$25	$40	$50	$65

GA-3. $20— Ceres standing at center.

GOOD	VG	FINE	VF	XF	UNC.
$15	$20	$30	$40	$60	$90

GA-4. $50— Ceres standing at center, Governor Joseph E. Brown at sides. Justice holding scales at each end.

GOOD	VG	FINE	VF	XF	UNC.
$25	$35	$45	$60	$75	$90

GA-5. $100— Ceres standing at center. Sailor in oval at each end.

GOOD	VG	FINE	VF	XF	UNC.
$30	$45	$55	$60	$75	$110

Act of December 5, 1862

Small denomination notes dated January 1, 1863.
These bear imprint of Howell, Engraver or Eng'd by R. H. Howell.

GA-6. 5 cents— Printed inscription. This and the following notes were redeemable in "Confederate Treasury Notes, when presented in sums of Five Dollars and upwards." Plate letters A to R.

GOOD	VG	FINE	VF	XF	UNC.
$5	$10	$13	$16	$20	$50

GA-7. 10 cents— Printed inscription. Plate letters A to R.

GOOD	VG	FINE	VF	XF	UNC.
$6	$10	$13	$16	$20	$30

GA-8. 15 cents— Printed inscription. Plate letters A to R.

GOOD	VG	FINE	VF	XF	UNC.
$15	$20	$30	$50	$70	$100

GA-9. 20 cents— Printed inscription. Plate letter A.

GOOD	VG	FINE	VF	XF	UNC.
$70	$120	$160	$225	$300	$525

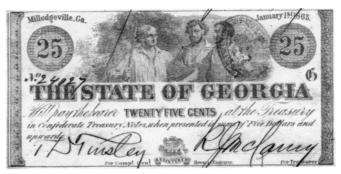

GA-10. 25 cents— Three workmen. Price is for green Treasury seal. Red seals are worth double. Also without seal (scarce). Plate letters A to K.

GOOD	VG	FINE	VF	XF	UNC.
$7	$10	$15	$20	$35	$45

GA-11. 50 cents— As above. Green Treasury seal. Value doubles for red seal. Plate letters A to P.

GOOD	VG	FINE	VF	XF	UNC.
$7	$10	$15	$20	$30	$40

GA-12. 75 cents— Indian maiden at left. Plate letter A.

GOOD	VG	FINE	VF	XF	UNC.
$100	$200	$350	$600	$850	$1200

GA-13. $1— Railroad train. Red or green Treasury seal. Value triples for no seal. Plate letters A to K.

GOOD	VG	FINE	VF	XF	UNC.
$15	$35	$50	$75	$100	$145

GA-14. $2— Ship at sea. Red or green Treasury seal. Value triples for no seal.

GOOD	VG	FINE	VF	XF	UNC.
$15	$35	$50	$80	$115	$175

GA-15. $3— Horses and farm animals. Minerva standing at left, Justice at right. Treasury seal in green.

GOOD	VG	FINE	VF	XF	UNC.
$700	$1200	$2000	$3200	$4500	$6000

GA-16. $4— Moneta seated with treasure. Slaves carrying cotton at left, wheat at right. Treasury seal in green.

GOOD	VG	FINE	VF	XF	UNC.
$1500	$3000	$5000	---	---	---

Act of December 12, 1862

Printed by Howell, Savannah.

These notes have the inscription changed to read that they will be paid "in Specie or six per cent Bonds of this state six months after a Treaty of peace shall have been ratified between the United States and the Confederate States."

GA-17. $10— State arms within a coiled snake at center, helmeted heads at sides with Minerva at left end, Ceres at right. Red Treasury seal. Dated February 2d, 1863.

GOOD	VG	FINE	VF	XF	UNC.
$7	$12	$20	$30	$50	$65

GA-18. $50— Similar except Roman numeral "L" (for "50") within coiled snake at center, state arms at left. Red overprint on spelled-out denomination. Treasury seal in black on back of note. Dated February 2d, 1863.

GOOD	VG	FINE	VF	XF	UNC.
$10	$20	$30	$45	$60	$90

GA-19. $100— Similar, except state arms within coiled snake at center, Governor Joseph E. Brown at left. Red overprint on spelled-out denomination. Treasury seal in black on back of note. Dated February 1st, 1863.

GOOD	VG	FINE	VF	XF	UNC.
$15	$35	$50	$75	$100	$125

Important

Where more than one variety was issued of a note, the prices listed are for the more common kinds, not a rare minor variety. Where no value is indicated, the price is speculative due to such notes being rare in higher grades and seldom offered. Most of the illustrations in this catalog are either larger or smaller than the actual specimens.

Act of December, 1863

Howell, Eng'r.

Small denomination notes dated January 1st, 1864. More notes of lower values were apparently needed and these are of the same type as those dated January 1, 1863. Prices are for signed notes.

GA-20. 50 cents— Same type as GA-11.

GOOD	VG	FINE	VF	XF	UNC.
$7	$12	$20	$35	$50	$65

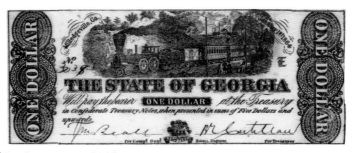

GA-21. $1— Same type as GA-13.

GOOD	VG	FINE	VF	XF	UNC.
$10	$20	$35	$50	$70	$100

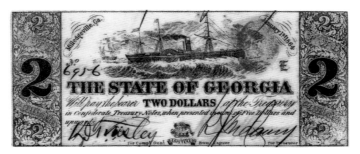

GA-22. $2— Same type as GA-14.

GOOD	VG	FINE	VF	XF	UNC.
$10	$20	$35	$50	$70	$100

GA-23. $3— Same type as GA-15.

GOOD	VG	FINE	VF	XF	UNC.
$150	$250	$600	$650	$700	$750

GA-24. $4— Same type as GA-16.

GOOD	VG	FINE	VF	XF	UNC.
$10	$20	$35	$50	$100	$175

Prices of Rarities

Rare notes that are in strong demand tend to rise continuously in price. This is particularly true of the Montgomery issue and certain other notes.

Dated April 6th, 1864

GA-25. $5— Moneta seated with treasure and State arms. Green Treasury seal. Plate letters A to K.

GOOD	VG	FINE	VF	XF	UNC.
$5	$10	$20	$30	$40	$55

GA-26. $10— As above. Large or small serial letters. Green Treasury seal. Plate letters A to K.

GOOD	VG	FINE	VF	XF	UNC.
$7	$13	$25	$35	$50	$75

GA-27. $20— As above. Green Treasury seal.

GOOD	VG	FINE	VF	XF	UNC.
$10	$20	$30	$50	$70	$100

GA-28. $50— As above. FIFTY in red.

GOOD	VG	FINE	VF	XF	UNC.
$15	$30	$45	$70	$100	$150

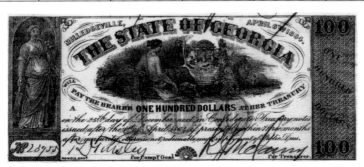

GA-29. $100— As above. Minerva standing at left, 100 in red.

GOOD	VG	FINE	VF	XF	UNC.
$20	$35	$60	$100	$135	$190

GA-30. $500— As above. 500 in red.

GOOD	VG	FINE	VF	XF	UNC.
$250	$400	$650	$1725	$2000	$3000

The notes no longer contain any mention of specie, but perhaps that was made up by having them redeemable on Christmas Day, December 25, 1864, although this date was later extended to March, 1865.

GA-31. $5— James Oglethorpe. Same type as GA-1. Black Treasury seal on back of note. Dated January 15th, 1865. Printed by Howell, Eng'r, Savannah.

GOOD	VG	FINE	VF	XF	UNC.
$25	$50	$75	$90	$125	$140

GA-32. $50— Ceres standing at center. Similar to GA-3 except denomination. It even includes the inscription about 8% interest and redemption in specie. FIFTY DOLLARS is overprinted in red. Black Treasury seal on back of notes. Printed by Howell, Eng'r, Savannah. Dated January 15, 1865.

GOOD	VG	FINE	VF	XF	UNC
$20	$40	$60	$85	$110	$150

GA-33. $10— State arms at center, train at left. Dated March 20th, 1865, and contains redemption date of December 25th. Black Treasury seal on back of note. R.H. Howell, Eng'r. (Notes without printer's name are worth double.)

GOOD	VG	FINE	VF	XF	UNC.
$15	$30	$45	$60	$75	$100

Georgia issued about $20 million in State currency but the exact amount is unknown, since part of it was exchanged for large denomination Treasury Certificates and part was destroyed as Sherman's army approached the capital at Milledgeville, Ga. However, all types are among the most readily available of Southern states issues.

INDIAN TERRITORY

From the first, the Confederacy recognized the importance of having the Indian Territory as an ally to help protect its western flank. It was assumed that the Five Civilized Tribes (Cherokees, Chickasaws, Choctaws, Creeks and Seminoles) who had been moved from the South by the Federal Government in the 1830s would be pro-Southern, since many of the Indians had adopted the ways of the white man and now owned slaves.

As early as February 7, 1861, the Choctaw Nation passed a resolution in favor of the South. Albert Pike of Arkansas, who had previously aided the Indians in legal matters with the Federal Government, was appointed to travel to the Indian Territory to arrange treaties. Having been authorized by the Confederate Government to spend $100,000 in this effort, Pike journeyed in late May 1861 to the Indian Territory but was only partially successful in his treaty making. It turned out that only part of the Indians favored the South while others were still loyal to the Union. This led to a "little civil war" within the Indian Territory that was not helpful to the Confederate cause.

The story is too long and complicated to be covered briefly, but John Ross, Chief of the Cherokee Nation since 1839, offers an example. He wished to maintain neutrality, but he was swayed by early victories of the Confederates in the East. Later, when some of his forces were defeated and he was captured by a Northern army, he journeyed to Washington where he tried to prove that he was coerced into joining the Confederates. He was still pleading his case when he died in 1866. On the other hand, General Stand Watie of the pro-South Cherokees, was the last Confederate military leader to surrender in 1865.

The treaties had stipulated that the Indians were only required to fight within the borders of the Indian Territory, but they also fought in Arkansas and Missouri. Albert Pike, who had been made a Brigadier General, ordered uniforms and supplies for the Indians, but these were largely taken by others. All in all, retaining the loyalty of the Indians was an expensive proposition since the Confederacy agreed to pay in gold and silver the amounts that had formerly been due from the U.S. Government.

Both the Cherokee and Choctaw Nations had a Representative in the Confederate Congress at Richmond, as did the Creek and Seminole Nations later in the war (1864), which means that the Confederacy recognized the need of Indian aid.

Cherokee Nation

Since the Cherokee Nation is known to have issued currency in June 1862, all in low denominations, which state that they are redeemable in "Notes of the Confederate States, whenever the sum of $20, $50 or $100 is presented at the Office of the Treasurer, Tahlequah" (the Cherokee capital), it appears that these notes may represent the denominations of the Confederate currency that Albert Pike had delivered earlier in the year. The need for fractional and low denomination notes apparently resulted because they were unavailable from the Confederate States. In any case, the following notes are known to have been issued in specific denominations. All are of similar design.

IT-I.   25 cents. (?)

IT-2.   50 cents— Typeset. Very rare.

IT-3. $1— As above. Very rare.

IT-4. $2— As above. Very rare.

IT-5. $5— As above. Very rare.

Choctaw Nation

IT-6.   50cents — Typeset. Written dates of 1863. Very rare.

IT-7. $1— As above. Very rare.

IT-8. $2.50— As above. Very rare.

IT-9. $5— As above. Very rare. The five "1" at lower left stands for $5.

Warrants with written amounts are also known. There may be other types not reported. The above notes are printed on colored papers and most of the known specimens bear an endorsement that they have been reissued under an Act of October 17th, 1865, with interest at 5%. In 1866, the Federal Government penalized the Indians for having supported the Confederate States.

KENTUCKY

The border State of Kentucky wished to remain neutral when the Civil War began, but it was pulled apart by the anti-slavery and pro-slavery factions. The winner in the presidential election of 1860 was not Lincoln (Republican) or Breckinridge (Democrat), it was John Bell of the Constitutional Union Party who gained the most votes in Kentucky. Governor Beriah Magoffin refused Lincoln's call for volunteers (but thousands of men were later to fight for both sides) and warned both the Union and the Confederacy not to invade the state, but he was ignored. General Albert S. Johnston, born in Kentucky, occupied the southern part of the State; while he was there, an irregular Ordinance of Secession was passed at Russellville on November 18, 1861. George W. Johnson was selected Provisional Governor and Bowling Green was made the State Capital. Actually, the Confederate government already had members in its Congress from Kentucky prior to its supposed secession but the state was not considered a part of the Confederacy by the Union and after the war was not subject to Reconstruction. However, the State suffered no less from invasions led by Generals E. Kirby Smith and Braxton Bragg during August to October 1862 and the cavalry raids of John Hunt Morgan of 1862-1863.

While not entirely a part of the Confederacy, Kentucky's attachment to the South remains strong. Jefferson Davis, the Confederate President, was born at Fairview, near Hopkinsville, Ky., in 1808. Although his family moved to Mississippi shortly after his birth, and Davis later represented that state in Congress, his connection with Kentucky was not forgotten. In 1907 it was proposed that a park be set aside at Fairview where a monument would be erected in his memory. The monument, in the form of a concrete obelisk, was completed in 1924 and represents one of the tallest in the United States. It is 351 feet in height above its foundation of Kentucky limestone.

No state currency of the Civil War was issued by Kentucky.

LOUISIANA

As early as December 1860, after learning of Lincoln's election, the Governor convened the legislature that passed an act calling for a convention to consider secession. The convention met at Baton Rouge on January 23, 1861, with 130 delegates in attendance. An Ordinance of Secession was drafted and submitted on January 26, which was adopted by a vote of 113 against 17. Like most other states, a motion to submit the ordinance to popular vote was defeated.

Louisiana proved vulnerable to Union forces and New Orleans fell to the naval squadron of Captain David G. Farragut on April 25, 1861. General Benjamin F. Butler's forces entered the city on May 1. As a result, the North largely controlled the Mississippi River except for blockade runners. The South continued to hold Western Louisiana where a capital was established at Shreveport under Governor Thomas O. Moore (1860-64). A major victory for the Confederates in Western Louisiana was at Sabine Crossing on April 8, 1864. Louisiana raised about 1,000 military companies comprising 56,000 troops that included black regiments (see U.S. National Archives, Microcopy No. 320, C.S. Soldiers of Louisiana).

General Butler originated many orders to the people of Louisiana, and one of the first proclamations contains a paragraph that concerns the currency: "The circulation of Confederate bonds, evidences of debt, except notes in the similitude of bank notes issued by the Confederate States, or scrip, or any trade in the same, is strictly forbidden. It having been represented to the Commanding General by the city authorities that these Confederate notes, in the form of bank notes, are, in a great measure, the only substitute for money which the people have been allowed to have, and that great distress would ensue among the poorer classes if the circulation of such notes were suppressed, such circulation will be permitted as long as any one may be inconsiderate enough to receive them, till further orders."

This proclamation was revoked a year later by Order No. 30, May 19, 1862, which ordered banks to make payments in bank notes of the banks, U.S. Treasury notes, gold or silver, but no further Confederate notes. For this reason, Bank of Louisiana notes will often be found stamped "Forced Issue." Other orders of General Butler's unpopular military rule concerned conduct of the citizens, curfews etc.

Like some of the other states, Louisiana was subjected to a wasteful Reconstruction government after the war that let no expense stand in the way of securing high quality printing from New York bank note firms. Even Louisiana's readmission to the Union on July 9, 1868, failed to end unnecessary projects, bloated travel expenses and other things that cost the state millions of dollars before Federal troops were withdrawn after the election of 1876.

Authorized by Act of January 23, 1862

Dated February 24, 1862

The first Louisiana State note of the Civil War issued by the Confederates indicate that they originated from the capital at Baton Rouge and were printed by Douglas in New Orleans. This was just a few months before both New Orleans and the eastern half of Louisiana were occupied by Northern troops. Regardless of where the currency was issued, the notes of Louisiana indicate that they will be paid "Twelve months after a definitive Treaty of Peace between the Confederate States and the United States." There generally remained some civility of this nature on Confederate currency.

These notes were printed on the backs of New Orleans or Texas notes and often bear the denominations overprinted in red or blue.

LA-1. $1 — Ceres seated at center. No overprint.

GOOD	VG	FINE	VF	XF	UNC.
$35	$65	$100	$150	$225	$325

LA-1A. $1— As above. ONE overprint in red. (Notes exist with TWO overprints or inverted.)

GOOD	VG	FINE	VF	XF	UNC.
$15	$30	$75	$100	$125	$150

LA-1B. $1— As above. Overprint in blue.

GOOD	VG	FINE	VF	XF	UNC.
$25	$50	$85	$110	$160	$275

LA-2. $2— As above. No overprint.

GOOD	VG	FINE	VF	XF	UNC.
—	—	—	—	—	—

LA-2A. $2— As above. TWO overprint in red.

GOOD	VG	FINE	VF	XF	UNC.
$20	$30	$75	$100	$125	$150

LA-2B. $2— As above. TWO overprint in blue.

GOOD	VG	FINE	VF	XF	UNC.
$40	$70	$100	$150	$200	$275

LA-3. $3— As above. Very rare. May not exist.

LA-4. $1— Typeset inscription. Beehive at bottom. "1" and "ONE" overprinted in green.

GOOD	VG	FINE	VF	XF	UNC.
$15	$35	$50	$65	$80	$100

LA-5. $2— As above. Denomination overprints in green.

GOOD	VG	FINE	VF	XF	UNC.
$15	$30	$40	$65	$80	$105

LA-6. $3— As above. Denomination overprints in green.

GOOD	VG	FINE	VF	XF	UNC.
$40	$70	$100	$150	$195	$260

LA-7. $5— "South Striking Down Union" as on some Confederate States $2 notes. "Lazy 5" at bottom. Ornate green back. Dated October 10th, 1862 and printed by B. Duncan, Columb. (New Orleans had fallen to Union forces in April.)

GOOD	VG	FINE	VF	XF	UNC.
$12	$25	$40	$45	$60	$75

Authorized by Act. of February 8th, 1863

Issued at Shreveport, Louisiana and dated March 10th, 1863. Printed by B. Duncan, Columbia, S.C.

LA-8. $5— "South Striking Down Union" as on LA-7 but without "Lazy 5." Ornate green back. Plate letters A to M.

GOOD	VG	FINE	VF	XF	UNC.
$12	$25	$35	$50	$75	$100

LA-9. $20— Bust of General P.G.T. Beauregard. Black with red overprint. Ornate blue back. Plate letters A to K.

GOOD	VG	FINE	VF	XF	UNC.
$45	$90	$110	$165	$220	$250

LA-10. $50— Bust of General Leonadis Polk. Liberty seated at right. Ornate green back. Plate letters A to K.

GOOD	VG	FINE	VF	XF	UNC.
$35	$65	$100	$130	$180	$290

LA-11. $100— Bust of Governor Thomas O. Moore at left. Large building at center. Liberty seated at right. Ornate blue-green back. Plate letters A to K.

GOOD	VG	FINE	VF	XF	UNC.
$25	$40	$65	$100	$150	$375

Issued from Shreveport, Louisiana and printed by South-Western Print with date of March 1st, 1864.

These notes are of small denominations and are typeset.

LA-12. 25 cents— Inscription only. Plain paper, with or without ONE or TWO in red or blue. Also found printed on backs of New Orleans notes or bills of exchange. Plate letters A, B, C.

GOOD	VG	FINE	VF	XF	UNC.
$25	$50	$75	$110	$160	$210

LA-13. 50 cents— Inscription only. Same varieties and plate letters as LA-12. A rare variety is printed on paper watermarked T.M. Saunderson & Co.

GOOD	VG	FINE	VF	XF	UNC.
$20	$40	$60	$85	$115	$150

LA-14. 50 cents— Shipping scene. Liberty seated coin design at left. Various plate letters.

GOOD	VG	FINE	VF	XF	UNC.
$7	$12	$17	$25	$40	$55

LA-15. 50 cents— Shipping scene. Eagle at left. Various plate letters.

GOOD	VG	FINE	VF	XF	UNC.
$7	$12	$17	$25	$40	$55

LA-16. $1— Ship at center, locomotive at left. Various plate letters.

GOOD	VG	FINE	VF	XF	UNC.
$7	$15	$20	$25	$40	$60

LA-17. $1— Commerce leaning on cotton bale, Washington standing at left. Various plate letters.

GOOD	VG	FINE	VF	XF	UNC.
$7	$15	$20	$25	$40	$60

LA-18. $1— Commerce leaning on cotton bale, ship at left. Various plate letters.

GOOD	VG	FINE	VF	XF	UNC.
$7	$15	$20	$25	$40	$60

About Prices

Genuine Confederate and Southern states currency in exceptionally choice condition may command a higher price than indicated by the valuations. General economic changes or the popularity of certain notes may also affect prices.

LA-19. $1— Mississippi River-type steamboat at center, Minerva at left. Various plate letters.

GOOD	VG	FINE	VF	XF	UNC.
$7	$15	$20	$25	$40	$60

LA-20. $1— Ship vertically in oval at left. Overprinted ONE or TWO in red or blue on front or back. Printed on plain paper or backs of New Orleans notes. Plate letters A, B.

GOOD	VG	FINE	VF	XF	UNC.
$30	$60	$100	$125	$145	$170

LA-21. $1— Train vertically in oval at left. Overprinted ONE or TWO in red or blue on front or back. Printed on plain paper or backs of New Orleans notes. Plate letters A, B. A rare variety is on paper watermarked T.H. Saunderson & Co.

GOOD	VG	FINE	VF	XF	UNC.
$30	$60	$90	$125	$150	$175

Reconstruction Period Notes
Act of February 9th, 1866

Printed by the American Bank Note Co., New York

LA-22. $5— Heads of two maidens; President Andrew Johnson at lower right. Green and black. Fancy green back. Plate letters A to D.

GOOD	VG	FINE	VF	XF	UNC.
$50	$100	$160	$225	$275	$400

LA-23. $10— Dog with chest at upper right, Washington at left, cotton ball at right. Green and black. Fancy green back. Plate letters A, B.

GOOD	VG	FINE	VF	XF	UNC.
$125	$250	$350	$450	$600	$850

LA-24. $20— Ships at dock at upper right, Thomas Jefferson at lower right. Fancy green back. Plate letters A, B.

GOOD	VG	FINE	VF	XF	UNC.
$100	$200	$300	$425	$550	$750

MARYLAND

The border State of Maryland was important to both the North and the South. The U.S. capital at Washington in the District of Columbia is within the borders of Maryland. Had the South been successful in securing Maryland for the Confederate States, either through secession or by military force, the U.S. government would have been disrupted by being forced to move to Philadelphia or another city in the North.

When troops to defend Washington were routed through Baltimore during April 1861, there were riots. Like many Southern states, Maryland had its pro-North and pro-South sections. Baltimore and the Eastern Shore with its planters favored the South, while the Western part of the State, which had fewer slaves, favored the North.

The riots in Baltimore had one notable aftermath that may have swayed the state to join the South but failed. When James Ryder Randall, a native of Baltimore, read the news while a teacher in New Orleans, he dashed off a stirring Civil War song, "Maryland, My Maryland!" that called attention to the casualties during the riots and beseeched the state to join the South. The song contains nine stanzas, of which the first and last are quoted:

> The despot's heel is on thy shore,
> Maryland!
> His torch is at thy temple door,
> Maryland!
> Avenge the patriotic gore
> That flecked the streets of Baltimore,
> And be the battle-queen of yore,
> Maryland, my Maryland!

> I hear the distant thunder-hum,
> Maryland!
> The Old Line's bugle, fife, and drum,
> Maryland!
> She is not dead, nor deaf, nor dumb;
> Huzza! she spurns the Northern scum—
> She breathes! She burns! She'll come!
> She'll come!
> Maryland, my Maryland!

In 1939, these lines were adopted as the State song but usually only the first few stanzas are sung today.

The legislators at Maryland's State House acted quickly before fervor built up for secession; on April 29, 1861, they voted 53 to 13 to remain with the Union. Thus assured, Governor Thomas H. Hicks refused to call a convention to consider secession. Later, in 1864, Maryland adopted a new Constitution that abolished slavery. Citizens with Confederate sympathies were also disenfranchised, but this repression was removed by a revised Constitution in 1867.

MISSISSIPPI

Although distant from South Carolina, Mississippi became the second state to secede. In November 1860, the Legislature provided for an election of delegates to a convention to be held on January 7, 1861, to decide upon secession. Delegates from South Carolina and Alabama were also present. While a significant number of delegates preferred to compromise or maintain a "wait and see attitude," those that favored secession intimidated those who were against with the result that the vote was 84 to 15. When the Ordinance of Secession was passed on January 9, the state established an independent republic, but that changed when Mississippi ratified the Constitution of the Confederate States on March 30. By that time, Jefferson Davis of Mississippi had already been selected to be President.

It wasn't as easy to return to the Constitution of the United States at the end of the war. President Johnson appointed William L. Sharkey as Provisional Governor on June 13, 1865, and he ordered a convention in August that amended the State Constitution to abolish slavery and repeal secession on August 21, 1865. However, when Benjamin G. Humphreys was elected governor in October, the U.S. Congressmen that were also chosen would not be seated and military rule took the place of civil government.

It was not until January 1868 that another convention was assembled to adopt a new Constitution. It remained in session until May 18, but its work was rejected by an election held on June 22, despite General Adelbert Ames having replaced Humphreys as governor a few days earlier. On April 12, 1869, Congress authorized the President to again submit the Constitution to vote; in November it was accepted after the clauses disenfranchising former Confederates were removed. In January 1870, the state legislature ratified the 14th and 15th Amendments to the U.S. Constitution, and Mississippi was readmitted to the Union on February 23, 1870. On March 10, 1870, James L. Alcorn (whose portrait appears on Reconstruction paper money) was inaugurated.

Acts of January 24, 1861,
November 29, 1861,
January 29, 1862

Printed by the American Bank Note Co., N.Y. & N.O.

These notes were first authorized before hostilities broke out in April 1861, and even before the Confederate States decided to issue currency. The notes were issued from the State Capital at Jackson, Mississippi, with written dates of 1861 through 1864. All of the notes were "on account of the Military Fund bearing Ten per cent interest per annum."

MS-1. $10— Slave with two horses at center, Governor John J. Pettus (1859-63) at left, woman at right. Black with red overprint.

GOOD	VG	FINE	VF	XF	UNC.
$150	$300	$500	$800	$210	$275

MS-2. $20— Mules pulling wagonload of cotton at center. Woman at left, Governor Pettus at right. Black with red overprint.

GOOD	VG	FINE	VF	XF	UNC.
$150	$300	$500	$900	$1350	$2000

MS-3. $50— Mules pulling wagon (frontal view), Governor Pettus at upper left, slave in cotton field at lower right. Black with red overprint.

GOOD	VG	FINE	VF	XF	UNC.
$150	$300	$500	$700	$850	$1000

MS-4. $100— Slaves picking cotton at center, Prosperina at upper left, Governor Pettus at lower right. Black with red overprint.

GOOD	VG	FINE	VF	XF	UNC.
$150	$300	$500	$700	$850	$1000

1862 Cotton Pledged Notes

This issue of notes resulted from the demands of the cotton planters that stored cotton be pledged for the eventual redemption of the currency. Various written dates of 1862. Green or blue overprints. Notes with inverted "Cotton Pledged" overprint or lacking the overprint are rare. Some of these notes are printed on the back of auditor's bills or bills of exchange, with or without orange tint. These notes were "receivable in payment of all Dues to the State and Counties, except the Military Tax."

MS-5. $1— Railroad train at center, Commerce seated at left, fanner with wheat at right. "Cotton Pledged" in green.

GOOD	VG	FINE	VF	XF	UNC.
$20	$30	$50	$80	$125	$175

MS-5A. $1 — As above. "Cotton Pledged" in blue.

GOOD	VG	FINE	VF	XF	UNC.
$20	$30	$50	$80	$125	$175

MS-6. $2.50— Farmer with wheat at left, Indian warrior standing at right. "Cotton Pledged" in green.

GOOD	VG	FINE	VF	XF	UNC.
$25	$40	$60	$125	$175	$225

MS-6A. $2.50— As above. "Cotton Pledged" in blue. Light orange background.

GOOD	VG	FINE	VF	XF	UNC.
$25	$45	$75	$125	$185	$275

MS-7. $3— Small vignette of train at center, ship in oval at left, sailor with oar at right. Large blue 3 in center. "Cotton Pledged" in green. Light orange background.

GOOD	VG	FINE	VF	XF	UNC.
$25	$40	$60	$135	$200	$300

MS-7A. $3— As above. "Cotton Pledged" in blue.

GOOD	VG	FINE	VF	XF	UNC.
$25	$45	$65	$100	$125	$175

MS-8. $5— Railroad train at center, Indian at left, sailing ship at right. "Cotton Pledged" in olive. Light gray background.

GOOD	VG	FINE	VF	XF	UNC.
$50	$75	$100	$175	$225	$350

MS-8A. $5— As above. "Cotton Pledged" in olive. Light orange background.

GOOD	VG	FINE	VF	XF	UNC.
$25	$40	$60	$100	$150	$220

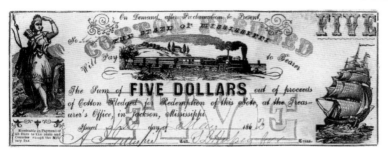

MS-8B. $5— As above. "Cotton Pledged" in green.

GOOD	VG	FINE	VF	XF	UNC.
$20	$30	$50	$50	$75	$200

MS-9. $10— Justice with scales standing at left. Plow and rural scene at right. "Cotton Pledged" in olive. Light gray background.

GOOD	VG	FINE	VF	XF	UNC.
$50	$75	$135	$200	$350	$500

MS-9A. $10— As above. "Cotton Pledged" in olive. Light orange background.

GOOD	VG	FINE	VF	XF	UNC.
$30	$50	$75	$125	$175	$275

MS-9B. $10— As above. "Cotton Pledged" in green.

GOOD	VG	FINE	VF	XF	UNC.
$30	$50	$75	$125	$175	$275

MS-10. $20— Small vignette of train at center, two Indian braves at left, Commerce seated at right. "Cotton Pledged" in olive. Light gray background.

GOOD	VG	FINE	VF	XF	UNC.
$75	$140	$200	$275	$400	$600

MS-10A. $20— As above. "Cotton Pledged" in olive. Light orange background.

GOOD	VG	FINE	VF	XF	UNC.
$35	$70	$100	$150	$225	$325

MS-10B. $20— As above. "Cotton Pledged" in green.

GOOD	VG	FINE	VF	XF	UNC.
$30	$50	$75	$100	$175	$225

MS-11. $50— Indian at left, slaves picking cotton at right. "Cotton Pledged" in olive. Light gray background.

GOOD	VG	FINE	VF	XF	UNC.
$100	$175	$250	$350	$450	$650

MS-11A. $50— As above. "Cotton Pledged" in olive. Light orange background.

GOOD	VG	FINE	VF	XF	UNC.
$50	$85	$135	$200	$275	$425

MS-11B. $50— As above. "Cotton Pledged" in green.

GOOD	VG	FINE	VF	XF	UNC.
$200	$250	$300	$350	$650	$850

MS-12. $100— Statue of "America" at left, small ship in center, Indian at right. "Cotton Pledged" in olive. Light gray background.

GOOD	VG	FINE	VF	XF	UNC.
$200	$250	$300	$350	$650	$850

MS-12A. $100— As above. "Cotton Pledged" in gray. Light orange background. Rare.

MS-12B. $100— As above. "Cotton Pledged" in green. Light orange background.

GOOD	VG	FINE	VF	XF	UNC.
$50	$75	$100	$200	$300	$500

1862 Faith of the State Pledged Notes

Notes with various dates of 1862 were also issued with "Faith of the State Pledged." This overprint is in red or blue. Some notes are printed on the back of Mississippi Cotton Company fractional notes or have a green tint. Many notes were also stamped "Re-Issue," which are worth about one-third more.

MS-13. $5— Railroad train at center, plow and rural scene at left, farmer with wheat at right. "Faith of the State Pledged" in red.

GOOD	VG	FINE	VF	XF	UNC.
$20	$35	$50	$75	$100	$175

MS-13A. $5— As above. "Faith of the State Pledged" in blue.

GOOD	VG	FINE	VF	XF	UNC.
$25	$40	$60	$100	$150	$200

MS-14. $10— Railroad train at center, Commerce at left, farmer with wheat at right. "Faith of the State Pledged" in red.

GOOD	VG	FINE	VF	XF	UNC.
$20	$35	$50	$75	$125	$225

MS-14A. $10— As above. "Faith of the State Pledged" in blue.

GOOD	VG	FINE	VF	XF	UNC.
$30	$50	$100	$200	$250	$350

MS-15. $20— Railroad train at center, plow and rural scene at left, two women at right. "Faith of the State Pledged" in red.

GOOD	VG	FINE	VF	XF	UNC.
$25	$40	$60	$90	$150	$225

MS-15A. $20— As above. "Faith of the State Pledged" in blue.

GOOD	VG	FINE	VF	XF	UNC.
$35	$65	$100	$165	$250	$400

MS-16. $50— Railroad train at center, tw owomen at left, commerce at right. "Faith of the State Pledged" in red.

GOOD	VG	FINE	VF	XF	UNC.
$30	$60	$70	$90	$100	$300

MS-17. $50— As above. "Faith of the State Pledged" in blue.

GOOD	VG	FINE	VF	XF	UNC.
$30	$65	$90	$125	$250	$385

MS-18. $100— Same design as MS-12. "Faith of the State Pledged" in red. Rare.

MS-18A. $100— As above. "Faith of the State Pledged" in blue, rare.

Important

Where more than one variety was issued of a note, the prices listed are for the more common kinds, not a rare minor variety. Where no value is indicated, the price is speculative due to such notes being rare in higher grades and seldom offered. Most of the illustrations in this catalog are either larger or smaller than the actual specimens.

Notes with printed date of May 1st, 1864

"By authority of law".
Printed by J. T. Paterson & Co., Augusta, Ga.
Notes are known without printer's name. Prices of both are about the same.

MS-19. 25 cents— Cotton boll at lower left. Plate letters A to P. Value in red. A rare variety also exists with the denomination inverted.

GOOD	VG	FINE	VF	XF	UNC.
$30	$60	$90	$150	$250	$325

MS-20. 50 cents— Slave hoeing at lower left. Plate letters A to P. Value in red.

GOOD	VG	FINE	VF	XF	UNC.
$10	$20	$30	$40	$65	$85

MS-21. $1— Railroad train at center, Ceres at lower left. Plate letters A to M. Value in red.

GOOD	VG	FINE	VF	XF	UNC.
$15	$25	$40	$50	$75	$125

MS-22. $2— Sailing ship at center, sailor at left. Plate letters A to G. Value in red.

GOOD	VG	FINE	VF	XF	UNC.
$15	$25	$40	$50	$60	$75

MS-23. $3— Guard standing at center, Indian at left. Plate letters A to E. Value in red.

GOOD	VG	FINE	VF	XF	UNC.
$25	$40	$60	$80	$110	$150

Certain other notes exist that have blanks for handwritten dates. These were printed by J.T. Paterson & Co., Augusta, Georgia, and indicate the "Faith of the State Pledged." Some notes are hand dated 1865-1867.

MS-24. $20— Eagle and shield. Seated Indian at right. "20" in red. Fancy green back. Plate letters A to H.

GOOD	VG	FINE	VF	XF	UNC.
$100	$200	$250	$300	$400	$550

MS-24A. $20— As above but with green "XX" added to face of note. Rare.

MS-25. $50— Intricate design with Commerce and Ceres seated, Indian at left. Green overprint. Fancy green back. Plate letters A to H.

GOOD	VG	FINE	VF	XF	UNC.
$90	$175	$250	$300	$375	$500

MS-26. $100— Harbor scene. Black with orange overprint. Fancy green back. Plate letters A to H. The harbor scene is of Wilmington, N.C. and appeared on $5 notes of that State printed by Paterson.

GOOD	VG	FINE	VF	XF	UNC.
$500	$600	$800	$1000	$1250	$1650

Reconstruction Period Notes

Printed by American Bank Note Co., New York.
Dated September 1st. 1870

All notes are green and black with green back. Prices are for notes that are usually found canceled with a large hole. Very scarce uncanceled and worth five to six times more.

MS-27. $1— Farmer with horses and plow at center, unidentified man at left, locomotive at right.

GOOD	VG	FINE	VF	XF	UNC.
$20	$30	$45	$70	$100	$125

MS-28. $2— Blacks loading cotton on wagon at center, unidentified man at right.

GOOD	VG	FINE	VF	XF	UNC.
$20	$30	$45	$70	$100	$125

MS-29. $3— Steamship at center, unidentified man at left, eagle at right.

GOOD	VG	FINE	VF	XF	UNC.
$30	$50	$80	$100	$130	$175

MS-30. $5— Govenor Alcorn at center, woman at left, cotton boll at right.

GOOD	VG	FINE	VF	XF	UNC.
$20	$30	$45	$65	$90	$130

About Sizes

The sizes of Confederate States notes may vary slightly, due to differences when the sheets were cut apart, but most are approximately 3 to 3¼ inches by 7 to 7¼ inches in size except Nos. 43-46, which are 2¾ by 61/8 inches. The 50-cent notes (Nos. 57 and 65) are approximately 2¼ by 4¼ inches.

MISSOURI

When Alabama was admitted to the Union as a State in 1819, the result was an equal number of free and slave states, which meant equal representation in the U.S. Senate. That would soon change but the Missouri Compromise of 1820-21 delayed the bitter dispute that was one of the causes of the Civil War. In brief, a decision was finally made that permitted Missouri to enter the Union as a slave State (with restrictions) while Maine in the North entered as a free State and the balance was maintained until repealed in 1854.

Missouri was the most Northern of the Confederate States. It may have been a bulwark protecting the Mississippi River but a huge vote against Lincoln's election in 1860 did not materialize in secession when pro-South Governor Claiborne F. Jackson called for a convention in March, 1861. The best Governor Jackson could do was to refuse Lincoln's call for troops. Not until October 21, after conflict between Southern and Union troops, did a remnant of Jackson's legislature meet at Nesho and approve secession. On November 28, Missouri was admitted to the Confederacy and members of Congress were seated early in December 1861. During 1862 and 1863, when the State was largely in the hands of Union forces, there was limited conflict but that changed in 1864 when Major General Sterling Price fought over 40 engagements in an attempt to gain all of Missouri for the Confederacy. He failed but guerrilla activity continued.

Although Missouri was in Northern hands during most of the war and was accepted as a Union State, it experienced Reconstruction measures that in some instances exceeded those of other Southern states. Until after the election of 1870, the Radicals had insisted on a "test" oath of anyone suspected of being a former Confederate, which severely suppressed the rights of many people. The Constitutional Convention of 1865 had already abolished slavery without compensation and apparently the Radicals were against payment of any other war claims as well. That was to change in 1874 when the Legislature passed an Act whereby the Federal Government would make payment to the State for audited and approved claims. In lieu of these claims, War Claim Certificates were issued but not all were honored due to irregularities of which an opposition political circular of 1876 may offer an explanation: "The State of Missouri has already audited and allowed Confederate war claims amounting to more than $2 million. These claims are based upon the cotton tax, damages to land and property during the war, the emancipation of slaves, and Confederate losses of all kinds."

Confederate Issue of Jan'y 1st, 1862

Engraved by A. Malus, New Orleans.
Issued at Jefferson City, Missouri

These notes sometimes have the printed date overwritten to 1863 or 1864. All are payable three years after date unless otherwise stated.

MO-1. $1— Jefferson Davis at center, gladiator at left, hunter and dog at right. ONE in red. Cream colored paper.

GOOD	VG	FINE	VF	XF	UNC.
$75	$100	$150	$200	$275	$360

MO-1A. $1— As above. Cream colored paper on back of bill of exchange.

GOOD	VG	FINE	VF	XF	UNC.
$75	$100	$150	$200	$275	$350

MO-1B. $1— As above. Blue tinted paper.

GOOD	VG	FINE	VF	XF	UNC.
$75	$100	$150	$200	$275	$375

MO-1C. $1 — As above. Blue tinted paper on back of bill of exchange.

GOOD	VG	FINE	VF	XF	UNC.
$40	$75	$100	$150	$200	$275

MO-2. $2— Farmer with plow and horses at center, girl at left, State arms at right. TWO in green. Cream colored paper.

GOOD	VG	FINE	VF	XF	UNC.
$40	$75	$100	$150	$200	$275

MO-2A. $2— As above. Cream colored paper on back of bill of exchange.

GOOD	VG	FINE	VF	XF	UNC.
$75	$100	$150	$200	$275	$375

MO-2B. $2— As above. Blue tinted paper. Rare.

MO-2C. $2— As above. Blue tinted paper on back of bill of exchange. Rare.

MO-3. $3— Governor Claiborne F. Jackson at center, gladiator at left, hunter and dog at right. THREE in green. Cream colored paper. Rare.

MO-3A. $3— As above. Cream colored paper on back of bill of exchange.

GOOD	VG	FINE	VF	XF	UNC.
$150	$250	$400	$500	$700	$850

MO-3B. $3— As above. Blue tinted paper.

GOOD	VG	FINE	VF	XF	UNC.
$70	$140	$180	$225	$300	$400

MO-3C. $3— As above. Blue tinted paper on back of bill of exchange.

GOOD	VG	FINE	VF	XF	UNC.
$40	$75	$100	$150	$200	$275

About Prices

Genuine Confederate and Southern states currency in exceptionally choice condition may command a higher price than indicated by the valuations. General economic changes or the popularity of certain notes may also affect prices.

The $5 and $10 notes are found with and without imprint of D. Weil, Eng.

MO-4. $5— Commerce seated on bale of cotton at center. Cream colored paper. With or without printer's name.

GOOD	VG	FINE	VF	XF	UNC.
$50	$80	$135	$175	$225	$325

MO-4A. $5— As above. Blue tinted paper. With or without printer's name.

GOOD	VG	FINE	VF	XF	UNC.
$50	$80	$135	$175	$225	$325

MO-5. $10— Ceres with horn of plenty at center, ship in oval at left. Cream colored paper. With or without printer's name.

GOOD	VG	FINE	VF	XF	UNC.
$50	$80	$125	$160	$200	$275

MO-5A. $10— As above. Blue tinted paper. With or without printer's name.

GOOD	VG	FINE	VF	XF	UNC.
$40	$65	$90	$125	$150	$225

MO-6. $20— Woman with trumpet flying at center, Liberty standing at left. Payable three years after date. Cream colored paper.

GOOD	VG	FINE	VF	XF	UNC.
$70	$110	$150	$180	$225	$300

MO-6A. $20— As MO-6 above. Blue tinted paper.

GOOD	VG	FINE	VF	XF	UNC.
$90	$150	$200	$250	$300	$400

Some notes have date changed by hand to 1863.

MO-6B. $20— As above. Payable five years after date. Cream colored paper. Rare.
MO-6C. $20— As MO-6B above. Blue tinted paper.

GOOD	VG	FINE	VF	XF	UNC.
$40	$65	$100	$140	$180	$250

The five-year notes with date changed by hand to 1863 are very rare.

Missouri Defence Bonds (Confederate)
Authorized by Act of November 5, 1861
Printed by Keatinge & Ball, Colombia, S.C.

By this time the Confederates had been pushed out of the capital at Jefferson City and these notes apparently arrived too late for many of them to be signed. Prices are for unsigned notes. When signed, signatures should be authenticated. The notes are finely engraved and printed on unwatermarked paper or paper bearing watermarks of W.T. & Co. or T.C.C. & Co. All are of approximately the same value.

MO-7. $1— Cattle in pasture, State arms at left, maiden at right. ONE in red. Plate letters A, B or C.

GOOD	VG	FINE	VF	XF	UNC.
$20	$40	$65	$80	$125	$175

MO-8. $3— Woman with cape flying, State arms at upper left, maiden at lower right. THREE in red. Plate letter A.

GOOD	VG	FINE	VF	XF	UNC.
$30	$50	$75	$100	$150	$225

MO-9. $4— Mississippi River boat at upper left, State arms below. Red and black. Plate letters A or B.

GOOD	VG	FINE	VF	XF	UNC.
$15	$25	$50	$100	$150	$250

MO-10. $4.50— Ceres seated between Commerce and Navigation at left. State arms at lower right. Red and black. Plate letters A or B.

GOOD	VG	FINE	VF	XF	UNC.
$65	$110	$175	$235	$275	$450

In addition to collectors of Southern states currency, the $4.50 note is in demand by those assembling different denominations of bank notes and script. These notes were printed in the denomination of $4.50 instead of $5.00 to make it unnecessary to pay the 10% interest ordered on all obligations of $5.00 or more that was set by the Act of November 5, 1861. In other words, the interest was "pre-paid," thereby avoiding accounting work on this denomination of that issue, had it entered general circulation, which it did not.

Requisitions for Missouri Defence Bonds

Printed by Keatinge & Ball, Columbia, S.C.

MO-11. $20— Small Mississippi River boat at center, Liberty seated at upper left, State arms at lower right. TWENTY in red, back in green.

GOOD	VG	FINE	VF	XF	UNC.
$30	$50	$75	$125	$200	$300

MO-12. $50— Slaves gathering cotton at upper left, Ceres at lower right. "50" in red, back in green.

GOOD	VG	FINE	VF	XF	UNC.
$40	$80	$125	$175	$250	$375

MO-13. $100— Jefferson Davis at center, woman standing at lower left, State seal at lower right. "100" in red, back in green.

GOOD	VG	FINE	VF	XF	UNC.
$50	$100	$150	$200	$300	$475

Defence Warrants (Union Government)

Printed by A. McLean Lith. St. Louis

MO-14. $10— State seal at left, girl at right. TEN in green. Written dates of 1862. Rare.

MO-15. $10— Similar to preceding but with ornate TEN in green and different arrangement of inscription. Written or stamped dates of 1862. Rare. Printed by R. P. Studley & Co. Lith. St. Louis

MO-16. $5— State seal at left, General Robert Allen (?) at right. General Allen was Chief Quartermaster in Missouri. June 25, 1864. Very rare.

MO-17. $10— State seal at left. General Isaac F. Shepard (?) at right. June 25, 1864. Very rare.

MO-18. $20— State seal At left. General John Polk at right. June 25, 1864. Very rare.

MO-19. $20— State seal at left. Governor Willard P. Hall (1864-65) at right. June 25, 1864. Very rare.

Union Military Bonds

Printed by American Bank Note Co., Philadelphia, PA.

These bonds were printed in the form of bank notes under an Act approved March 9, 1863. The Act of February 20, 1865, covered the re-issue of these bonds with 1865 and 1866 dates. The years of 1863, 1865 or 1866 are printed on the bonds.

MO-20. $1— General Nathaniel Lyon (?) at upper left, Liberty with eagle and globe at right. Ornate green back. Rare.

MO-21. $3— Major General Joseph A. Mower (?) at upper left, head of Liberty in wreath at center. Ornate green back. Very rare.

MO-22. $5— Hunters with slain deer on horseback at upper left. General James Craig (?) at right. Ornate green back. Very rare.

MO-23. $10— Brig. General Francis P. Blair, Jr. at upper left, three women reclining at right. Ornate green back. Rare.

MO-24. $20— Rural scene with Pilot Knob in background at upper left. Hamilton R. Gamble, who was governor of Missouri during 1861-64 at center. Ornate green back. Very rare.

MO-25. $50— No information available. Very rare.

The foregoing notes were in payment for military service and were almost entirely redeemed.

War Claim Certificates Act of May 19, 1874

Printed by the R. P. Studley Co. Lith. St. Louis

Since the Missouri Defence Fund was exhausted, no further payments could be made to veterans or for other claims until arrangement was made with the Federal Government to reimburse the State. Generally, these certificates are for military service but may also be found for other purposes. The dollar amount and other data is written.

MO-26. Handwritten denomination. Military Service. Liberty standing at left, State arms at center. Green. Fancy green back.

GOOD	VG	FINE	VF	XF	UNC.
$60	$90	$120	$150	$200	$275

MO-27. Handwritten denomination. As above but for Civil Service. Brown. Fancy green back.

GOOD	VG	FINE	VF	XF	UNC.
$60	$90	$120	$150	$200	$275

NORTH CAROLINA

The people of North Carolina were not really in favor of secession; in February 1861 they voted by a small majority not to approve a convention for its consideration. That was to change after the attack on Fort Sumter and President Lincoln's call for troops. Not only that, North Carolina was positioned between South Carolina and Virginia, both of which had seceded.

John W. Ellis was governor in 1861, and he favored secession as did a number of Legislators who authorized a convention of delegates on May 13, 1861. The convention assembled on May 20 and issued an Ordinance of Secession the same day by an unanimous vote. At the same time, the governor approved the enrollment of 30,000 men. In all, North Carolina contributed between 125,000 and 130,000 men to the Confederate services, fed and clothed its own soldiers and sustained about one quarter of all Confederate losses. This was a high number in excess of its relative population.

North Carolina led the Southern states in blockade running, and it was largely through supplies received at Wilmington that Confederate forces in the East were enabled to remain in the field as long as they did. Wilmington was the last important port to fall in February 1865. The port is pictured on a $5 note of January 1, 1863 (NC-33).

Zebulon B. Vance, who succeeded Ellis in office, was a determined war governor (1862-1865). His portrait appears on $20 and $50 notes of January 1, 1863. After the distasteful Reconstruction was over, he again became governor in 1877-1879.

The state did not have great success with its paper money, which resulted in a large variety that is estimated to have totaled over $10 million by the end of the war. Even listing the basic types is complicated. Apparently there was such a quantity of it that no further issues were considered appropriate during the Reconstruction.

Act of May 11, 1861

Imprint of N.C. Inst. Deaf & Dumb Print
Printed on back of earlier North Carolina bank notes. No plate letters.

NC-1. $1— Minerva standing at left, watchdog and safe at center. "One Dollar" in red on back. Dated October 1st through October 5th, 1861.

GOOD	VG	FINE	VF	XF	UNC.
$20	$40	$65	$100	$150	$200

Error notes with no "For" before Pub. Treas'r and those printed on paper watermarked T. C. C. & Co. are rare and worth five to six times as much. If printed on backs of North Carolina bonds these notes double in value. No printer's name.

NC-2. $1— Minerva standing at left, small ship at center. Plain paper with red back. Plate letters A, B. Dated October 10th through October 21st, 1861.

GOOD	VG	FINE	VF	XF	UNC.
$5	$10	$20	$25	$40	$70

NC-2A. $1— As above. Watermarked TEN. Dated October 16th through October 21st, 1861.

GOOD	VG	FINE	VF	XF	UNC.
$10	$20	$30	$50	$75	$100

NC-2B. $1— As above. Watermarked FIVE. Dated October 16th through October 21st, 1861.

GOOD	VG	FINE	VF	XF	UNC.
$50	$100	$250	$300	$350	$450

NC-2C. $1— As above. Watermarked T. C. C. and Co. Dated October 16th through October 21st, 1861.

GOOD	VG	FINE	VF	XF	UNC.
$20	$30	$45	$65	$90	$130

Error notes with January misspelled "Jonuary" are rare.

Were treasury officers of North Carolina omniscient? All of the currency dated between 1861 and 1863 is redeemable on January 1 of 1865 or 1866, near the end of the Civil War.

NC-3. $2— Liberty standing at left, dog with safe at center. "Two Dollars" in red on back. Date of October 2d, 1861, has been noted. All dates are rare.

Important

Where more than one variety was issued of a note, the prices listed are for the more common kinds, not a rare minor variety. Where no value is indicated, the price is speculative due to such notes being rare in higher grades and seldom offered. Most of the illustrations in this catalog are either larger or smaller than the actual specimens.

Imprint of F. W. Bornemann, Charleston, S. C.

NC-4. $2— Inscription only. "By Authority of Law." Dated October 1st through October 6th, 1861. "Two Dollars" in red on back. Plate letters A to E.

GOOD	VG	FINE	VF	XF	UNC.
$15	$30	$50	$90	$135	$200

NC-4A. $2— As above. Plain back.

GOOD	VG	FINE	VF	XF	UNC.
$10	$20	$35	$50	$80	$110

NC-4B. $2— As above. Watermarked FIVE.

GOOD	VG	FINE	VF	XF	UNC.
$40	$65	$100	$150	$250	$350

NC-4C. $2— As above. Printed on back of North Carolina bond.

GOOD	VG	FINE	VF	XF	UNC.
$35	$50	$85	$125	$225	$325

Notes with "Two Dollars" inverted on back are rare. Those without "For" before Treasurer are worth six times as much.

Prices of Rarities

Rare notes that are in strong demand tend to rise continuously in price. This is particularly true of the Montgomery issue and certain other notes.

Act of June 28th, 1861

J. Spelman, Public Printer
Dated October 1st, 1861

NC-5. 5 cents— Typeset. With or without plate letters A or B.

GOOD	VG	FINE	VF	XF	UNC.
$5	$10	$20	$30	$45	$55

NC-5A. 5 cents— As above. Watermarked TEN.

GOOD	VG	FINE	VF	XF	UNC.
$40	$60	$90	$135	$195	$260

NC-5B. 5 cents— As above. Watermarked FIVE.

GOOD	VG	FINE	VF	XF	UNC.
$40	$60	$90	$135	$195	$260

NC-5C. 5 cents— As above. Watermarked T. C. C. and Co. Rare.

Notes printed without plate letters on blue paper or on back of North Carolina bonds are scarce.

NC-6. 10 cents— Typeset. With or without plate letters A or B.

GOOD	VG	FINE	VF	XF	UNC.
$10	$15	$25	$35	$50	$75

NC-6A. 10 cents— As above. Watermarked TEN.

GOOD	VG	FINE	VF	XF	UNC.
$40	$60	$90	$135	$185	$250

NC-6B. 10 cents— As above. Watermarked FIVE.

GOOD	VG	FINE	VF	XF	UNC.
$40	$60	$90	$135	$185	$250

NC-6C. 10 cents— As above. Watermarked T. C. C. and Co. Rare.

NC-7. 20 cents— Typeset. With or without plate letters A or B.

GOOD	VG	FINE	VF	XF	UNC.
$20	$40	$65	$90	$120	$175

NC-7A. 20 cents— As above. Watermarked TEN.

GOOD	VG	FINE	VF	XF	UNC.
$50	$75	$100	$150	$200	$300

NC-7B. 20 cents— As above. Watermarked FIVE.

GOOD	VG	FINE	VF	XF	UNC.
$50	$75	$100	$1505	$200	$300

NC-7C. 20 cents— As above. Watermarked T. C. C. and Co. Rare.

NC-8. 25 cents— Typeset. With or without plate letters A or B.

GOOD	VG	FINE	VF	XF	UNC.
$10	$20	$30	$40	$50	$75

NC-8A. 25 cents— As above. Watermarked TEN.

GOOD	VG	FINE	VF	XF	UNC.
$40	$60	$90	$135	$185	$250

NC-8B. 25 cents— As above. Watermarked FIVE.

GOOD	VG	FINE	VF	XF	UNC.
$40	$60	$90	$135	$185	$250

NC-8C. 25 cents— As above. Watermarked T. C. C. and Co. Rare.

Notes printed on blue paper are rare.

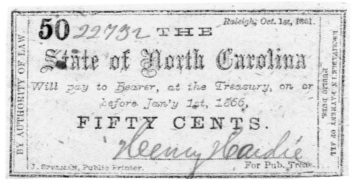

NC-9.   50 cents— Typeset. With or without plate letters A or B.

GOOD	VG	FINE	VF	XF	UNC.
$10	$20	$30	$40	$50	$75

NC-9A.   50 cents— As above. Watermarked TEN.

GOOD	VG	FINE	VF	XF	UNC.
$40	$60	$60	$135	$185	$250

NC-9B.   50 cents— As above. Watermarked FIVE.

GOOD	VG	FINE	VF	XF	UNC.
$40	$60	$90	$135	$185	$250

NC-9C.   50 cents— As above. Watermarked T. C. C. and Co. Rare.

About Sizes

The sizes of Confederate States notes may vary slightly, due to differences when the sheets were cut apart, but most are approximately 3 to 3¼ inches by 7 to 7¼ inches in size except Nos. 43-46, which are 2¾ by 61/8 inches. The 50-cent notes (Nos. 57 and 65) are approximately 2¼ by 4¼ inches.

Authorized by Act of December 1st, 1861

Printed by J. T. Paterson & Co., Augusta, Ga.
There are many printing varieties. Only the basic types are listed.

NC-10.   10 cents— Beehive. September 1st, 1862. Plate letters A to U.

GOOD	VG	FINE	VF	XF	UNC.
$10	$15	$25	$35	$50	$60

NC-11.   10 cents— Slave plowing. September 1st, 1862. Plate letters A to U.

GOOD	VG	FINE	VF	XF	UNC.
$20	$30	$45	$60	$85	$110

NC-12. 25 cents— Ceres at left. September 1st, 1862. Plate letters A to O or without plate letters.

GOOD	VG	FINE	VF	XF	UNC.
$40	$60	$90	$135	$200	$275

NC-12A. 25 cents— As above. Printed on back of bonds.

GOOD	VG	FINE	VF	XF	UNC.
$25	$40	$60	$75	$95	$120

NC- 12B. 25 cents— As above. Printed on back of North Carolina notes.

GOOD	VG	FINE	VF	XF	UNC.
$50	$75	$100	$130	$160	$200

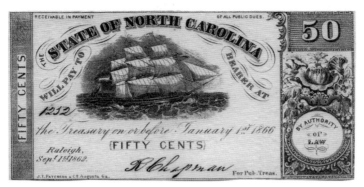

NC-13. 50 cents— Sailing ship. September 1st, 1862. Plate letters A to O or without plate letters.

GOOD	VG	FINE	VF	XF	UNC.
$10	$15	$25	$30	$40	$50

NC-13A. 50 cents— As above. Printed on back of bonds.

GOOD	VG	FINE	VF	XF	UNC.
$20	$100	$200	$400	$450	—

NC-14. $1— Typeset. Inscription only. September 1st, 1862. Plate letters A to K.

GOOD	VG	FINE	VF	XF	UNC.
$15	$25	$35	$50	$70	$90

NC-14A. $1—As above. Watermarked FIVE. Rare

NC-14B. $1 — As above. Red fiber paper. Very Rare

NC-15. $5— Steamship at center, Ceres at left. With or without "Fundable" inscription in red. Written dates of July 1st, 1862, or January 1st, 1863. Plate letters A to D.

GOOD	VG	FINE	VF	XF	UNC.
$20	$30	$40	$50	$75	$125

NC-16. $20— Railroad Train at center as on Confederate $100 notes of 1862. Written dates of May 1st, 1862, or January 1, 1863. "Fundable" inscription overprinted in red. Plate letters A to D. Usually trimmed to eliminate "Fundable" inscription, worth double or more with inscription intact.

GOOD	VG	FINE	VF	XF	UNC.
$20	$30	$40	$50	$75	$125

Printed by J. Manouvrier, New Orleans
With or without imprint

NC-17. $3— Entirely typeset. Dated May 1, June 8, and August 6, 1862. Rare.
NC-18. $4— Typeset. Dated August 1, 1862. Rare.

The authenticity of Nos. 17 and 18 has been questioned.

NC-19. $5— Ceres seated at center. Train vertically at right. Written date of February 15th, 1862. With or without "Fundable" overprint in red. Plate letters A to D.

GOOD	VG	FINE	VF	XF	UNC.
$50	$75	$100	$175	$300	$425

NC-19A. $5— As above. Printed on back of bill of exchange. Rare

NC-20. $5— Liberty standing, Ceres seated at center. Train vertically at right. Written date March 1st, 1862. With or without "Fundable" overprint in red. Plate letters A to D.

GOOD	VG	FINE	VF	XF	UNC.
$50	$75	$100	$175	$300	$425

NC-21. $10— Train. "Ten Dollars" in red on back, Written dates of January, February, or March 1862. With or without "Fundable" overprint. Plate letters A to D.

GOOD	VG	FINE	VF	XF	UNC.
$50	$75	$100	$150	$230	$340

NC-21A. $10— As above. Printed on back of North Carolina bonds.

GOOD	VG	FINE	VF	XF	UNC.
$75	$150	$250	$400	$500	$675

NC-21B. $10— As above. Printed on back of bill of exchange.

GOOD	VG	FINE	VF	XF	UNC.
$65	$100	$175	$275	$400	$550

NC-21C. $10— As above. Paper watermarked TEN.

GOOD	VG	FINE	VF	XF	UNC.
$65	$100	$175	$275	$400	$550

NC-22. $20— Woman with trumpet flying to left. Written dates of February or March 1862. With or without "Fundable" overprint. Plate letters A to D.

GOOD	VG	FINE	VF	XF	UNC.
$40	$65	$90	$135	$180	$250

NC-22A. $20— As above. Printed on back of North Carolina bonds.

GOOD	VG	FINE	VF	XF	UNC.
$100	$150	$250	$350	$500	$675

NC-22B. $20— As above. Printed on back of bill of exchange.

GOOD	VG	FINE	VF	XF	UNC.
$50	$75	$100	$150	$225	$325

NC-23. $50— Liberty standing, Ceres seated. "Fifty Dollars" in red on back. Written dates of 1861 or 1862. With "Fundable" overprint in red. Plate letters A to D. Printed on back of North Carolina bond.

GOOD	VG	FINE	VF	XF	UNC.
$500	$1000	$2000	—	—	—

NC-23A. $50— As above. Without "Fundable" overprint.

GOOD	VG	FINE	VF	XF	UNC.
$300	$600	$1000	$1500	$2000	$3000

About Prices

Genuine Confederate and Southern states currency in exceptionally choice condition may command a higher price than indicated by the valuations. General economic changes or the popularity of certain notes may also affect prices.

NC-24. $100— Agricultural tools at center, Commerce at lower right. Written dates of 1861 or 1862. Plate letters A to D. Printed on back of North Carolina bonds. With "Fundable" inscription.

GOOD	VG	FINE	VF	XF	UNC.
$300	$600	$1000	$1500	$2000	$3000

NC-24A. $100— As above. Without "Fundable" inscription. Very rare.

Authorized by Act of December 20th, 1862

Printed by J. T. Paterson & Co., Augusta, Ga.
Dated January 1, 1863

NC-25. 5 cents— Liberty and Peace within circle. Plate letters A to U.

GOOD	VG	FINE	VF	XF	UNC.
$5	$10	$15	$20	$35	$45

NC-26.   10 cents— Beehive. Plate letters A to U.

GOOD	VG	FINE	VF	XF	UNC.
$5	$10	$15	$20	$35	$45

NC-27.   25 cents— Ceres standing at left. Plate letters A to O.

GOOD	VG	FINE	VF	XF	UNC.
$4	$7	$9	$12	$15	$20

NC-27A.   25 cents— As above. 25 cents or 25 Cts. in red on back.

GOOD	VG	FINE	VF	XF	UNC.
$10	$15	$20	$30	$45	$55

NC-27B. 25 cents— As above. Printed on back of state or bank notes.

GOOD	VG	FINE	VF	XF	UNC.
$20	$30	$40	$65	$90	$110

NC-27C. 25 cents— As above. Printed on paper watermarked WHATMAN.

GOOD	VG	FINE	VF	XF	UNC.
$50	$75	$100	$140	$185	$235

NC-28. 50 cents— Sailing ship. Plate letters A to O. Position of serial numbers varies. Similar to NC-13.

GOOD	VG	FINE	VF	XF	UNC.
$10	$30	$40	$50	$75	$80

NC-29. 75 cents— Industry beside beehive. Plate letters A to O.

GOOD	VG	FINE	VF	XF	UNC.
$20	$30	$40	$50	$65	$85

NC-30. $1— Commerce and industry holding figure "I." Plate letters A to M and AB to MB.

GOOD	VG	FINE	VF	XF	UNC.
$10	$15	$20	$25	$35	$45

NC-31. $2— State capitol at Raleigh. Plate letters A to M.

GOOD	VG	FINE	VF	XF	UNC.
$15	$20	$28	$35	$50	$60

NC-32. $3— Liberty standing, Ceres seated. Center vignette same as NC20, NC23. THREE at each side. Plate letters A to H.

GOOD	VG	FINE	VF	XF	UNC.
$20	$30	$40	$50	$65	$85

NC-32A. $3— As above. Paper watermarked TEN.

GOOD	VG	FINE	VF	XF	UNC.
$50	$75	$125	$175	$250	$325

NC-32B. $3— As above. Paper watermarked FIVE.

GOOD	VG	FINE	VF	XF	UNC.
$50	$75	$125	$175	$250	$325

NC-32C. $3— As above. Paper watermarked T. C. C. and Co.

GOOD	VG	FINE	VF	XF	UNC.
$75	$135	$200	$300	$400	$525

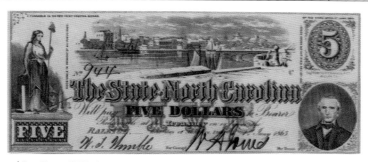

NC-33. $5— Port of Wilmington, N. C. Liberty at left, portrait of D. W. Courts at right. He was State Treasurer, 1852-1863. "Five" in red. (Notes without "Five" are rare.) Plate letters A to H.

GOOD	VG	FINE	VF	XF	UNC.
$20	$40	$60	$100	$150	$175

NC-34. $10— State capitol at center, portrait of D. W. Courts at right. "X" and "Ten" in red. (Notes without red overprints are rare.) Plate letters A to F.

GOOD	VG	FINE	VF	XF	UNC.
$20	$40	$60	$100	$145	$175

NC-35. $20— Governor Zebulon B. Vance (1862-65) at center. Beehive at lower right. Red overprint. Plate letters A to L. Plain paper.

GOOD	VG	FINE	VF	XF	UNC.
$40	$75	$110	$150	$200	$300

NC-35A. $20— As above. Watermarked J. Whatman, 1861.

GOOD	VG	FINE	VF	XF	UNC.
$40	$65	$100	$135	$185	$250

NC-35B. $20— As above. Watermarked 1862. Very scarce.

GOOD	VG	FINE	VF	XF	UNC.
$100	$150	$200	$275	$350	$450

NC-36. $50— Governor Zebulon B. Vance (1862-1865) at center. Justice standing at left. Red overprint. Plate letters A to L. Plain paper. Rare.

GOOD	VG	FINE	VF	XF	UNC.
$100	$200	$300	$400	$500	$700

NC-36A. $50— As above. Watermarked J. Whatman, 1861.

GOOD	VG	FINE	VF	XF	UNC.
$50	$75	$135	$150	$175	$200

NC-36B. $50— As above. Watermarked 1862. Very scarce.

Authorized by Act of December 12th, 1863

Printed by J. T. Paterson & Co., Augusta, Ga.
Dated Jan'y 1st, 1864

NC-37. 25 cents— Ceres standing at left. Same type as NC-27 except printed date. 25 Cts overprinted in blue. Plate letters A to P.

NC-37A. 25 cents— As above. 25 Cts overprinted in green.

GOOD	VG	FINE	VF	XF	UNC.
—	—	$1500	$2500	—	—

NC-38. 50 cents— Sailing ship. Same type as NC-28 except printed date. 50 Cts overprinted in red. Plate letters A to P.

GOOD	VG	FINE	VF	XF	UNC.
—	—	$1500	$2500	—	—

SOUTH CAROLINA

South Carolina was not only the first Southern state to secede on December 20, 1860, nearly 30 years earlier the state had passed a Nullification Act to force repeal of high Federal tariffs that it considered an infringement upon States' Rights. The threat of secession at that time was alleviated by compromise, but no compromise was forthcoming in 1860 and Governor Francis W. Pickens (1860-62) immediately demanded all Federal property within the state. That included Fort Sumter, which was taken by force (April 12-14, 1861), setting off the Civil War. It was exactly four years later on April 14, 1865, that the U. S. flag was again flown over the fort.

Obviously, April 14th was selected as a commemorative date since Charleston, where Fort Sumter was located, had been evacuated by the Confederates on February 18 after the destruction of the state capital at Columbia a day earlier. Columbia was the objective of General William T. Sherman and his 60,000 troops who had previously cut a swath of devastation over 50 miles in width during the famous march through Georgia. General Sherman was then determined to punish South Carolina for having set off the Civil War by seceding in 1860. The reason that Columbia was the primary objective in South Carolina is explained by Major George W. Nichols who was Sherman's aide-de-camp and wrote about the march near the end of the war. He stated that Columbia contained the "largest printing establishment in the Rebel States," and that "manufactures of powder, arms, cloths and other materials are there," which made it, "a richer and more important capture than any other city in the South. "While the city could have been the Southern states capital, in the end its vulnerability would have been no less.

Having been the first state to secede, one might expect that after being joined by other states in the South, that the Confederate States would establish its capital in South Carolina. However, for political reasons, which included the selection of a President, South Carolina's leaders recommended that each state send delegates to a convention in Montgomery, Ala., in February 1861. Thus, Montgomery not only became the provisional capital of the Confederacy, but also the place where the Confederate Constitution was adopted.

Unlike other Southern states that issued their own currency to finance Civil War needs, South Carolina used a more conventional and conservative approach. It relied on taxes and bonds of which the Bank of the State of South Carolina was the agent.

The bank, in turn, issued Civil War currency, primarily in fractional denominations, most of which depict a palmetto tree. While these notes indicate that they are issued by the Bank of the State of South Carolina, the state's name is much larger than any other inscription, except the denomination. Although this gave the impression that they were issued by the state, it wasn't until after the war, during the Reconstruction, that state notes were issued by a wasteful government.

Reconstruction Period

Acts of December 1865; March 2, 1872; and November 19, 1873

Printed by American Bank No Co., New York

SC-1. $1— Oxen pulling cart, two children in oval, maiden at right. Green and black. Ornate green back. January _, 1866. Series A, B. Very rare.

SC-1A. $1 — As above. Revenue Bond Scrip. March 2nd, 1872.

GOOD	VG	FINE	VF	XF	UNC.
(Usually collected in Unc.)			$75	$100	$150

SC-1B. $1— As above. Certificate of Indebtedness. December 1st, 1873. Very rare.

SC-2. $2— Harbor scene at center, girls gathering grain at left, woman wearing wreath at right. Green and black. Ornate green back. January _, 1866. Series A, B. Very rare.

SC-2A. $2— As above. Revenue Bond Scrip. March 2nd, 1872.

GOOD	VG	FINE	VF	XF	UNC.
(Usually collected in Unc.)			$40	$50	$75

SC-2B. $2— As above. Certificate of Indebtedness. December 1st, 1873. Very rare.

SC-3. $5— General Francis Marion's "Sweet Potato Dinner" at center. General Thomas Sumter at left, General William Moultrie at right. Green and black. Ornate green back. January _, 1866. Series A, B. Very rare.

SC-3A. $5— As above. Revenue Bond Scrip. March 2nd, 1872.

GOOD	VG	FINE	VF	XF	UNC.
(Usually collected in Unc.)			$50	$75	$100

SC-3B. $5— As above. Certificate of Indebtedness. December 1st, 1873. Very rare.

SC-4. $10— Revolutionary War rescue scene. General Daniel Morgan at left. Young woman at right. Green and black. Ornate green back. Series A, B. Very rare.

SC-4A. $10— As above. Revenue Bond Scrip. March 2nd, 1872.

GOOD	VG	FINE	VF	XF	UNC.
(Usually collected in Unc.)			$50	$75	—

SC-4B. $10— As above. Certificate of Indebtedness. December 1st, 1873. Very rare.

SC-5. $20— Liberty, angel and soldier with state arms. Revenue Bond Scrip. Green and black. Ornate green back. Series A, B.

GOOD	VG	FINE	VF	XF	UNC.
(Usually collected in Unc.)			$65	$85	$100

SC-5A. $20— As above. Certificate of Indebtedness. December 1st, 1873. Very rare.

SC-6. $50— George Washington at center, horses pulling cart at left, slaves in cotton field at right. Revenue Bond Scrip. Green and black. Ornate green back. Series A, B.

GOOD	VG	FINE	VF	XF	UNC.
(Usually collected in Unc.)			$50	$75	—

SC-6A. $50— As above. Certificate of Indebtedness. December 1st, 1873. Very rare.

About Sizes

The sizes of Confederate States notes may vary slightly, due to differences when the sheets were cut apart, but most are approximately 3 to 3¼ inches by 7 to 7¼ inches in size except Nos. 43-46, which are 2¾ by 61/8 inches. The 50-cent notes (Nos. 57 and 65) are approximately 2¼ by 4¼ inches.

Act of March 2, 1872
No printer's name

SC-7. $5— Typeset with train in vertical oval at left end. Denominations in green. Revenue Bond Scrip.

GOOD	VG	FINE	VF	XF	UNC.
$20	$30	$35	$40	$65	$75

SC-8. $10— As above except denomination TEN and "10" in green. Revenue Bond Scrip.

GOOD	VG	FINE	VF	XF	UNC.
$15	$20	$25	$30	$50	$70

Act of March 1872
No printer's name

SC-9. $100— Palmetto tree at center, small dog and safe at lower right.

GOOD	VG	FINE	VF	XF	UNC.
$50	$100	$150	$200	$275	$425

SC-10. $1000— As above. Rare.

SC-11. $5000— As above. Very rare.

TENNESSEE

Unlike most Southern states, Tennessee held popular referendums to decide whether to secede. The first one held on February 9, 1861, failed, but after the attack on Fort Sumter, Governor Isham G. Harris, who favored secession, campaigned throughout the state for a second referendum. On June 8, 1861, secession was approved by a two-thirds majority. The vote against secession came primarily from East Tennessee, which was strongly pro-Union. If any state can be said to be brother against brother, it was Tennessee. The state supplied 165,000 soldiers of which 50,000 fought for the Union.

Tennessee authorized currency during 1861-1863, but since large portions of the state were occupied almost from the beginning by Union forces, it is not known if any genuine notes were issued. The state relied primarily on local scrip, notes of the various banks and Federal "Greenbacks." Confederate currency was also used, depending on which portions of the heavily fought-over state were in Southern hands. A considerable number of the bank issues were also redeemable in Confederate money.

While Tennessee continued to suffer the pains of war after it was over, the state was not subjected to the same Reconstruction Acts that were employed in the other states that had been a part of the Confederacy. Consequently, Tennessee was restored to the Union early, on July 24, 1866. However, animosity continued between former Confederates and those that had supported the Union. One result was the formation of the Ku Klux Klan in 1865, which endeavored to maintain white supremacy by force.

The fact that Andrew Johnson had been Military Governor of Union-held areas of Tennessee prior to succeeding Lincoln as President in April, 1865, and the quick adoption of the 13th and 14th Amendments to the U. S. Constitution undoubtedly contributed toward saving the state from a Reconstruction government. Somehow, the 15th Amendment was overlooked and not adopted until 1997.

However, the state was not saved from the governorship of William A. Brownlow (1865-1869) who instituted his own version of the Reconstruction, nor the issue of bonds during those years. Since the sale of bonds was insufficient to meet all of the needs of an impoverished state, notes of lower denominations were also issued in 1875. Another issue, dated 1883, is also related to Civil War debts since it was intended to be used to redeem the notes of the Bank of Tennessee that had been left in financial straits due to having been the state's banker during the Civil War. The bank was liquidated on February 16, 1866.

Post-war Issues

Dated May 1st, 1875
Printed by American Bank Note Co., N. Y.
Prices are for punch canceled notes

TN-1. $1— Wagonload of cotton at center, children at left, seated woman at right. Green and black. Fancy green back.

GOOD	VG	FINE	VF	XF	UNC.
$100	$200	$300	$400	$550	$1000

TN-2. $2— Chickens at left, woman at right. Green and black. Fancy green back.

GOOD	VG	FINE	VF	XF	UNC.
$100	$200	$300	$40	$550	$1000

About Prices

Genuine Confederate and Southern states currency in exceptionally choice condition may command a higher price than indicated by the valuations. General economic changes or the popularity of certain notes may also affect prices.

TN-3. $5— Agricultural implements at center, man picking cotton at upper left, James Polk, former Governor and U.S. President, at lower right. Green and black.

GOOD	VG	FINE	VF	XF	UNC.
$75	$200	$300	$400	$550	$1000

TN-4. $10— Andrew Jackson at center, boy gathering corn at left, dog with safe at right. Green and black. Green back.

GOOD	VG	FINE	VF	XF	UNC.
$75	$200	$300	$400	$550	$1000

TN-5. $20— Man picking cotton at left, Ceres at right. Green and black.

GOOD	VG	FINE	VF	XF	UNC.
$150	$300	$375	$500	$800	$1250

TN-6. $50— Boy with plow and horses at center, girl at left, woman at right. Green and black.

GOOD	VG	FINE	VF	XF	UNC.
$100	$200	$300	$500	$750	$1100

Printed by Louisville Lithographic Co.

Dated July 1, 1883, and redeemable over a five-year period. These notes indicate that they are for the redemption of notes of the Bank of Tennessee and may be used for taxes or other debts to the state.

TN-7. $1— Governor William B. Bates at left. Denomination in green. Vignette of state capitol on back. Series A to E. Rare.

TN-8. $5— As above. Series A to E. Rare.

TN-9. $20— As above. Series A to E. Rare.

Additional notes were needed to supplement the issue of 1883. The following are dated October, 1, 1885, and redeemable over a five-year period.

TN-10. $1— State arms at left. Denomination in green. Vignette of state capitol on back. Series F to J. Very rare.

TN-11. $5— As above. Series F to J. Very rare.

TN-12. $20— As above. Series F to J. Very rare.

People who resided in Northern-held portions of the South and who considered themselves having been loyal to the Union sought compensation for their losses, of which this claim in Tennessee is an example.

TEXAS

Sam Houston, who became President of Texas in 1836 after its independence from Mexico, was governor of the state when the Civil War began. He opposed a Secession Convention that passed an Ordinance of Secession on February 1, 1861, by a vote of 168 to 8. The convention's action was legitimized by submitting the ordinance to the people who ratified it on February 23 by vote of 46,129 to 14,697. Shortly afterward, on March 2, 1861, Texas was declared a part of the Confederacy. Houston declined to take an oath of allegiance to the new government and the office was assumed by Lt. Governor Edward Clark.

Most of the military action in Texas was limited to its borders and coastal areas, but Union forces were unable to prevent supplies to the Confederates entering the state from Mexico. Supplies such as cloth and similar needs came from home industries, while a wide variety of other war materials, ranging from kettles to wagons, were produced at quartermaster shops established by the Confederate government. Control of the Mississippi River by the Union in 1863 curtailed delivery of supplies to the East but not completely since the Federal troops could not guard every foot of this great waterway.

Texas supplied between 50,000 and 60,000 troops, of which a quarter fought in the East. These included Hood's Texas Brigade and Terry's Texas Rangers, who fought throughout the war and who were considered among the hardest fighting units on either side, but their bravery and daring often resulted in heavy losses.

The finances of Texas during the Civil War differed somewhat from other states. Specie could be obtained from Mexico in payment for cotton but it was never enough. For that reason, the state was forced to rely heavily on Confederate paper money and its own currency, known as Treasury Warrants, which are in two forms, Military Service and Civil Service. In addition, there were many county and local issues such as were prevalent in other states, especially for smaller denominations that were unavailable from the Confederacy.

Texas was admitted to the Union on March 30, 1870, after experiencing Reconstruction similar to that of other Southern states. No postwar Reconstruction currency was issued.

Civil War Issues

The Civil War notes of Texas are a challenge to complete should one wish to assemble every denomination and date of the Acts authorizing their issue. A list of the many acts is given below for both Military and Civil Service notes, but remember that the dates of these acts are handwritten on the notes, not printed. Therefore, even if all dates exist for a denomination, the type remains the same. The date of the act should not be confused with the issue date, which is also given. There are also printing varieties such as a single or double scroll on a letter, with or without "Q" after the appropriation number. Only the major types and varieties are listed. Occasionally, notes will be found on which "Military" is written over "Civil." "While this increases value slightly, notes that have "Civil" written over "Military" are much scarcer and valued higher.

Military Service	Civil Service
Feb. 3, 1860	Feb. 11, 1860
Feb. 8, 1861	April 8, 1861
April 5, 1861	Jan. 8, 1862
April 8, 1861	Jan. 13, 1862
Jan. 4, 1862	March 2, 1863
Jan. 12, 1862	March 3, 1863
Jan. 13, 1862	March 5, 1863
Jan. 14, 1862	Dec. 15, 1863
March 5, 1863	Dec. 16, 1863
March 6, 1863	May 28, 1864
April 11, 1863	Nov. 15, 1864
Dec. 16, 1863	

TX-1. $1— Milkmaid at left. Orange lace overprint. Military Service.

GOOD	VG	FINE	VF	XF	UNC.
$40	$50	$60	$75	$100	$140

TX-2. $1— As above. Civil Service.

GOOD	VG	FINE	VF	XF	UNC.
$30	$50	$70	$85	$100	$120

TX-3. $1— Typeset. Green and black. Military Service.

GOOD	VG	FINE	VF	XF	UNC.
$40	$60	$80	$100	$120	$140

TX-4. $1— As above. Civil Service.

GOOD	VG	FINE	VF	XF	UNC.
$40	$60	$80	$100	$120	$140

TX-5. $1— Typeset, less intricate design. Military Service.

GOOD	VG	FINE	VF	XF	UNC.
$50	$75	$100	$125	$160	$200

TX-6. $1— As above. Civil Service.

GOOD	VG	FINE	VF	XF	UNC.
$50	$75	$100	$125	$160	$200

TX-7. $2.50— Typeset. Blue network on back. Military Service.

GOOD	VG	FINE	VF	XF	UNC.
$20	$40	$60	$90	$120	$175

TX-7A. $2.50— As above. Blank space for signature within network. Military Service.

GOOD	VG	FINE	VF	XF	UNC.
$35	$50	$80	$125	$175	$250

TX-8. $2.50— As above. Red network on back. Civil Service.

GOOD	VG	FINE	VF	XF	UNC.
$35	$50	$80	$125	$175	$250

TX-9. $3— THREE DOLLARS on ribbon. Green and black. Military Service.

GOOD	VG	FINE	VF	XF	UNC.
$20	$40	$60	$90	$120	$175

TX-10. $3— As above. Civil Service.

GOOD	VG	FINE	VF	XF	UNC.
$30	$50	$70	$100	$150	$200

TX-11. $5— Washington standing at left. Black with green lace overprint. Bluish gray paper. Military Service.

GOOD	VG	FINE	VF	XF	UNC.
$20	$40	$60	$90	$125	$175

TX-11A. $5— As above. White paper. Military Service.

GOOD	VG	FINE	VF	XF	UNC.
$30	$50	$70	$100	$150	$200

Prices of Rarities

Rare notes that are in strong demand tend to rise continuously in price. This is particularly true of the Montgomery issue and certain other notes.

TX-12. $5— As above. Black with green lace overprint. Civil Service

GOOD	VG	FINE	VF	XF	UNC.
$30	$50	$70	$100	$150	$200

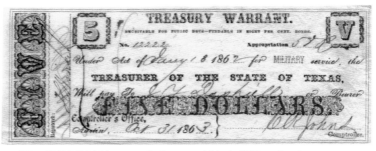

TX-13. $5— FIVE DOLLARS on scroll. Green and black. Military Service.

GOOD	VG	FINE	VF	XF	UNC.
$30	$50	$70	$100	$150	$200

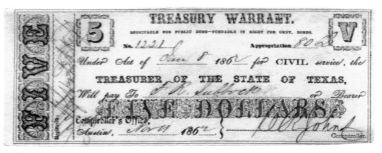

TX-14. $5— As above. Civil Service.

GOOD	VG	FINE	VF	XF	UNC.
$30	$50	$70	$100	$150	$200

TX-15. $5— Typeset, less intricate design. Military Service.

GOOD	VG	FINE	VF	XF	UNC.
$40	$60	$75	$100	$140	$175

TX-16. $5— As above. Civil Service

GOOD	VG	FINE	VF	XF	UNC.
$50	$75	$100	$150	$200	$250

TX-17. $10— Sailing ship at left. Black with red lace overprint. Military Service.

GOOD	VG	FINE	VF	XF	UNC.
$30	$50	$70	$100	$150	$200

TX-18. $10— As above. Civil Service.

GOOD	VG	FINE	VF	XF	UNC.
$50	$75	$100	$150	$210	$275

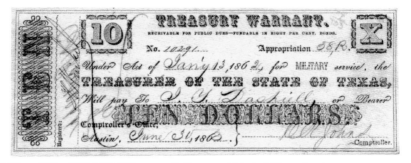

TX-19. $10— TEN DOLLARS on scroll. Green and black. Military Service.

GOOD	VG	FINE	VF	XF	UNC.
$30	$50	$70	$100	$150	$200

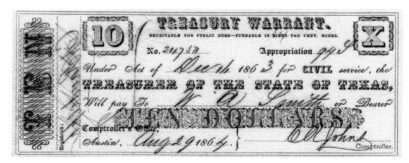

TX-20. $10— As above. Civil Service.

GOOD	VG	FINE	VF	XF	UNC.
$30	$50	$70	$100	$150	$200

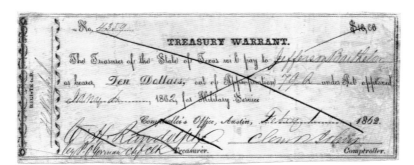

TX-21. $10— Typeset, less intricate design. Military Service.

GOOD	VG	FINE	VF	XF	UNC.
$50	$80	$110	$165	$225	$300

TX-22. $10— As above. Civil Service.

GOOD	VG	FINE	VF	XF	UNC.
$40	$60	$80	$125	$175	$250

TX-23. $20— Ceres standing on pedestal at left. Steamboat in oval at upper right. Black with red lace overprint. Military Service.

GOOD	VG	FINE	VF	XF	UNC.
$35	$40	$60	$100	$250	$325

TX-24. $20— As above. Civil Service.

GOOD	VG	FINE	VF	XF	UNC.
$45	$60	$80	$150	$310	$400

TX-25. $20— TWENTY DOLLARS on ribbon. Green and black. Military Service.

GOOD	VG	FINE	VF	XF	UNC.
$60	$85	$125	$175	$250	$325

TX-26. $20— As above. Civil Service.

GOOD	VG	FINE	VF	XF	UNC.
$60	$85	$125	$175	$250	$325

TX-26A. $20— As above with blue-green back. Civil Service.

GOOD	VG	FINE	VF	XF	UNC.
$80	$125	$175	$235	$300	$400

TX-27. $20— Typeset, less intricate design. Military Service.

GOOD	VG	FINE	VF	XF	UNC.
$60	$80	$115	$175	$250	$325

TX-28. $20— As above. Civil Service.

GOOD	VG	FINE	VF	XF	UNC.
$60	$80	$115	$175	$250	$325

TX-29. $50— Train in vertical oval at left, ships passing lighthouse at upper right. Denomination in green. Yellow network on note. Military Service.

GOOD	VG	FINE	VF	XF	UNC.
$75	$150	$225	$300	$400	$500

TX-30. $50— As above. Civil Service

GOOD	VG	FINE	VF	XF	UNC.
$75	$150	$225	$300	$400	$500

TX-31. $50— Typeset with fancy green back. Military Service.

GOOD	VG	FINE	VF	XF	UNC.
$50	$75	$100	$150	$200	$275

TX-32. $50— As above. Civil Service.

GOOD	VG	FINE	VF	XF	UNC.
$50	$75	$100	$150	$200	$275

TX-33. $50— Typeset, less intricate design. Military Service.

GOOD	VG	FINE	VF	XF	UNC.
$500	$800	$1000	—	—	—

TX-34. $50— As above. Civil Service.

GOOD	VG	FINE	VF	XF	UNC.
$500	$800	$1000	—	—	—

About Prices

Genuine Confederate and Southern states currency in exceptionally choice condition may command a higher price than indicated by the valuations. General economic changes or the popularity of certain notes may also affect prices.

TX-35. $100— Ships passing lighthouse. Denomination in dark red. Red network on face of note. Military Service.

GOOD	VG	FINE	VF	XF	UNC.
$100	$175	$250	$350	$525	$675

TX-36. $100— As Above. Civil Service.

GOOD	VG	FINE	VF	XF	UNC.
$100	$175	$250	$350	$525	$675

TX-37. $100— Typeset. Fancy green back. Military Service.

GOOD	VG	FINE	VF	XF	UNC.
$50	$75	$100	$150	$225	$300

TX-38. $100— As above. Civil Service.

GOOD	VG	FINE	VF	XF	UNC.
$50	$75	$100	$150	$200	$275

TX-39. $100— Typeset, less intricate design. Military Service. Rare.

TX-40. $100— As above. Civil Service. Rare.

TX-41. Written denominations. Liberty standing at left, beehive at upper right. Black with blue network. Military Service.

GOOD	VG	FINE	VF	XF	UNC.
$40	$60	$85	$125	$175	$225

TX-42. As above. Civil Service.

GOOD	VG	FINE	VF	XF	UNC.
$40	$60	$85	$125	$175	$225

TX-43. Written denominations. Ceres seated at center, Indian maiden standing at left. Green and black. Military Service.

GOOD	VG	FINE	VF	XF	UNC.
$40	$60	$90	$135	$200	$250

TX-44.   As above. Civl Service.

GOOD	VG	FINE	VF	XF	UNC.
$60	$85	$125	$175	$235	$300

TX-45.   Written denominations. Typeset, Military Service.

GOOD	VG	FINE	VF	XF	UNC.
$75	$100	$150	$200	$275	$400

TX-46.   As above. Civil Service.

GOOD	VG	FINE	VF	XF	UNC.
$75	$100	$150	$200	$275	$400

Texas also had warrants with 18__ printed, which have written amounts but these resemble checks more than currency.

Since the warrants could be used to pay taxes and other debts due to the State, which frequently were not in even dollar amounts, the excess was refunded by Treasury Warrants with written denominations. Thus, if the amount of tax was $18.74 and a warrant of $20 was tendered in payment, the payer received in return a Treasury Warrant with a written amount of $1.26 that represented the excess. While this may seem unusual, it was a convenient way to get around the shortage of coins. Warrants with written denominations were also used by the state to pay for goods or services that were priced in odd amounts. Think what Texas could have done if credit cards had been invented.

VIRGINIA

If one were asked to name three of the most important States of the Confederacy, one of them would surely be Virginia. Not only was Virginia the state where the Confederate capital was located, it was the home state of Generals Robert E. Lee, Stonewall Jackson and J.E.B. Stuart. In addition, Richmond was the location of the Tredegar Iron Works, a major supplier of military equipment. Even Confederate currency was printed in Richmond at first.

While circumstances made Virginia one of the most determined of the Confederate States, secession did not come easily. Seven Southern states had already seceded when Virginia called for a conference at Washington on February 4, 1861, to see if a compromise could be worked out. In all, 21 states, both Northern and Southern, were to send delegates but on the 27th, they disbanded without solving the problem peacefully. Instead, there would be war.

In the meantime, a state convention assembled at Richmond on February 13, 1861, to consider secession, but it was making no more progress than the convention at Washington. As late as April 4, the delegates were still voting against secession despite strong pressure and threats from those in favor. Finally, some of those against secession gave way; on April 17, Virginia voted to secede by a margin of 85 to 55. Even then, the decision was reserved by putting the ordinance to popular vote but that mattered little due to the strong emphasis that those against secession should not vote. While that failed to discourage everyone, the final vote for secession was heavily in favor.

After Virginia joined the Confederacy, it meant that communications were shortened by having Confederate forces nearer the Northern states and military action, but it also meant that the state would become a major battleground. No complete history of the Civil War can be written without including the contribution of Virginia. After the war, Virginia was governed as a military district but succeeded in being readmitted to the Union on January 26, 1870.

Like most of the Southern states, Virginia scaled down its war and Reconstruction debts. Since the state was unable to afford them, it is unknown how many people were reimbursed for their losses after the act quoted here was passed: "Be it enacted by the General Assembly that it shall be the duty of the several county and corporation clerks to keep a record of such papers relating to the loss of property due to the late war as they may be required to do by this act. Any person who has suffered losses by the operations of the war since the 17th day of April 1861, may make a statement of such losses, stating the kind and description of property, including Negroes emancipated; at what time taken, damaged, or destroyed, by the army of which belligerent and in whatever manner by either army, and the amount of loss sustained, making the value of said property on January 1, 1861, the standard of valuation, and offer the same, proven by affidavit of one or more citizens to the clerk of the county or corporation in which said property was taken, damaged, or destroyed who shall receive and record same in a book kept for that purpose. The original papers shall be safely kept by the clerk, but they may be withdrawn at any time after they have been recorded."

Virginia did not issue a deluge of state notes during the Civil War and all except the $1 note are decently printed. Unfortunately, while the series is fairly brief, it will be difficult or impossible to obtain several of the notes due to their cost or rarity.

Authorized by Acts of March 14, April 30 and June 28, 1861

Printed by Hoyer & Ludwig, Richmond, Va.
Written dates of 1861

These notes state that "The Faith of the Commonwealth is Pledged" and that "Twelve months after date, the Commonwealth of Virginia will pay the bearer at the Treasury with interest at the rate of Six Per Cent per annum until redeemed or advertised for redemption."

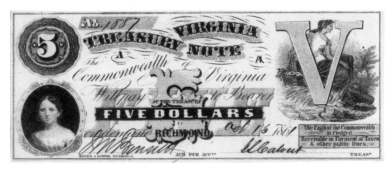

VA-1. $5— Girl at lower left, Ceres seated in large "V" at right. Plate letters A to D.

GOOD	VG	FINE	VF	XF	UNC.
$50	$75	$100	$200	$325	$425

VA-2. $10— Liberty standing at left. Plate letters A to D.

GOOD	VG	FINE	VF	XF	UNC.
$50	$75	$100	$200	$325	$425

VA-3. $20— Bust of Washington at center, Minerva at left, man seated with tablet at right. Green overprint.

GOOD	VG	FINE	VF	XF	UNC.
$50	$75	$125	$200	$550	$750

VA-4. $50— Ceres and Commerce with an urn at center, state arms in oval at left, John Tyler at upper right. Denomination in red. Plate letters A, B. Rare.

GOOD	VG	FINE	VF	XF	UNC.
$1500	$2000	$2500	$3000	$4000	$7000

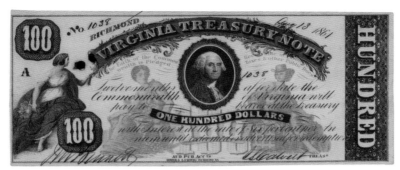

VA-5. $100— Bust of Washington at center between two seated women, Ceres at left. Denomination in red. Plate letter A. Rare.

GOOD	VG	FINE	VF	XF	UNC.
$2500	$3500	$4500	$6000	$8000	$15000

VA-6. $500— Three women representing Commerce, Ceres and Navigation at left, Washington at upper right. Denomination in red. Plate letter A. Very rare.

Authorized by Acts of December 30, 1861 and March 31, 1862

*Printed by Hoyer & Ludwig, Richmond, Va.
The following notes do not bear interest.*

VA-7. $1— Woman seated at center, Governor John Letcher (1860-64) at lower left. Dated May 15, 1862. Red and black. Plate letters A, B.

GOOD	VG	FINE	VF	XF	UNC.
$12	$20	$30	$50	$75	$100

VA-7A. $1— As above. Printed date of July 21, 1862.

GOOD	VG	FINE	VF	XF	UNC.
$7	$12	$20	$30	$40	$50

VA-7B. $1— As above. Printed date of October 21, 1862.

GOOD	VG	FINE	VF	XF	UNC.
$10	$15	$25	$35	$55	$75

Printed by Keatinge & Ball, Richmond, Va.
Dated March 13, 1862

VA-8. $5— J. M. Bennett, Auditor of Public Accounts at center, state arms at right. Green and black. Plate letters A to D.

GOOD	VG	FINE	VF	XF	UNC.
$20	$30	$45	$60	$90	$110

VA-8A. $5— As above. Paper watermarked Hodgkinson & Co. Wookey Hole Mill.

GOOD	VG	FINE	VF	XF	UNC.
$100	$150	$200	$250	$400	$500

VA-8B. $5— As above. Paper watermarked CSA in block letters.

GOOD	VG	FINE	VF	XF	UNC.
$20	$30	$40	$75	$175	$250

VA-8C. $5— As above. Paper watermarked J. Whatman.

GOOD	VG	FINE	VF	XF	UNC.
$100	$150	$200	$250	$400	$500

Printed by Keatinge & Ball, Columbia, S.C.
Dated October 15th, 1862

VA-9. $10— Ceres at center, Vulcan at left, Governor John B. Floyd (1849-52) at lower right. Denominations in green. Plate letters A to D.

GOOD	VG	FINE	VF	XF	UNC.
$30	$50	$70	$100	$125	$145

VA-9A. $10— As above. Paper watermarked TEN.

GOOD	VG	FINE	VF	XF	UNC.
$30	$50	$75	$110	$145	$175

VA-9B. $10— As above. Paper watermarked FIVE.

GOOD	VG	FINE	VF	XF	UNC.
$75	$125	$200	$350	$500	$600

VA-9C. $10— As above. Paper watermarked W.T.C.C. & Co.

GOOD	VG	FINE	VF	XF	UNC.
$30	$50	$80	$135	$200	$300

VA-9D. $10— As above. Paper watermarked J. Green & Sons. Scarce.

GOOD	VG	FINE	VF	XF	UNC.
$100	$200	$300	$400	$500	$600

VA-10. $50— James M. Mason at left, Commerce, Ceres and Navigation at right. Orange or red overprint. Plate letters A to D. (Mason was U.S. Senator from 1847 until expelled in 1861.)

GOOD	VG	FINE	VF	XF	UNC.
$30	$50	$70	$175	$250	$350

VA-11. $100— Governor John Letcher at center, Washington at left, Indian maiden at right. Orange or red overprints. Plate letters A to D.

GOOD	VG	FINE	VF	XF	UNC.
$50	$100	$150	$225	$350	$500

Important

Where more than one variety was issued of a note, the prices listed are for the more common kinds, not a rare minor variety. Where no value is indicated, the price is speculative due to such notes being rare in higher grades and seldom offered. Most of the illustrations in this catalog are either larger or smaller than the actual specimens.

WEST VIRGINIA

The secession of the Southern states from the Union is well known. Apparently because the South was considered to be a part of the Union, although in revolt, secession from the Confederate States is not given recognition. For example, in June 1861, the strongly pro-Union counties of Eastern Tennessee petitioned the U.S. Congress for admission as a separate state but was ignored. More successful was the western portion of Virginia. This mountainous area had few slaves among its farmers and differed in many other ways from the plantation owners of the eastern lowlands.

For many years, the people of Western Virginia felt that they were unfairly treated by the eastern half of the state but it was not until Virginia seceded in 1861 that an opportunity arose to part ways. A number of meetings were held, which resulted in an ordinance for a new state that was put to popular vote on October 24, 1861 (18,489 in favor, 781 against). In 1862, application was made to Congress for admission to the Union and in December, President Lincoln approved, providing that the state constitution included a provision for the gradual abolition of slavery. It may be of interest to quote this provision since it offers an idea how Lincoln proposed to end slavery before he felt it necessary to issue his Emancipation Proclamation:

"The children of slaves born within the limits of this state after the fourth day of July, eighteen hundred and sixty-three, shall be free, and that all slaves within the said State, who shall at the time aforesaid be under the age of ten years, shall be free when they arrive at the age of twenty-one years; and all slaves over ten and under twenty-one years shall be free when they arrive at the age of twenty-five years; and no slave shall be permitted to come into the State for permanent residence therein."

On April 20, 1863, President Lincoln issued a proclamation that 60 days from that date West Virginia should enter the Union on June 20, 1863. After the Civil War, Virginia sought to regain Berkeley and Jefferson Counties in the Eastern Panhandle of West Virginia, which were East of the mountains. That question was decided by the Supreme Court in 1871 in favor of West Virginia. It took much longer to decide how the debt of Virginia prior to the Civil War was to be divided. Negotiations began in 1870 but, when they were unsuccessful, Virginia funded the debt in 1871 and arbitrarily assigned one-third to West Virginia. West Virginia replied that it had paid the same taxes as the eastern counties and had received no comparable benefit. In addition to bonds, Virginia issued interest-bearing auditor's warrants that specifically name the expected settlement between the two states. A couple kinds are known from 1879 and there may be others since it was not until 1911-1919 that the debt was finally settled in the favor of Virginia.

AFTERWORD

On May 29, 1865, President Johnson of the United States issued an Amnesty Proclamation to former Confederates, providing that they took an oath of Allegiance. Not accepted were civil and diplomatic officers of the Confederate States; Confederates who had left U. S. judicial posts; officers above the rank of Colonel in the Army, or Lieutenant in the Navy; Confederates who had been U. S. Congressmen; Confederates who had left the armed forces of the United States; Confederates who mistreated war prisoners; Confederates who fled to other countries; Confederates who had attended West Point or the Naval Academy; Confederates who had served as Governors of Confederate states; those of the North who had fought for the South; and persons whose taxable property was worth over $20,000.

While this Amnesty Proclamation enabled most "ordinary persons" to regain their rights and citizenship, there were exceptions. There was a tendency among Southern states during the period the Reconstruction governments held power to disenfranchise anyone that had aided the Confederacy. That was to change as were some of President Johnson's restrictions; not long afterward former Confederates elected to the U.S. Congress included Alexander H. Stephens, who had been Vice President of the Confederate States; four Confederate Generals; five Colonels; six Cabinet officers; and 58 former Congressmen.

TOGETHER AGAIN

Today, in a dangerous world, we may be thankful that the United States is again "one and inseparable," a union of both the North and the South.

EPILOGUE

Could the Civil War have been prevented? Many students of the subject are convinced that this bloody conflict need never have happened. But we have the advantage of hindsight and time. Those closely involved in the events that led to the outbreak of hostilities did not have that advantage. Events moved very rapidly. Southern leaders had already warned that if Lincoln and the Republicans won the election in November 1860, the South would secede. Before the end of the year, South Carolina had followed through.

Slavery was supposed to have been the paramount issue of the Civil War but in reality it was only one issue. Moreover, while blacks living in the North might be "free men," it did not mean that all of them were living better than in the South, nor were they equal, despite the sanctimonious claims of abolitionists. (This has held true to this day.) Maryland law even permitted free men to renounce their freedom and become slaves. One cannot take a wide brush and say that race relations were all bad or all good in either the North or the South — it was a mixture in both sections depending upon the people involved.

Although generally buried under the banner of slavery, there were other reasons why the South wanted to part ways with the North. Not only were state rights an issue, there was the matter of tariffs that favored the North and a feeling of oppression among cotton growers and businessmen that the North was exploiting the South like a fiefdom. And to a large extent that was true. It was a "rich man's war and a poor man's fight" writ large since most of the wealth was in the North. There are times when people feel that they have no recourse but to fight.

By the time of Lincoln's inaugural address of March 4, 1861, several Southern states in addition to South Carolina had seceded and he tried to be conciliatory in his message. While Lincoln insisted that secession was illegal and previously stated that "government cannot endure permanently half slave, half free," he relented to the extent that he would not interfere with slavery where it was already in existence and had even agreed to support a constitutional amendment to that effect (Crittenden Compromise, December 1860) if it would prevent secession. At the urging of Virginia, a peace convention met in Washington during February 1861, but the participants failed to agree on a compromise to save the Union. Time was obviously running out and any statement by Lincoln would not reverse it.

Lincoln had concluded in his address that "there needs to be no bloodshed or violence, and there shall be none unless it be forced upon the national authority." The South forced the issue when Fort Sumter was attacked and other Federal properties were seized. Thus began the contest that Lincoln feared would be fatal to "free government upon the earth," if the United States should be dissolved. It is unlikely that the result would have been that bad had the Confederate States succeeded in becoming an independent nation. More likely, slavery would have been phased out at a slower pace under the authority of the states (as in the North) rather than having to endure the disruptive effect of sudden emancipation before the majority of the slaves were ready to subsist on their own. In a desperate effort to gain British recognition of the Confederacy, President Davis even offered in 1864 to free the slaves, but it was too late. In any case, world opinion would surely have effected gradual emancipation if nothing else. Brazil accomplished this by laws adopted in 1871, 1885 and 1888. Emancipation was proper but because there was insufficient economic and educational aid to former slaves, there was a general breakdown that would require many years to correct.

Both sides made mistakes, politically and militarily. And these are among the things that make the study of the Civil War so fascinating. It has even been called "the last gentlemen's war" but I think it more correct to call it the first modern war — large areas of the South saw a preview of total destruction that has been wrought many times since. Yet, the Confederate States in defeat lives on, alive as ever, through its currency. Few, if any, other countries that arose and fell in a civil war, have left a comparable legacy.

History of Collecting Confederate Money 1865-1945
By Pierre Fricke and Fred Reed
Well Illustrated 340 pages, quality hard back, color, DVD.

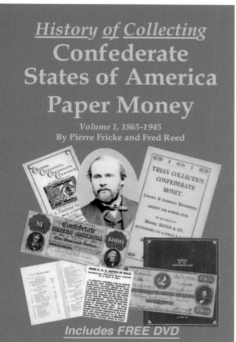

- Easy-to-use guide to types of Confederate paper money
- Confederate finance history
- Dealers, auctions, books, and collectors of 1865 to 1945
- Typical and major collections
- Price history
- Research material on DVD
- Many supplemental articles on DVD
- Checklists of collections
- Condition census of rare Confederate notes
- Census of Montgomeries, Indian Princess and Eagle & Shield notes
- Presentation of the history of collecting 1865—2012

"The book is well researched and gives a wonderful history of various collections, the collectors who investigated the mysteries of many of the notes, and discussion and emphasis on early catalogs and sales. As such, it should interest anyone…" Marvin Ashmore

Please send $49 ppd. to:
Pierre Fricke,
P.O. Box 1094,
Sudbury, MA 01776

Personalized and Signed by Author
www.csaquotes.com

Email — pfricke@attglobal.net

Buy * Sell * Auctions * New Varieties * Research